Cassell Dictionary of Clichés

Cassell Dictionary of Clichés

NIGEL REES

CASSELL

A CASSELL BOOK
First published 1996 by Cassell
Wellington House
125 Strand, London WC2R 0BB

Distributed in the United States
by Sterling Publishing Co., Inc.
387 Park Avenue South, New York, NY 10016–8810

Distributed in Australia
by Capricorn Link (Australia) Pty Ltd
2/13 Carrington Road, Castle Hill, NSW 2154

British Library Cataloguing-in-Publication Data
A catalogue record for this book may be obtained from the British Library

ISBN 0–304–34698–5

Typeset by Gem Graphics, Trenance, Cornwall
Printed and bound by Biddles Ltd, Guildford and King's Lynn

Contents

Introduction   ix

How to Use This Dictionary   xiii

The Dictionary   1

Policeman to burglar: 'And what, if you'll pardon the cliché, is all this 'ere?'
Caption to *Punch* cartoon by J.W. Taylor (23 November 1938)

On a long-winded memorandum by Anthony Eden: 'As far as I can see, you have used every cliché except "God is love" and "Please adjust your dress before leaving".'
Attributed to Winston Churchill in *Life* Magazine (*c.*1941), though disowned by him

On the cliché-ridden content of a speech by another politician (possibly also Anthony Eden): 'It was clitch after clitch after clitch.'
Ernest Bevin (attributed)

'I had fewer verbal prejudices but I always found Robert [Byron's] exhilarating. He had an abomination for clichés, whereas I thought that under careful control clichés could achieve amusing effects like old-fashioned music-hall tunes.'
Harold Acton, *Memoirs of an Aesthete* (1948)

'Let's have some new clichés.'
Samuel Goldwyn, quoted in the *Observer* (24 October 1948)

On being a Foreign Secretary: 'Nothing he can say can do very much good, and almost anything he may say may do a great deal of harm. Anything he says that is not trite is risky. He is forever poised between the cliché and the indiscretion.'
Harold Macmillan, speech, House of Commons (27 July 1955)

On discussions with the Prince and Princess of Wales prior to marrying them: 'My advice was delicately poised between the cliché and the indiscretion.'
Robert Runcie, Archbishop of Canterbury, quoted in *The Times* (14 July 1981)

'The truths of the past are the clichés of the present.'
Ned Rorem, 'Listening and Hearing', *Music from Inside Out* (1967)

'The cliché is dead poetry. English, being the language of an imaginative race, abounds in clichés, so that English literature is always in danger of being poisoned by its own secretions.'
Gerald Brenan, *Thoughts in a Dry Season* (1978)

Introduction

The *Oxford Companion to English Literature* defines a cliché as: 'A stock expression which by constant use has lost its sharp edge.' The *Longman Dictionary of Contemporary English* ventures rather: 'An unchanging idea or expression used so commonly that it has lost much of its expressive force.' Indeed, there can be little doubt what is meant by the word 'cliché'. It is a worn-out phrase. But bestowing the slur upon precise examples is more problematic. Hitherto, the only major attempt to list examples of the breed has been Eric Partridge's *Dictionary of Clichés*, first published in 1940, with the fifth edition appearing in 1978, the year before he died. The curious thing about Partridge's work is that I have not felt inclined to include in this present book very many of the scores of clichés he listed. This is largely because what Partridge considered to be undoubted clichés in the 1940s and 1950s, do not always seem to be that way today.

In some cases, what may have been tiresome phrases then – 'to have two strings to one's bow' is a random example – is now no more than what I would call an idiom or popular phrase and hardly worthy of condemnation. Then again, when Partridge lists 'love in a cottage' as a cliché, my reaction is that nowadays, when used at all, it is no more than a quaint saying and possibly only used in a self-consciously archaic way.

So, what I am saying about Partridge's 'GROUND-BREAKING' or 'SEMINAL WORK' (and those, I think, are current clichés) boils down to two points. First, he may have fallen into the trap of condemning popular phrases or 'vogue terms' on the grounds that they were familiar rather than that they were worn out. I am also aware, on this point, that a book published in Britain as the *Methuen Dictionary of Clichés* (1992) is not that at all. It is a book of popular phrases and catchphrases as is shown by its original American title *Have a Nice Day – No Problem!*

Second – and more importantly – what Partridge's book serves to remind one is that 'once a cliché' is not 'always a cliché'. Additionally, hackneyed quotations (which Partridge noticed rather a lot) do not remain hackneyed quotations if no one uses them much nowadays. It is possible, then, for a phrase to be rehabilitated – not least when it has been ridiculed into temporary retirement – and it is possible for a clichéd expression to reappear and be used acceptably even if it is spoken or written with invisible quotation marks. Some might argue that a phrase used self-consciously in this way remains in essence a cliché, but I am not so sure that it does.

The charm, if you like, of formerly clichéd phrases is nowhere more enjoyably on display than in Jonathan Swift's little work known briefly as *Polite Conversation* (1738) and, in full, *A Complete Collection of Genteel and Ingenious Conversation According to the Most Polite Mode and Method Used at Court, and in the Best Companies of England.* Here he worked about a thousand conversational clichés into short dialogues which now read only charmingly:

> *Neverout*: Well, miss . . .
> *Miss Notable*: Ay, ay; many a one says well, that thinks ill.
> *Neverout*: Well, miss; I'll think of this.
> *Miss Notable*: That's rhyme, if you take it in time.
> *Neverout*: What! I see you are a poet.
> *Miss Notable*: Yes; if I had but the wit to show it.
>   (A puff of smoke comes down the chimney.)
> *Lady Answerall*: Lord, madam, does your ladyship's chimney smoke?
> *Colonel*: No, madam, but they say, smoke always pursues the fair, and your ladyship sat nearest.
> *Lady Smart*: Madam, do you love bohea tea?
> *Lady Answerall*: Why, madam, I must confess I do love it; but it does not love me.

If any of Swift's famous 'savage indignation' had prompted him to list the inevitably second-hand nature of people's conversation, he ended up by bequeathing a delightful celebration of a habit that would barely merit a condemnation these days.

In 1984 and 1985 I wrote two books *The Joy of Clichés* and *The Gift of the Gab* which sought to do for contemporary speech and writing what Swift had done for conversation in the 1730s. They took the form of language guides *encouraging* readers to use clichés rather than to avoid them. It is not for me to say whether they succeeded or not, though the word 'facetious' springs to mind when I read them now. But writing them did put me in a state of permanent alert as to the changing status of individual phrases in and out of clichédom. The present dictionary is the result of having maintained that watch and, in particular, of having continued to compile citations of clichés in use.

These examples of clichés caught on the wing, so to speak, need to be treated with care. I would not wish to be thought to be ridiculing the writers or speakers whose words I am quoting. They may, after all, be poking fun at the clichés they are themselves using and any irony may not be apparent from the short extracts taken. Or, especially if they are journalists, they may feel that the journalese to which they resort is a legitimate shorthand and that only a pedant would deny them use of these tools of their trade. Or again, especially if they are journalists, they may feel that using a cliché is a convenient way of getting an idea over in a small space with the advantage of off-the-peg familiarity.

So, yes, there is plenty of scope for argument as to whether any particular phrase is a cliché. This dictionary is inevitably very subjective (I would be inclined to say 'personal' if that word hadn't been diluted by such use as 'Your personal invitation to join our special private tours of Kensington Palace'*), and I must confess that there are times when I have included a phrase purely on the basis of my dislike of it rather than any perceived over-use by others (CARING AND SHARING being one). At other times I have allowed my extreme irritation at some much-used new phrase to become apparent even if the phrase cannot yet really be described as over-used or worn.

I have also tended to be kind towards other phrases that another compiler might have included in a book like this. Someone asked if I was going to include 'user-friendly' and all the other '-friendlies', but I have decided not to. There may be a lot of it about but I am not sure that this suffix construction amounts to a worn phrase (yet). For me, it is still a useful phrase to play with and it retains an entertaining aspect. Somebody else begged me to include the phrase 'an item' (used when referring to whether two people are a couple in the sense of having some sort of relationship). But no. It may be irritating but it is not yet worn to tatters. I have also been a little less hard on spoken clichés (not least because there are so many of them). This is because rather more thought goes (or should go) into what we write than what we say and, therefore, the fall from grace, when it occurs, is more reprehensible.

*Advertising Leaflet, July 1995.

Which brings me to the point at which I must state how I have defined what constitutes a cliché for the purposes of this dictionary. How have I selected the phrases for inclusion from the hundreds of thousands of phrases that do get used rather a lot and possibly too much?

For me a cliché is a phrase that, when I come across it in speech or writing, makes my heart sink a little or encourages me to exclaim, 'Here we go again!' This has been my chief yardstick. This sinking feeling derives usually from the dreadful *inevitability* of the phrase or expression occurring when and where it does. When I am told that someone is away 'ENJOYING A WELL-DESERVED REST', I groan inwardly at the obviousness of the thought. (I also begin to wonder whether the rest has genuinely been well-deserved or whether the speaker has just said it because that is what an off-the-peg phrase like that dictates.)

When, however, an obituarist writes of some recently departed friend that 'HE WAS A BIG MAN IN EVERY WAY', I do temper my inward groaning with the knowledge that, in bereavement, the clichés of comfort and sorrow may have their place. I remember at the first funeral I ever attended being advised by one of the elderly mourners, 'THAT'S ANOTHER PAGE TURNED IN THE BOOK OF LIFE' – a frightful cliché, but quite understandable in the circumstances.

Accordingly, I would advise readers of this selection not to see it as a withering condemnation of lazy speech or writing but as a gentle nudge towards the advisability of avoiding the inevitable, the worn and the faded phrase. This dictionary is not written in the spirit of 'Thou Shalt Not Utter Clichés Under Any Circumstances Whatsoever'. Its purpose is not to root out and strangle clichés wherever they are to be found. All it is urging is an awareness of the response that an unthinking use of clichés can prompt in the hearer or reader.

Some clichés are perfectly good phrases – that is why they have become clichés, because people like them too much – and it would be foolish to chuck them out of the window. All I am suggesting is that, if they are to be used, they should be used with a little care and discrimination.

This dictionary confines itself to clichés of language but it is worth remembering that there is another sort of book waiting to be written about clichés of thought and idea. There is clichéd behaviour, action and situations, and though the origin of the word *cliché* has to do with printing and words, there are even visual clichés (think of the inevitable shots you get in films). But that task is for someone else.

In this Introduction I have probably allowed in several constructions that others might consider clichés (I have a feeling that 'a little care and discrimination' in the paragraph before last has a certain inevitability about it). But that is what I am saying: a cliché is in the ear of the beholder and it is quite easy to become over-sensitive on the matter. The result could be that you neither said nor wrote anything for fear of offending the members of the ClichéWatch Patrol. IN THE FINAL ANALYSIS, that would surely be a FATE WORSE THAN DEATH.

How to Use This Dictionary

Each entry contains the following information in this order:

1. The cliché as a headword or phrase in **bold** letters. Headwords or phrases are given in word-by-word order.
2. Where the cliché is most likely to be encountered – journalism, films, obituaries, etc.
3. The origins of the phrase with approximate date of its first use in its original sense.
4. A *very* approximate date when the phrase may be said to have achieved cliché status. Some of these dates may be very wide of the mark but are included in order to provoke the offer of more precise references.
5. Comment on the use of the cliché (where available).
6. Citations – examples of the cliché being used as such in newspapers, books, film dialogue, etc.

Cross-references are given in SMALL CAPITALS.

Quotations from Shakespeare are as in *The Arden Shakespeare* (2nd series). Citations are printed as they appeared in the original publication named.

= A =

—— **abhors a vacuum.** General but especially journalistic use. Referring to the maxim 'Nature abhors a vacuum' which François Rabelais quotes in its original Latin form *natura abhorret vacuum* in *Gargantua* (1535). Galileo (1564–1642) asserted it as the reason mercury rises in a barometer. The earliest appearance in the *Oxford English Dictionary* (2nd edition) is in the form, 'The Effatum, That Nature abhors a Vacuum', a citation from Robert Boyle's *A Free Enquiry Into the Vulgarly Receiv'd Notion of Nature* (1685). 'Nature abhors a straight line' was a saying of the English garden landscaper, Capability Brown (1715–83). Clare Boothe Luce, the American writer and socialite (1903–87), said, 'Nature abhors a virgin'. A cliché by the 1950s either as a quotation or in some variant form. Listed in the *Independent* (24 December 1994) as a cliché of newspaper editorials.

> Nature abhors a vacuum and what appears ultimately to concern the Reagan Administration most of all is the possibility that President Mitterrand's France will gradually abandon its traditional military protection of central Africa and the Sahara.
> *Financial Times* (12 August 1983)

> Though I like Scalia's principles better, I prefer Wilkey's conclusions. Law, like nature, abhors a vacuum. It seems wise to extend the protection of the law to those who are left out in the cold of a legal no-man's land.
> *Financial Times* (14 March 1985)

> I quickly developed a pearshaped figure that testified to my indolent lifestyle. I became the archetypal also-ran that PE masters could barely bring themselves to talk to without risk of life-threatening apoplexy: they abhorred my idleness as Nature abhors a vacuum.
> *Guardian* (24 June 1986)

abject apology. General use but especially wherever faintly pompous politicians and legally minded persons are to be found. Date of origin not known. Probably a cliché by the 1950s.

1

Newscaster Nicholas Witchell issued an abject apology last night for describing the Irish venue for the Eurovision Song Contest as 'a cow shed'. He went on national radio station RTE after a storm over his 'misjudged' remark about the 4.4 million arena.
Daily Mail (15 May 1993)

'I have written to Gillian Shephard (Employment Secretary) telling her what has happened and demanding she orders Mr Forsyth to deliver to me a public and abject apology and withdrawal'.
Herald (Glasgow) (27 May 1993)

This is the first of the 'inevitable pairings' or 'two-word clichés' to be found in this book. They were largely drawn to my attention by Matthew Barnes and Dr Martin Barnes in 1989. The Barneses are keen collectors of such things – indeed, their annual compilations list hundreds.

about. *See* THAT'S WHAT —— IS ALL . . .

accident waiting to happen. Chiefly journalistic use, often reflecting expert or popular opinion. A cliché frequently uttered in the wake of a disaster is that it was 'an accident waiting to happen'. This is the survivors' and experts' way of pointing to what, to them, seems the foreseeable and inevitable result of lax safety standards which will now probably be corrected only *as a result* of the tragedy. Much used in relation to the late 1980s spate of UK disasters (Bradford City football ground fire, Zeebrugge ferry overturning, Piper Alpha oil-rig explosion, Kings Cross Tube fire, Hillsborough football stadium crowd deaths). Used as the title of a 1989 book on the subject by Judith Cook.

Ignorance and neglect cost 51 lives [in the *Marchioness* boat disaster] . . . 'You don't need the benefit of hindsight to say this was an accident waiting to happen,' he said.
Today (16 August 1991)

Achilles' heel. General use, referring to Achilles, the foremost warrior in the Trojan war, who sulked in his tent, was hero of the *Iliad*, and was vulnerable only at the heel (in allusion to the story of the dipping of Achilles' heel in the river Styx). Hence, the phrase is used to describe the vulnerable point of any person or thing. A cliché probably by 1900, it was cited as a 'dying metaphor' by George Orwell in 'Politics and the English Language' (*Horizon*, April 1946).

Divorce is the Achilles' heel of marriage.
G.B. Shaw, letter (2 July 1897)

2

If Oppenheimer has an 'Achilles' heel, it is his overriding loyalty to his friends.
Arthur Holly Compton, *Atomic Quest* (1956)

It is the refusal to condemn which is the Achilles heel of contemporary Christian psychology.
Catholic Herald (28 January 1972)

acid test. General use, but especially journalistic. Originally an 'acid test' involved the use of aqua fortis to test for gold but the term has come to be applied to any crucial test. A cliché by the 1920s/30s. Cited as a 'lump of verbal refuse' by George Orwell in 'Politics and the English Language' (*Horizon*, April 1946).

The treatment accorded Russia by her sister nations in the months to come will be the acid test of their good will.
President Woodrow Wilson, quoted in *The Times* (9 January 1918)

The acid test of any political decision is, 'What is the alternative?'
Lord Trend, quoted in *Observer* (21 December 1975)

'Let's get South Africa working. For we must together and without delay begin to build a better life for all South Africans. This is going to be the acid test of the government of national unity.'
Nelson Mandela, quoted in *Financial Times* (3 May 1994)

If the same weight is not given to the improvement of human capital as to market share, profit and other organisational priorities, small wonder the human resources function is often viewed as unrelated to the 'real' goals of the company. The acid test here is: do the job descriptions of all staff (board of directors, executive, administration) include meaningful percentages of weights and time spent in subordinate development with examples of what this means in practice?
Financial Times (6 May 1994)

acquired taste. General popular use, but often literally with regard to food and drink. Meaning 'any thing or person for whom one has acquired a liking' – as distinct from a natural or spontaneous taste. Probably a cliché by 1939.

He would have loved me in time. I am an acquired taste.
W.S. Gilbert, *The Mikado* (1885)

Most French asparagus is completely white, with a hard skin which must be

scraped off. The flavour is quite different, too, delicate but well defined. 'It's an acquired taste,' says Paske. 'I'd liken it to chewing iron bars.'
Independent on Sunday (9 May 1993)

active consideration. Bureaucratic use, often when an idea or project is being subjected to quite the reverse. Possibly a cliché by the 1950s.

Ken Vowles, Scottish Power's managing director in the generation division, said the installation of flue gas desulphurisation (FGD) equipment – to reduce sulphur pollution – was under active consideration and could be installed by the end of the century.
Scotsman (7 May 1993)

added bonus. *See* WITH THE ADDED . . .

[adjective][national/regional origin]. Sports journalism and broadcasting. Appalling style in which the writer avoids re-using the athlete's name (especially if it is a difficult foreign one) by dreaming up a sobriquet (sometimes alliterative). Adopted from a well-established sporting tradition: Paavo Nurmi, the Finnish runner successful at the 1924 Olympics, was known as 'the Flying Finn', as later was Hannu Mikkola, the World Rally Champion in 1983. A cliché by the 1960s.

Since then Marvin Hagler has crushed [Sibson] and another American, Don Lee, stopped him in the eighth round of a seesaw struggle when the muscular Midlander was floored four times.
Sunday Express (25 November 1984)

ado. *See* WITHOUT FURTHER . . .

advertise. *See* IT PAYS TO . . .

after I've shampooed my hair . . . Conversational use. In *Are You a Bromide?* (1907), the American writer Gelett Burgess castigated people who spoke in clichés. Among the 'Bromidioms' he listed was: 'After I've shampooed my hair, I can't do a thing with it!'

after/for more years than I care to remember. General use, to describe the passage of time. Date of origin unknown. A cliché by the mid-twentieth century.

'Having been an habitué of racecourses and betting shops for more years than I care to remember, I am absolutely determined to improve, indeed I

hope perfect, the availability of information relevant to the public's needs,' he said yesterday.
The Times (29 June 1994)

It is a long way removed from the techniques available when Dr Macleod started to work with the cream of Scottish rugby, 'more years ago than I care to remember'.
Scotsman (12 October 1994)

agenda-setting. Media and political usage, since the 1980s. Meaning 'that which establishes the important issues to be dealt with'. Date of origin not known. Identified as a current cliché in *The Times* (17 March 1995).

In those days the media approached their role as servants of democracy with more self-effacement. They were less determined to set the agenda than is the case thirty years later.
John Cole, *As It Seemed To Me* (1995)

Radio 4's *Today*, which has been under fire from the Cabinet, won the speech-based breakfast show award, remaining 'the most authoritative, agenda-setting programme available on British radio'.
Guardian (27 April 1995)

'Setting the agenda' has become one of the sacred phrases of the age, especially among politicians . . . [seeming] to mean 'getting oneself, or one's thoughts, talked about' – or 'being the first to come out with some mindless nonsense or opinion, which is so controversial that people are forced to take it seriously.'
Observer (24 September 1995)

agonizing reappraisal. Politics, journalism. Describing a reassessment of position that has probably been forced on the reappraiser. Originally, an allusion to a speech that John Foster Dulles, US Secretary of State, made to the National Press Club, Washington, in December 1953: 'When I was in Paris last week, I said that . . . the United States would have to undertake an agonizing reappraisal of basic foreign policy in relation to Europe.' A cliché by the late 1950s but hardly much in evidence nowadays.

As in response to new directions from an agonising reappraisal in MCC's room at lunch, the scoring spurted as Cowdrey twice swung Benaud to the leg fence.
Star (9 December 1958)

The nation's rogue elephants rampage, shattering complacency and compelling many to an agonizing reappraisal.
Kenneth Gregory, *The First Cuckoo* (1978)

He forecast a period of agonizing reappraisal for Nato. The flexible response strategy was now clearly untenable for many reasons, so a new approach would be essential.
The Times (27 June 1987)

Aladdin's cave (in there). *See* IT WAS LIKE AN . . .

alarm bells. *See* SET ALARM BELLS . . .

alive and well (and living in ——). Mainly journalistic use. The short phrase 'alive and well' was known by 1866, the longer form by the 1960s. It probably began in a perfectly natural way – 'What's happened to old so-and-so?' 'Oh, he's alive and well and living in Godalming' etc. In the preface to *His Last Bow* (1917) Conan Doyle wrote: 'The Friends of Mr Sherlock Holmes will be glad to learn that he is still alive and well . . .' The extended form may have been used in religious sloganeering, possibly prompted by *Time* Magazine's famous cover (*c*.1966), 'Is God Dead?' (see 1966 citation). However, in a letter to the *Independent* Magazine (13 March 1993), M.H.I. Wright wrote: 'When I was a medical student and young house physician 50 years ago, we had to write very detailed case-sheets on every patient admitted. Under the heading "Family History", we detailed each member of his family – for example, "Father, died of heart disease in 1935; Mother, alive and well and living in London." One pedantic consultant insisted we drop the word "alive" because, as he said, how could the relative be "dead and well"?'

The extended form was also given a tremendous fillip when the Belgian-born songwriter and singer Jacques Brel (1929–78) became the subject of an off-Broadway musical show entitled *Jacques Brel is Alive and Well and Living in Paris* (1968–72). A cliché from that point.

God is alive and living in Argentina.
Graffito, quoted in *New Statesman* (26 August 1966)

'The *Goon Show* is not dead. It is alive and well, living in Yorkshire and operating under the name of BBC Radio Leeds.'
Listener (3 October 1968), quoting the *Daily Mail*

The last English eccentric is alive and well and living comfortably in Oakland.
Time Magazine (5 September 1977)

God is not dead – but alive and well and working on a much less ambitious project.
Graffito, quoted in *Graffiti Lives, OK* (1980)

Jesus Christ is alive and well and signing copies of the Bible at Foyles.
Graffito, quoted in *Graffiti 2* (1980)

The GOLDEN AGE detective story is alive and well.
Review in *The Times* of Ruth Rendell's *Put On By Cunning* (1981)

Socialism is alive and well and living in Moscow.
Independent (25 June 1990)

all good men and true.   General use, now in a consciously archaic fashion. 'Are you good men and true' occurs in Shakespeare's *Much Ado About Nothing*, III.iii.1 (1598). Dogberry puts the question, and, being a constable, would naturally use legal terminology so it presumably relates to the longer '*twelve* good men and true', referring to the composition of a jury. 'It is a maxim of English law that legal memory begins with the accession of Richard I in 1189 ... with the establishment of royal courts ... The truth of [witnesses'] testimony [was] weighed not by the judge but by twelve "good men and true" ' (Winston Churchill, *A History of the English-Speaking Peoples*, Vol.1). Identified as a still current cliché in *The Times* (17 March 1995).

12 good men and true, glumly spruce, resigned to a long haul and bored, bored out of their skulls.
Listener (7 December 1967)

Tognazzi's anger at the way good men and true are killed, or sidelined by Italian bureaucracy out of fear of retribution or even complicity with the predatory Mafiosi, comes strongly across. But the movie otherwise doesn't travel too well.
Evening Standard (London) (5 May 1994)

'How can this man get a fair trial?' he demanded of the experts. They chorused: 'It all comes down to the 12 good men and true, the ladies and gentlemen of the jury.' But not just any old jury. No, to ensure a fair trial for OJ, it seems, the jury itself must be tried first.
Independent (8 October 1994)

all-time low.   General, particularly journalistic use – meaning 'to the lowest point on record'. Probably American in origin, by the early twentieth century. Could it have first referred to weather temperatures? A cliché by the 1950s. 'British prestige sunk to yet another all-time low' is included in the parody of sportswriters' clichés by David Frost and Peter Cook included in the book *That Was The Week That Was* (1963). Also **all-time high**, but less so.

Brings cost of power to new all-time low.
Saturday Evening Post (10 June 1933)

A new all-time low in political scurviness, hoodlumism.
Germaine Greer, *The Female Eunuch* (1970)

Tory MP Phil Gallie was even prompted to predict the party could gain a seat, despite pundits' claims of likely Tory losses and the party's crushing all-time low of 13% in the polls.
Sunday Times (1 May 1994)

What is also significant about BP's share rise to 386p last week is that it has brought the prospect of a serious assault on the all-time high of 418p much nearer the day.
Observer (1 May 1994)

ample opportunity.   General use. The Rev. Sydney Smith wrote in *Letters on the Subject of the Catholics, by Peter Plymley* (1807): 'An addition of polemics ... which must highly gratify the vigorists, and give them an ample opportunity of displaying that foolish energy upon which their claims to distinction are founded.' A cliché by 1900?

Mr Martens and his colleagues feel that the greatest danger to its programme, and to the stability of the country, will come when the measures begin to bite and they are acutely aware that the country's divided political and social structure presents ample opportunity for serious quarrels to erupt at any time.
Financial Times (11 January 1982)

analysis.   *See* IN THE FINAL/LAST/ULTIMATE ...

Anatomy of (a) ——.   Book title format, of which the first notable use was *The Anatomy of Melancholy* (1621) by Robert Burton. That book used the word 'anatomy' in an appropriate manner, its subject being a medical condition (*anatome* is the Greek word for dissection). The modern vogue for 'anatomies' of this and that began with the film *Anatomy of a Murder* (US, 1959) and was followed by Anthony Sampson's *Anatomy of Britain*, first published in 1962 and revised a number of times thereafter.

and now, if you'll excuse me, I've got work to do. Drama. An invariable way of ending a conversation, observed by Fritz Spiegl in an article on drama cliché lines in the *Listener* (7 February 1985).

—— **and that's official.** Journalistic formula used when conveying, say, the findings in some newly published report. The aim, presumably, is to dignify the fact(s) so presented but also to do it in a not too daunting manner. A cliché by the 1960s. Condemned by Keith Waterhouse in *Daily Mirror Style* (1981).

> In America, there are no bad people, only people who think badly of themselves. And that's official. California has a state commission to promote self-esteem, there is a National Council for Self-Esteem with its own bulletin . . .
> *Independent on Sunday* (8 May 1994)

anguish turned to joy (and *vice versa*). Journalistic use, as a lead-in to a story. 'A young mother's anguish turns to joy . . .' and so on. A cliché noted by the 1970s.

> Joy has turned to anguish for the parents of British student Colin Shingler aged 20, who was trapped in the Romano during the earthquake. Only hours after hearing that he had been rescued they were told that surgeons had to amputate his left hand.
> *The Times* (23 September 1985)

> Meanwhile, that anguish had turned to joy among the 250 Brechin fans at Hamilton. The players took a salute and then it was Clyde's turn to be acclaimed, with the championship trophy being paraded round the ground.
> *Herald* (Glasgow) (17 May 1993)

Compare DREAM TURNED TO NIGHTMARE.

animal life. *See* LOWEST FORM OF . . .

anon. *See* OF WHICH MORE . . .

another page turned. *See* THAT'S ANOTHER PAGE TURNED . . .

arc lamps. *See* UNDER THE GLARE . . .

armed to the teeth. General use, conveying that a person or body is heavily armed, alluding to the fact that pirates are sometimes portrayed as carrying a knife or sabre held between the teeth. A cliché by 1900.

Is there any reason why we should be armed to the teeth?
Richard Cobden, *Speeches* (1849)

Mujahedin . . . played a major role in bringing down the Shah and armed to the teeth.
Daily Telegraph (21 August 1979)

Once upon a time it would have been pirates fighting over buried treasure. Nowadays it's redneck firemen (Bill Paxton and William Sadler) under siege from a posse of drug dealers (headed by rappers Ice T and Ice Cube) who are armed to the teeth with guns and mobile phones.
Sunday Telegraph (9 May 1993)

art. *See* I DON'T KNOW MUCH ABOUT . . .

as every schoolboy knows. General but now consciously archaic use. In *The Anatomy of Melancholy* (1621), Robert Burton wrote: 'Every schoolboy hath . . .' and Bishop Jeremy Taylor used the expression 'every schoolboy knows it' in 1654. In the next century, Jonathan Swift cited 'to tell what every schoolboy knows'. But the most noted user of this rather patronizing phrase was Lord Macaulay, the historian, who would say things like, 'Every schoolboy knows who imprisoned Montezuma, and who strangled Atahualpa' (essay on 'Lord Clive', January 1840). A cliché since that date.

as if/like there was/were no tomorrow. General conversational but some slangy journalistic use. Meaning 'recklessly, with no regard to the future' or 'with desperate vigour' (especially the spending of money), as Paul Beale glosses it in his revision of Eric Partridge's *Dictionary of Slang and Unconventional English* (1984), suggesting that it was adopted from the US in the late 1970s. However, it has been known since 1862. Identified as a current cliché in *The Times* (17 March 1995).

The free travel scheme aimed at encouraging cyclists to use trains unearthed a biking underground which took to the trains like there was no tomorrow.
Time Out (4 January 1980)

Oil supplies that Americans at home continue to consume as though there were no tomorrow.
Guardian Weekly (3 February 1980)

The evidence from the last major redrawing of council boundaries is mixed.

Some authorities did go for broke, and spent their capital reserves as though there were no tomorrow.
The Times (9 June 1994)

as sick as a parrot. General use, meaning 'very disappointed (at losing something)'. Often used in opposition to OVER THE MOON. What may be an early version of 'sick as a parrot' appears in Robert Southey's Cumbrian dialect poem *The Terrible Knitters e' Dent* (1834). There, 'sick as a peeate' (pronounced 'pee-at') means a feeling like a heavy lump of peat in the stomach – the equivalent of having a heart feeling 'as heavy as lead' perhaps? A more likely origin is in connection with psittacosis or parrot disease/fever. In about 1973 there was a number of cases of people dying of this in West Africa. It is basically a viral disease of parrots (and other birds) but can be transmitted to humans. Even so, there may be an older source. In the seventeenth and eighteenth centuries there was an expression 'melancholy as a (sick) parrot' (in the plays of Aphra Behn, for example). And Desmond Morris in *Catwatching* (1986) claims that the original expression was 'as sick as a parrot with a rubber beak', meaning that the animal was incapacitated without a sharp weapon, as also in the saying, 'no more chance than a cat in hell with no claws'. Another use for the phrase is to describe post-alcoholic dejection. Parrots will eagerly feed on rotting – and therefore alcoholic – fruit or fruit pulp. Hence 'pissed as a parrot' and, next day, 'sick as a parrot'.
A cliché by the late 1970s.

(as surely) as night follows day . . . General use when describing the inevitable. Origin untraced, but surely by the nineteenth century. A cliché by 1900?

Because, if incomes run ahead of production, it will follow as night follows day, that the only result will be higher prices and no lasting improvement in living standards.
British Prime Minister Harold Wilson, speech to Shopworkers' Union Conference (1965)

As surely as night follows day, the pompous, the pretentious and the politically-correct will seize the lion's share of the money available.
Leading article, *Daily Mail* (28 April 1995)

── as we know it. General use, but especially in portentous American contexts, particularly Hollywood ones. The simple intensifier has long been with us, however. From *Grove's Dictionary of Music* (1883): 'The Song as

11

we know it in his [Schubert's] hands . . . such songs were his and his alone.'
A cliché by the 1950s. From a David Frost/Peter Cook sketch on sport
clichés (BBC TV *That Was the Week That Was*, 1962–3 series): 'The ghastly
war which was to bring an end to organized athletics as we knew it.'

> Politics as we know it will never be the same again.
> *Private Eye* (4 December 1981)

See also END OF CIVILIZATION AS WE KNOW IT.

as wild as a stallion.   Cheap literary use, particularly when describing
sexuality. Date of origin not known. A cliché by the mid-twentieth
century.

> He captivated women with his fierce, proud face, his lean well-exercised
> body, and his aura of sexuality, wild as that of a stallion.
> Shirley Conran, *Lace* (1982)

as you may have heard in the news . . .   Broadcasting use, specifically
in BBC Radio where owing to a division between 'news' and 'current
affairs' (i.e. the presentation of the facts tends to be followed in a
separate programme by discussion and analysis), backward references are
continually made from the latter to the former. Rampant in the 1970s, and
when I was presenting the Radio 4 breakfast-time *Today* programme I
made a point of never saying it.

at daggers drawn.   General use. Meaning 'hostile to each other'.
Formerly, 'at daggers' drawing' – when quarrels were settled by fights with
daggers. Known by 1668 but common only from the nineteenth century.
'Three ladies . . . talked of for his second wife, all at daggers drawn with
each other' – Maria Edgeworth, *Castle Rackrent* (1801). A cliché by 1900.

> It just might be different this time, however, because of a dimension that,
> amid all the nuclear brouhaha, has received much less attention than it
> merits. The two Korean governments may be at daggers drawn, but this has
> not stopped their companies from doing business.
> *Independent* (28 June 1994)

> The trick will be shown on The Andrew Newton Hypnotic Experience
> which starts on BSkyB next Friday and will have fellow illusionist Paul
> McKenna glued to his seat – the pair have been at daggers drawn for
> years.
> *Today* (8 October 1994)

at five minutes past eight on Wednesday morning . . .   An example of an opening sentence from a certain type of British journalism. Unilluminating recital of facts (especially time, date, weather) was the hallmark of *Sunday Times* 'Insight' journalism in the 1970s and was recognized as a cliché almost as soon as the style was established. The above head phrase comes from mockery of the style by Tom Stoppard in the play *Night and Day* (1978).

at the end of the day. General use but particularly beloved of British trade unionists and politicians, and indeed anyone who wishes to tread verbal water. This must have been a good phrase once – alluding perhaps to the end of the day's fighting or hunting. It appeared, for example, in Donald O'Keeffe's 1951 song, 'At the End of the Day, I Kneel and Pray'. But in Britain it was used in epidemic quantities during the 1970s and 1980s, and was recognized as a cliché by 1974, at least. The *Oxford English Dictionary* (2nd edition) has the grace to define it as a 'hackneyed phrase'.

> Eschatological language is useful because it is a convenient way of indicating . . . what *at the end of the day* we set most store by.
> H. McKeating, *God and the Future* (1974)

> 'At the end of the day,' he stated, 'this verifies what I have been saying against the cuts in public expenditure.'
> *South Nottinghamshire Echo* (16 December 1976)

> At the end of the day one individual surely has to take responsibility, even if it has to be after the transmission has gone out?
> Anthony Howard interviewing a BBC official in *Radio Times* (March 1982)

> Many of the participants feel at the end of the day, the effects of the affair [the abortion debate in the Irish Republic] will stretch beyond the mere question of amendment.
> Patrick Bishop, *Observer* (4 September 1983)

And Queen Elizabeth II, opening the Barbican Centre in March 1982, also used it. But it *is* the Queen's English, so perhaps she is entitled to do whatever she likes with it.

at/from the grassroots. A political cliché, used when supposedly reflecting the opinions of the RANK AND FILE and the 'ordinary voter' rather than the leadership of the political parties 'at national level'. The full phrase is 'from the grassroots up' and has been used to describe anything of a fundamental nature since *c.*1900 and specifically in politics from *c.*1912 – originally in the US. A cliché in the UK since the late 1960s. A BBC Radio programme *From the Grassroots* started in 1970. Katherine

13

Moore writing to Joyce Grenfell in *An Invisible Friendship* (letter of 13 October 1973): 'Talking of writing – why have roots now always got to be *grass* roots? And what a lot of them seem to be about.'

> In spite of official discouragement and some genuine disquiet at the grassroots in both parties, 21 such joint administrations have been operating in counties, districts and boroughs over the past year.
> *Guardian* (10 May 1995)

> The mood of the grassroots party, and much of Westminster too, is for an end of big government, substantial cuts in taxation, cuts in public spending, toughness on crime, immigration and social-security spending, and as little Europe as possible.
> *Guardian* (10 May 1995)

at the psychological moment.   General use, but now rather loosely so, to describe an opportune moment when something can be done or achieved. It is a mistranslation of the German phrase *das psychologische Moment* (which was, rather, about momentum) used by a German journalist during the 1870 siege of Paris. He was thought to be discussing the moment when the Parisians would most likely be demoralized by bombardment. With or without the idea of a mind being in a state of receptivity to some persuasion, a cliché by 1900.

> The Prince is always in the background, and turns up at the psychological moment – to use a very hard-worked and sometimes misused phrase.
> *Westminster Gazette* (30 October 1897)

> *The Psychological Moment*
> Title of book (1994) by Robert McCrum

> Indeed, some would argue that the end of hanging in 1969 was the psychological moment at which we ceased to take crime as a whole seriously, putting the liberal-humanitarian 'conscience' first.
> *Daily Mail* (27 August 1994)

at this moment/point in time.   Ranks with AT THE END OF THE DAY at the top of the colloquial clichés poll. From its periphrastic use of five words where one would do (i.e. 'now'), it would be reasonable to suspect an American origin. Picked up with vigour by British trade unionists in ad lib wafflings, it was already being scorned by 1972/3. 'Thoroughly agree with you about the lowering of standards in English usage on the BBC. "At this moment of time" instead of "Now" is outrageous' – Kenneth

Williams, letter of 8 October 1976, in *The Kenneth Williams Letters* (1994). 'At this point in time' was described by Eric Partridge in the preface to the 5th edition of his *A Dictionary of Clichés* (1978) as the 'mentally retarded offspring' of IN THIS DAY AND AGE. Only occasionally to be found committed to paper. Most clichés, to qualify as such, must have been good phrases once. But there was never any point to this one.

> The usual stuff about meaningful relationships taking place . . . at this moment in time.
> *Guardian* (12 March 1973)

> There were five similar towers . . . but at this moment in time, they were only of passing interest.
> Clive Eagleton, *October Plot* (1974)

> The phrase 'at that point of time' . . . quickly became an early trademark of the whole Watergate affair.
> *Atlantic Monthly* (January 1975)

> At this point in time the private rented sector of the housing market was shrinking.
> *Irish Times* (8 June 1977)

> The Marines, of course, had other ideas, but fortune was not favouring them at this moment in time.
> R. McGowan and J. Hands, *Don't Cry for Me, Sergeant Major* (1983)

auspicious occasion. In speech-making or on any occasion when portentousness or pomposity is demanded. In fact, almost any use of the word 'auspicious' is a candidate for clichédom: 'An auspicious debut on the platform was made the other day by Mr Winston Churchill, elder son of the late Lord Randolph Churchill' – *Lady* (5 August 1897). A cliché by the 1850s.

> Drinking around the imposing stone in order to celebrate some auspicious occasion.
> Charles T. Jacobi, *The Printers' Vocabulary* (1888)

> 'What about a glass of sherry to celebrate the auspicious occasion?'
> 'Taffrail', *Pincher Martin* (1916)

> The longer the game wore on the more obvious it became that Forest could not even rise to this auspicious occasion, much as they yearned to give their manager the mother and father of all send-offs.
> *Sunday Times* (2 May 1993)

author. *See* BEST-SELLING . . .

avoid —— like the plague, to. General, mostly conversational, use. Meaning 'to avoid completely, to shun.' The *Oxford English Dictionary* (2nd edition) finds the poet Thomas Moore in 1835 writing, 'Saint Augustine . . . avoided the school as the plague'. The fourth-century St Jerome is also said to have quipped, 'Avoid as you would the plague, a clergyman who is also a man of business.' A well-established cliché by the mid-twentieth century.

It may have been Arthur Christiansen, one of the numerous former editors of the *Daily Express*, who once posted a sign in the office saying: 'All clichés should be avoided like the plague.'

> If you get a film over there called 'Don't Look Now' avoid it like the plague. I went last night and it was terrible . . . Truly decadent rubbish.
> Kenneth Williams, letter of 5 November 1973, in *The Kenneth Williams Letters* (1994)

award-winning ——. Promotional use, especially in theatre, films and publishing. Depressing because it does not describe its subject in any useful way. Almost any actor in a leading role is likely to have received one of the many theatrical awards at some time, just as any writer may (however illegitimately) be called a BEST-SELLING AUTHOR if more than just a few copies of his or her books have been sold. The phrase was in use by 1962. A cliché by the 1980s, at least.

> Giles Cooper, who died nearly twenty years ago, is described in today's *Times* as 'award-winning playwright Giles Cooper'. I'd have thought one of the few things to be said in favour of death was that it extinguished all that.
> Alan Bennett, diary entry for 30 June 1984, quoted in *Writing Home* (1994)

> Award-winning actor Michael Gambon can also be seen . . . David Hare has written many successful plays and screenplays, including his award-winning trilogy . . . the Pulitzer Prize winning author, John Updike . . .
> Royal National Theatre brochure (26 June – 28 August 1995)

> We also introduce some new writers this week. Allison Pearson, the award-winning TV Critic of the year, joins us from the *Independent on Sunday* . . . Kenneth Roy, another new award-winning voice . . . will be writing a personal weekly peripatetic notebook.
> *Observer* (27 August 1995)

away from it all. *See* GET AWAY . . .

axe to grind. *See* HAVE NO/AN AXE . . .

= B =

bachelor gay. General informal use, referring to someone who puts himself about in a way characteristic of the unmarried male. 'A Bachelor Gay (Am I)' is the title of a song by James W. Tate from *The Maid of the Mountains* (1917). An arch phrase, to be used only within quotation marks, even before the change in the meaning of 'gay' from the 1960s onwards.

> 'He was a bachelor gay,' says Diana. 'He left his first wife and small child, years before I knew him . . . After that he'd lived at separate times with two other women and walked out on both of them. He said to me: "You must appreciate I've been around a lot." It was part of the appeal.'
> *Daily Mail* (29 November 1993)

back to basics. A political cliché now, but the alliterative phrase (sometimes 'back to *the* basics') may first have surfaced in the US where it was the mid-1970s slogan of a movement in education to give priority to the teaching of the fundamentals of reading, writing and arithmetic. In 1993, however, John Major, the British Prime Minister, launched it as an ill-fated slogan in a speech to the Conservative Party Conference: 'The message from this Conference is clear and simple. We must go back to basics . . . The Conservative Party will lead the country back to these basics, right across the board: sound money, free trade, traditional teaching, respect for the family and the law.' A number of government scandals in the ensuing months exposed the slogan as hard to interpret or, at worst, suggesting rather a return to 'the bad old days'. Listed in the *Independent* (24 December 1994) as a cliché of newspaper editorials.

> Our national education and training targets are saying that we have to do better than we have ever done before. It is not a question of going back to the basics we once knew. Nor is it a question of restoring standards where standards may have slipped.
> *Times Higher Education Supplement* (4 November 1994)

17

bad. *See* —— CAN'T BE (ALL) . . .

baptism of fire. General use, but especially in journalism, describing a difficult initial experience. Originally a soldier's first time in battle (compare the French *baptême du feu*) and said to derive from ecclesiastical Greek. Matthew 3:11 has, 'I [John the Baptist] indeed baptize you with water . . . but he that cometh after me . . . shall baptize you with the Holy Ghost and with fire.' A cliché by the mid-twentieth century.

> The first American troops to receive a baptism of fire in Europe in this war were the men of the United States Ranger Battalion who fought in the Dieppe raid today.
> *New York Times* (20 August 1942)

> The past four months have been a baptism of fire for Mr Georges-Christian Chazot, Eurotunnel's chief executive. Appointed in January to turn a large construction project into a profitable transport undertaking, he has been faced with a succession of postponements to the start of commercial operations.
> *Financial Times* (6 May 1994)

> 'I was in the Dundee Repertory Theatre when I had a call asking me to test for *For Them That Trespass*. To my amazement I got the part and starred in the first film I ever made. It certainly was a baptism of fire but I was very lucky because my producer, Victor Skutezky, and the director Alberto Cavalcanti took me in hand.'
> Richard Todd, quoted in *Daily Telegraph* (14 May 1994)

Bard of Avon or simply **The Bard.** General use, but nowadays earnestly to be avoided. One of several sobriquets for William Shakespeare and alluding to the river running through his birthplace at Stratford in Warwickshire. A cliché by the early 1900s. Even worse was to come with a certain type of actor always talking about 'Bill'.

> Pen introduced [the topic of Shakespeare because he] professed an uncommon respect for the bard of Avon.
> William Thackeray, *Pendennis*, Chap. 6 (1848–50)

> But there may well be more subtle influences at work than the Bard of Avon was aware of. An American scientist has recently published results which suggest that the rate at which human beings procreate is influenced by variations in terrestrial magnetism no matter how constant the human or animal attractiveness may be.
> *Irish Times* (3 October 1994)

This man who killed two people in his former life as a numbers racketeer in Cleveland . . . acquired the rudiments of a classical education. I once heard him react to an English accent with the line: 'As yo' great Bard of Avon truly said, "To be or not to be – that's what they askin', baby".'
Mail on Sunday (26 March 1995)

bare necessities. General use, referring to the minimum requirements to keep alive – food, drink and possibly a roof over one's head. Known by 1913, when *Punch* (10 December) referred to 'The Bare Necessity Supply Association [having] the honour to announce their list of Daintiest Recencies for the Yule-Tide Season'. A cliché not so much in its original form but as a veiled allusion to the song 'Bare Necessities' in the Walt Disney film of Kipling's *The Jungle Book* (US, 1967) – which was sung by a *bear*.

Profits in the bare necessities of life.
Headline, *Independent* (13 May 1995)

barefaced cheek. General use, to describe any assertive behaviour that is accomplished without a blush of embarrassment. Date of origin unknown. A cliché by (maybe) the late 1980s.

Barefaced Cheek
Title of book about Rupert Murdoch by Michael Leapman (1983)

Garden-rustling is Britain's fastest-growing crime, as thieves twig that all you need to nurture a flourishing fortune is a spade – and a wheelbarrow-load of barefaced cheek.
Today (25 May 1993)

When it was announced recently that HM the Q had graciously consented to allow taxpayers to view their own property for £8 a head . . . It was left to newspaper cartoonists to characterize it as the kind of barefaced cheek which could only happen in a country which, as Cobbett observed, has a Royal Mint but a National Debt.
Observer (6 June 1993)

barge-pole. *See* I WOULD NOT TOUCH . . .

Barons of —— and Caliphs of ——. Journalistic headline format, open to much variation. A cliché parodied since the 1960s (see first citation):

This British soccerbluesday – there is no other word for it – drove another

19

NAIL into the tottering COFFIN of Britain's Barons of Ball and Caliphs of Kick.
From the parody of sportswriters' clichés by David Frost and Peter Cook included in the book *That Was The Week That Was* (1963)

The Caliph of Coal and the Paymaster of Terror.
Headline, *Daily Express* (29 October 1984) – over an article sub-titled 'Fury grows over the miners' mission of shame [led by Arthur Scargill] to the killer of Yvonne Fletcher [Colonel Kadhafi]'.

battle-scarred (veterans). General use, often journalistic. 'Our leaders battle-scarred' wrote Oliver Wendell Holmes in an open letter *To General Grant* (1865). A cliché by the 1920s/30s. In Nat J. Ferber, *I Found Out* (1939), it is related that once on the New York *American* the printing error 'battle-scared hero' was hastily corrected in a later edition and came out reading 'bottle-scarred hero'.

> Can a bunch of battle-scarred old pols ... gang up to stop a brash young lawyer named Brian Mulroney?
> *Toronto Star* (14 February 1976)

> The man who made it possible – bringing a new lease of life to his own political career in the process – was Mr Peres, one of the most battle-scarred veterans of Israeli politics.
> *Sunday Telegraph* (5 September 1993)

> 'Just be the benevolent old maestro, Bob, battle-scarred and wordly-wise in the ways of the biz,' Moir advised.
> Bob Monkhouse, *Crying With Laughter* (1993)

> Battle-scarred veterans of the women's movement can be forgiven for sighing wearily at some of this; like the youngsters who 'think sex was invented the year they reached puberty,' she seems unaware that the Sixties movement was greatly about women's right to love freely.
> *Observer* (5 December 1993)

beached whale. *See* LIKE A . . .

bear garden. *See* LIKE A . . .

bears eloquent testimony. Pompous use among writers of opinion and speech-makers. Date of origin unknown. Listed in the *Independent* (24 December 1994) as a cliché of newspaper editorials, and well-established as such by that date.

It is one of life's curiosities that most major champions do not know when enough is enough. Seve Ballesteros bears eloquent testimony to that. Their major victories, instead of satisfying them, fill them with the conviction that they are within a day or two's march of perfection, as they embark upon sweeping changes that frequently lead to their downfall.
Sunday Times (11 July 1993)

With sufficient fanaticism among his followers, a despot might need nothing more sophisticated than a Transit van to ensure a weapon of mass destruction reaches its intended target with complete accuracy. The recent Bishopsgate bomb bears eloquent testimony to the vulnerability of open societies to the zealot.
Letter to the editor, *Daily Telegraph* (20 July 1993)

beautiful. *See* BUT MISS ——, YOU'RE . . .

because the scenery is better.   Overworked and inevitable argument in promoting the superior imaginative qualities of radio as a medium. It apparently originated in a letter to *Radio Times* in the 1920s, quoting a child who had said rather: 'The pictures are better'. A cliché by the 1970s.

'Do you ever listen [to the radio]? I do. I like it best. As a child I know says: "I see it much better on radio than on TV." '
Joyce Grenfell in letter of 22 September 1962 and included in *An Invisible Friendship* (1981)

'I like the wireless better than the theatre,' one London child wrote in a now legendary letter, 'because the scenery is better.'
Derek Parker, *Radio: The Great Years* (1977)

By way of illustration a young lad was quoted as saying he preferred radio to television – because the scenery is better. A proof of the power of imagination!
Prayer Book Society *Newsletter* (August 1995)

before dealing with that (let me just say this . . .).   Mostly a phrase used by politicians when seeking to control the shape and content of a broadcast interview. Heard with suspicion by those anticipating that the politician will never get around to dealing with the 'that' and that the trope is a diversionary ploy. Identified by the 1970s? In *The Joy of Clichés* (1984) I wrote: 'The wise politician always uses this phrase when being interviewed on television in order to slip in a statement which he has learned off by heart and which has nothing to do with the interviewer's question. If used carefully, it can lead to the interviewer moving on to the second question without having obtained an answer to the first. Never say "and now let me answer your question". That will only throw the interviewer who will have forgotten what it was.' Cited as a current cliché in *The Times* (17 March 1995).

beggars all description.   General use. A light literary turn of phrase for 'is indescribable' and originating with the meaning of the verb 'to beggar' in the sense 'exhausting the resources of'. Apparently this was an original coinage of Shakespeare in *Antony and Cleopatra*, II.ii.197 (1607) where Enobarbus says of Cleopatra: 'For her own person,/It beggar'd all description'. A cliché by the mid-twentieth century.

> Let us begin the tale in 1755 when an entranced visitor to the park [Painshill] wrote: 'Pray follow me to Mr Hamilton's. I must tell you it beggars all description, the art of hiding art is here in such sweet perfection.'
> *Financial Times* (23 April 1988)

> A place which beggars all description.
> Mrs Piozzi, *Observations and Reflections Made in the Course of a Journey Through France &c.* (1789)

> Of the massacre itself that followed, where shall I begin and what shall I tell? It simply beggars all description. Occidentals of the 19th century cannot comprehend it. Still, I will try to give a few facts.
> *The Times* (29 March 1895)

believe it would be possible!   *See* YOU WOULD NEVER BELIEVE . . .

believed.   *See* I'VE NEVER . . .

bended knee.   *See* ON BENDED . . .

best mum in the world.   *See* FOR THE BEST MUM . . .

best shot.   *See* GIVE SOMETHING ONE'S . . .

best swordsman in all France or **finest swordsman in all France.**   A film cliché to be found in swashbuckling period pieces, consciously archaic. A relatively unself-conscious use occurs in Charles Dickens, *Barnaby Rudge*, Chap. 27 (1841): 'I have been tempted in these two short interviews, to draw upon that fellow, fifty times. Five men in six would have yielded to the impulse. By suppressing mine, I wound him deeper and more keenly than if I were the best swordsman in all Europe.' Even earlier, completely straightforward is John Aubrey's use in his *Lives* (*c.*1697): 'Sir John Digby yielded to be the best swordsman of his time.' A cliché by the 1930s/40s.

> 'Don't worry . . . my father was the best swordsman in France.'
> Line spoken in the film *Son of Monte Cristo* (US, 1940), though unverified

> *The Finest Swordsman in All France*
> Title of a book (1984) by Keith Miles on the subject of clichés in general

best-kept secret. Journalistic use, mostly. In its original form about any well-withheld information, a cliché by the mid-twentieth century, but as used by travel-writers to draw attention to a holiday destination, it was included in the 'travel scribes' armoury' compiled from competition entries in the *Guardian* (10 April 1993).

> Seeing that in the last month Lasmo's share price has drifted northwards from 114p to a peak of 169p (now 149.5p) this was hardly the world's best-kept secret.
> *Observer* (1 May 1994)

> If this punchy little two-hander from Footpaul Productions of South Africa has ambitions to being the best kept secret of this year's Mayfest, then it won't work because word-of-mouth will acclaim it for the gem it is.
> *Herald* (Glasgow) (11 May 1994)

> Once known as 'Europe's best kept secret', the secret leaked out and now much of [the Algarve's] wonderful Atlantic coast has been obscured by a wall of concrete – dense, high urbanisation around Quarteira, Vilamoura, and Albufeira, low cubist complexes sprouting from the rich red cliffs round Carvoeiro.
> *Herald* (Glasgow) (28 May 1994)

best-seller. *See* RUNAWAY SUCCESS.

best-selling author. Publishing and journalistic use. The phrase 'best-selling' had been applied to books (in the US) by 1889. The phrase 'best-selling author' was known by 1958. A cliché chiefly notable for its lack of any precise meaning by the 1970s. Note how this extract manages to combine the concept with that of AWARD-WINNING:

> He [John F. Kennedy] is the author of *Profiles of Courage*, a prize-winning and best-selling work of pop history.
> *Economist* (20 June 1959)

better half.   General use and pretty inoffensive except to the politically correct who might jib at any inequality in a married relationship (even if the better of the two people is invariably the woman). Of long standing: 'My dear, my better half (said he) I find I must now leave thee' – Argalus to his wife, Sir Philip Sidney, *Arcadia* (1580). A cliché by 1900? Or not until the self-conscious 1970s/80s?

big enough.   *See* THIS TOWN AIN'T . . .

big man.   *See* HE WAS A . . .

bigger than both of us.   *See* THIS THING IS . . .

birth pangs.   General use, denoting initial difficulties in any area. Date of origin unknown. A cliché by the 1950s.

> The inevitable transformation of universities everywhere into 'multi-versities' is being achieved with appalling birth pangs in the University of California.
> *Guardian* (30 November 1968)

> The boom in the DIY retailing in the 1980s had been fuelled by the growth in home ownership and the number of house moves. Once that engine was switched off, retail price wars and '20pc off everything' promotions followed. Do It All, still in its painful birth pangs, was thrust into the firing line.
> *Daily Telegraph* (7 May 1994)

bitter end.   General use, meaning 'the last extremity, the absolute limit', and a common phrase by the mid-nineteenth century. Bitterness doesn't really enter into it: the nautical 'bitt' is a bollard on the deck of a ship, on to which cables and ropes are wound. The end of the cable that is wrapped round or otherwise secured to the bollard is the 'bitter end'. On the other hand, ends have – for possibly longer – been described as bitter in other senses. Proverbs 5:4 has: 'But her end is bitter as wormwood, sharp as a two-edged sword.' A cliché by 1900.

> The rather shallow stretch of water we call 'la Manche' has always masked a gaping chasm of a different sort – between the island and the Continent (what a strange word!) in general, and France in particular. Right to the bitter end, some island fundamentalists have feared that the tunnel will bring some foreign plague or other, be it rabies, frogs' legs or garlic.
> *Guardian* (6 May 1994)

The maverick anti-Maastricht MP, Denzil Davies, indicated that he would continue fighting for nominations until the bitter end. The former Treasury minister and MP for Llanelli is not expected to attract more than a handful.
Independent (16 June 1994)

bitter experience. General use. An inevitable pairing. Date of origin unknown. A cliché by the 1920s/30s. Listed in the *Independent* (24 December 1994) as a cliché of newspaper editorials.

Breeders know from bitter experience that matings do not always 'nick' and that . . . they are sure to suffer many a disappointment.
Daily Telegraph (4 January 1971)

The bitter experience of 1960 affected Nixon deeply. Watergate was born in the way the Kennedys and the Kennedy money treated him then. Nobody was ever going to cheat him again.
Scotsman (2 May 1994)

The battery alone in my laptop weighs just marginally less than the combined weight of a Psion computer and modem – and I know from bitter experience you always have to carry at least one spare battery.
Lloyd's List (28 June 1994)

blame. *See* HAVE ONLY HIMSELF . . .

blazing inferno. Especially journalistic use. An inevitable pairing. Date of origin unknown. A cliché by the 1950s. Singled out as a media cliché by Malcolm Bradbury in *Tatler* (March 1980) in the form: 'As I stand here in the blazing inferno that was once called Saigon/Beirut/Belfast . . .'

Hex's favourite Stephen Jones hats remain the series of fabulous kitchen follies which included a frying-pan (complete with bacon and eggs) and a colander brimming with vegetables. Does Jones have a particular favourite? From a blazing inferno in his showroom he might try to save a gigantic layered tulle confection.
Scotsman (11 May 1994)

In June a 13-year-old schoolgirl died as she saved her two young sisters and brother after a massive gas explosion ripped through their home. The blast turned their home in Ramsgate, Kent, into a blazing inferno.
Daily Mirror (29 December 1994)

Blitz. *See* IT WAS WORSE THAN THE . . .

25

blonde bombshell. Journalistic use, to describe *any* (however vaguely) blonde woman but especially if a dynamic personality and usually a film star, show business figure or model. The original was Jean Harlow who appeared in the 1933 film *Bombshell*. In Britain – presumably so as not to suggest that it was a war film – the title was changed to *Blonde Bombshell*. A cliché by the 1950s. In June 1975 Margo Macdonald complained of being described by the *Daily Mirror* as 'the blonde bombshell M.P.' who 'hits the House of Commons today'.

bloodstained tyrannies. Political and journalistic use. Date of origin unknown. A cliché by the 1920s? Cited as the phrase of a 'tired hack' by George Orwell in 'Politics and the English Language' (*Horizon*, April 1946).

> The Prime Minister [Mrs Thatcher] welcomed Romania to 'the family of free nations' and promised help for its people. She praised the Romanian 'heroes' who had not been prepared to 'knuckle under in a bloodstained tyranny'.
> *Guardian* (23 December 1989)

bloody but unbowed. General use, often as an unascribed quotation, meaning 'determined after having suffered a defeat'. From W.E. Henley's poem 'Invictus. In Memoriam R.T.H.B.' (1888):

> In the fell clutch of circumstance,
> I have not winced nor cried aloud:
> Under the bludgeonings of chance
> My head is bloody but unbowed.

A cliché since the 1920s/30s.

> Bloody but unbowed, veteran discount retailers Gerald and Vera Weisfeld have hit out at the new £56m rescue deal agreed between struggling Poundstretcher owner Brown & Jackson and South African group Pepkor.
> *Daily Mail* (10 May 1994)

> Bloody but unbowed, Dungannon had several heroes. Johns lorded the lineouts; while Beggs and Willie Dunne scrapped for everything.
> *Irish Times* (17 October 1994)

> Charles Scott, acting chairman of Saatchi & Saatchi, now renamed Cordiant, survived his first shareholders' meeting since the upheavals at the top of the advertising combine bloody but unbowed, with investors' vitriol

shared out fairly equally between him, the Saatchi brothers and David Herro, the Chicago investor.
The Times (17 March 1995)

blue water. *See* PUT CLEAR BLUE WATER . . .

body. *See* YOU ONLY WANT ME FOR MY . . .

body blow. General use, derived from boxing, meaning 'a severe knock to one's esteem or activities'. 'That body-blow left Joe's head unguarded' – Thomas Hughes, *Tom Brown* (1857). A cliché by 1900.

Its latest action is a body-blow to the growers.
Daily Chronicle (24 August 1908)

Criminalizing squatters, New Age travellers and the like is hardly a body-blow to the well-established underworld. No matter how many times Mr Howard says the word 'people' (count it, next time you hear him), he will not convince me that he is really going to deal with the real problems of crime in this country.
Independent on Sunday (1 May 1994)

The conclusions of Lonrho's report . . . destroyed Bond's credibility. In unambiguous terms they declared he was technically bust, and so it proved. It was a body blow from which Bond never recovered.
Sunday Times (6 November 1994)

bonanza. Journalistic use, to describe any wildly lucrative deal. Of American origin and known since the 1840s, the derivation is from the Spanish word for 'fair weather, prosperity'. Initially used by miners with reference to good luck in finding a body of rich ore. Used figuratively a good deal later. A cliché by the mid-twentieth century. Specifically **pay bonanza** is listed as a cliché to be avoided by Keith Waterhouse in *Daily Mirror Style* (1981).

The show is still, as topical entertainment, a real bonanza.
Listener (10 January 1963)

Jobs bonanza for ex-ministers . . . Former Cabinet ministers who served under Margaret Thatcher and John Major hold a total of 125 directorships and 30 consultancies.
Independent (2 May 1995)

book. *See* EVERYBODY HAS ONE . . .

book of life. *See* THAT'S ANOTHER PAGE TURNED IN THE ...

boon companion. General use, slightly archaic. Literally, 'a good fellow' and used originally in a jovial bacchanalian sense. The clichéd use – say, by 1900 – now refers to a close companion of either sex.

> Only after Saudi pressure, it is said, did the president relent and two months ago allow Rifaat to return from six months in exile. The Saudi crown prince, Abdullah, is a brother-in-law and boon companion of Rifaat, and the Saudis like Rifaat's pro-western views.
> *Economist* (26 January 1985)

bottom line. Business, journalistic, political use. Originally an American expression for the last line of a profit and loss account showing the final profit or loss. The clichéd figurative use (by the 1960s) means the final analysis or determining factor; the point, the crux of the argument. Arthur Jacobs took an *Independent* editorial to task for a 'splendidly meaningless example [on 14 April 1995]: "The bottom line is that there are too many boats chasing too few fish". Surely this, as the statement of the problem, would be a top line and a true bottom line would be the solution.'

> 'George Murphy and Ronald Reagan certainly qualified because they have gotten elected. I think that's the bottom line.'
> *San Francisco Examiner* (8 September 1967)

> Our 'bottom-line' has always been to protect jobs and services in our boroughs. In London, with a good deal of help from the GLC, we should survive.
> *Guardian* (21 June 1985)

> The bottom line/Protecting Miami's heritage ... The billboard's pro-tan message in the era of thinning ozone layers is no longer consistent with Coppertone's new emphasis on sunscreens ... Baring little girls' bottoms is not so politically correct either.
> Headline and text, *Economist* (14 September 1991)

> According to a leaked memo seen by the *Independent* ... 'The bottom line is that the waste cannot be dumped at sea. The only option is to take ashore and treat.'
> *Independent* (20 June 1995)

> The IRA's bottom line is a united Ireland, so what happens when they realise they're not going to get that?
> *Independent* (1 September 1995)

bounden duty.   General, somewhat consciously archaic use, meaning 'conduct which is expected of one or to which one is bound by honour or position'. Best known from its use in the Anglican *Book of Common Prayer* (1662) – 'it is very meet, right, and our bounden duty, that we should at all times, and in all places, give thanks unto thee, O Lord' – though the phrase predates this. A cliché by the mid-twentieth century.

> Had Evan Hunter been dealing with the Lizzie Borden case under his other hat as Ed McBain it would have been one's bounden duty to keep the solution dark.
> *Guardian* (23 August 1984)

> These were the people who promoted and supported public libraries, municipal swimming baths and playing fields, museums and art galleries, free access to which was part of the spiritual provision the Victorians saw as their bounden duty towards their fellow citizens.
> *Sunday Telegraph* (6 May 1990)

> John Nott also wished to resign. But I told him straight that when the fleet had put to sea he had a bounden duty to stay and see the whole thing through.
> Margaret Thatcher, *The Downing Street Years* (1993)

boy.   *See* MY BOY IS A GOOD . . .

brave new world.   General use, meaning 'a future state, particularly one where progress has produced a nightmarish utopia'. Nowadays a slightly ironic term for some new or futuristically exciting aspect of modern life. It is taken from Miranda's exclamation in Shakespeare's *The Tempest*, V.i.183 (1612): 'O brave new world,/That has such people in't!' A cliché since Aldous Huxley used it as the title of his novel *Brave New World* in 1932. 'Perhaps as much a cliché as it is a vogue-term' – Eric Partridge, *Usage and Abusage* (1947).

> Consequently, when the pair signed to Virgin a couple of years back, the record company was keen to talk them up as a multimedia outfit, the kind of band best suited to the brave new world of interactive CDs.
> *Observer* (1 May 1994)

> Will there still be a [BBC radio] drama department in 10 years or, in the multi-skilled brave new world, will producers be billeted on different departments and everyone else be casualised?
> *Guardian* (13 March 1995)

bread and butter issue(s). Journalistic and political use to describe fundamental matters of direct concern to ordinary people – as important to them as the basic food they eat. Of quite recent origin and a cliché by about 1990.

> The second problem is more fundamental: what does the party stand for? The dilemma was highlighted in a thoughtful speech to a fringe meeting by Mr Matthew Taylor, MP for Truro, who pointed out that 'we have a higher profile on Bosnia than on any bread-and-butter domestic policy issue that determines how people vote'.
> *Financial Times* (14 March 1994)

> This is precisely why Tony Blair has devoted much time and thought to softening up the ground to be more fertile to accept the reasons for widespread change in the way the country is governed. It is very much a bread and butter issue.
> Letter to the editor, *Guardian* (3 January 1995)

bread is buttered. *See* KNOW WHICH SIDE ONE'S . . .

breakfast. *See* CONDEMNED MAN ATE A . . .

breath. *See* TAKE ONE'S . . .

breathing space. General use, to denote a pause in time for consideration and when some outside pressure has been taken off. Date of origin uncertain. A cliché by the 1980s.

> Their crowd expects results, speed and guts, and particularly results. Playing in Europe, where even the most demanding crowd realizes guile is all, has given Arsenal the breathing space to develop different ideas.
> *Sunday Times* (1 May 1994)

> Alexon Group, the women's wear retailer, has secured financial breathing-space by striking an agreement with its bankers for a new two-year facility. The shares responded by rising 4p to 26p.
> *Financial Times* (31 March 1995)

(bridge) too far. Journalistic use to describe a position reached which is considered to be ill-advised. Sometimes used allusively when warning of an unwise move. The clichéd use derives from the title of Cornelius Ryan's book *A Bridge Too Far* (1974; film UK/US, 1977) about the 1944 airborne landings in Holland. These were designed to capture eleven bridges needed for the Allied invasion of Germany – an attempt which came to grief at Arnhem, the Allies suffering more casualties than in the landing at Normandy. In advance of the action, Lieut.-General Sir Frederick Browning was reported to have protested to Field-Marshal Montgomery, who was in overall command: 'But, sir, we may be going a bridge too far.' More recent research has established that Browning never saw Montgomery before the operation and most likely never made this comment to him. A cliché by the 1980s.

> A bridge too near. A public inquiry opened yesterday into plans to re-span the Ironbridge Gorge in Shropshire.
> Headline and text, *The Times* (20 June 1990)

> Ratners: A bid too far?
> Headline, *Observer* (8 July 1990)

> In *The Path to Power* [Lady Thatcher] describes Maastricht as 'a treaty too far' and calls for the rolling back of European Union law.
> *Independent* (22 May 1995)

bronzed. *See* LOOKING BRONZED . . .

brought to a satisfactory conclusion. General use. 'Satisfactory conclusion' on its own was known by 1825. A cliché by 1900. Cited as a 'resounding commonplace' by George Orwell in 'Politics and the English Language' (*Horizon*, April 1946).

> There Richard Cattell, who had unique experience in repairing inadvertently damaged common bile ducts, brought this sad episode to a more or less satisfactory conclusion.
> *Daily Telegraph* (19 May 1994)

> Andrew Cohen, Betterware's chief executive says: 'Hopefully, this saga has been now brought to a conclusion satisfactory to all parties.'
> *Sunday Telegraph* (17 July 1994)

brute force. General use. A phrase known by 1736 and an inevitable pairing by the mid-twentieth century.

> It was in fact the combination of public service motive, sense of moral obligation, assured finance and the brute force of monopoly which enabled the BBC to make of broadcasting what no other country has made of it.
> Lord Reith, *Into the Wind* (1949)

> The brutality is part of the attraction, but it was not all mindless thuggery. The highlight of the entire match had nothing to do with brute force. Right

in the middle of the softening up period when the big men were knocking lumps out of each other, Martin Offiah collected a ball eight metres from his own goal-line.
Sunday Telegraph (1 May 1994)

The DUP would never enter dialogue with an organisation 'which is fascist in nature' and which in negotiations has the advantage of a 'threat of brute force'. Sinn Fein could not be regarded as a constitutional party until the IRA was 'demolished' and its weapons handed over.
Irish Times (28 September 1994)

buck. *See* YOU HAVE TO SPEND A . . .

buck stops here. General use, to show where the ultimate responsibility lies. Harry S. Truman (US President 1945–53) had a sign on his desk bearing these words, indicating that the Oval Office was where the passing of the buck had to cease. It appears to be a saying of his own invention. 'Passing the buck' is a poker player's expression. It refers to a marker that can be passed on by someone who does not wish to deal. A cliché by the 1970s. Listed in the *Independent* (24 December 1994) in the form 'the buck must stop here' as a cliché of newspaper editorials.

bull by the horns. *See* TAKE THE BULL BY . . .

bums on seats. *See* PUT BUMS . . .

buried their own. *See* THEY CAME —

burn the midnight oil, to. General use, meaning 'to sit up and work beyond midnight, to slave over something'. Known by 1744. A cliché by 1900. Listed as a cliché in *The Times* (28 May 1984).

Mr Moore, a council member since the mid-1970s, said: 'I have three partners (one of whom is about to be a council member of the Irish institute), and I get tremendous support from them. But it does mean that I have to burn a lot of midnight oil to keep my end going.'
Independent (3 May 1994)

At a time of year when students and staff used to be in the classroom, students are now wandering around like lost sheep while the staff burn the midnight oil trying to get marking completed in a week.
Letter to the editor, *Times Higher Education Supplement* (24 February 1995)

burner. *See* PUT AN ISSUE ON . . .

burning question. General use, meaning 'the subject of the hour, what really needs to be addressed'. Popular from the nineteenth century onwards. Benjamin Disraeli used the phrase in 1873. 'The source of the Boulangist election expenditure is a burning question in France' – *St James's Gazette* (16 January 1889). A cliché by 1900.

> The burning question of the week has been whether a school teacher, now dead, beat boys during the 1960s. More than a quarter of the Times's letters page was devoted to this urgent subject on Thursday, and nearly as much again on Friday.
> *Independent on Sunday* (1 May 1994)

bustling nightlife/trade. General use. 'Bustling trade' was probably the forerunner of the travel writer's cliché 'bustling nightlife'. Dates of origin unknown. 'Bustling nightlife' was listed in the *Independent* 'DIY travel writers' cliché kit' (31 December 1988).

> I had now seen both sides of Ibiza – the bustling nightlife for which it is justly famed, and the less well-known northern coastline where white sandy beaches, hidden coves, beautiful countryside and clean shallow waters makes it an ideal family holiday haven.
> *Today* (8 May 1993)

> Suffering businesses have hit on a plan to restore Asakusa's bustling trade and jazzy nightlife. They have pooled £300,000 to open a geisha school.
> *Daily Telegraph* (29 December 1993)

but first . . . Broadcasting use: 'Hello! Later in the programme we'll be . . ., but first . . . '; 'More on that in a moment, but first . . . ' Noticed in the 1970s and a cliché since then.

but Miss ——, you're beautiful! Film script use, uttered by the boss when his hitherto bespectacled secretary reveals her natural charms. No citation to hand, but one feels that Cary Grant or Clark Gable was probably around at the time. From the Hollywood of the 1930s/40s. Cited in the song 'I Love a Film Cliché' by Dick Vosburgh and Trevor Lyttelton from the show *A Day in Hollywood, A Night in the Ukraine* (1980) in the form, 'Why, Miss Murray, without your glasses, you're . . . BEAUTIFUL!'

by hook or by crook/I'll be last in this book.   The cliché you append to the final page of an autograph book when asked to contribute a little something more than your signature. Noticed in the 1970s.

bygone era.   General use, meaning simply a period in the past. Date of origin unknown. A cliché, especially in tourist promotions, by the 1980s.

> 'I was probably born at the wrong time. I have a passion for the gentler, more rustic days of a bygone era.'
> Susan George, quoted in *Hello!* (13 May 1995)

= C =

Caliphs. *See* BARONS OF —— AND . . .

call(ing). *See* —— THEY CALL IT ——

callow youth. General, slightly archaic use, meaning an 'immature, inexperienced young person'. 'One overhears a callow youth of twenty address a still fascinating belle of forty' – A.M. Binstead, *More Gal's Gossip* (1901). A cliché by the 1920s/30s.

> There is a slightly awkward father-and-son relationship here between the gullible, disapproving, callow youth who lived and the sophisticated man who writes, and it is the open unresolvability of this tension which makes the book so recognisable and so true.
> *Guardian* (17 May 1994)

> On his first ever visit to the regal ski resort of St Moritz, King Farouk of Egypt, then a callow youth, felt a sartorial fool. He had arrived at the Suvretta House Hotel wearing a black morning suit and nervelessly flicked back the tails as he helped his mother.
> *Daily Mail* (24 December 1994)

came. *See* THEY CAME ——

—— can't be (all) bad. General slangy use, meaning that something about which doubt has been expressed is really rather good. Date of origin not known. 'Any man who hates dogs and babies can't be all bad' – Leo Rosten about W.C. Fields at a Masquer's Club dinner (16 February 1939). Compare 'She loves you . . . and you know that can't be bad' – song, 'She Loves You' by Lennon and McCartney (1963) and the congratulatory phrase 'Can't be bad!' A cliché by the 1960s/70s.

Colin Montgomerie three-putted for the first time in the week as he shot a

72 for 279, but he insisted: 'After taking four weeks off and tying for 17th place in America, that can't be bad.'
Daily Record (6 March 1995)

Further up the pecking order is the 27-ish woman who left to set up a gilt-trading operation at a rival for £300,000. 'She's nothing special, but she'll stay three years and do an okay job for them, and from her point of view it can't be bad.'
Independent (13 May 1994)

Uncomfortable parallels between Dracula and Nicolae Ceausescu, the former Stalinist dictator, meant that such a gathering was impossible in the Communist era. But now Europe's second poorest country after Albania can cash in on the legend. Can't be bad for garlic growers either.
Financial Times (22 May 1995)

All the same, Garland and Rooney as *Babes In Arms*. . . plus long-lost tracks from *Band Wagon* and *Good News* and *Brigadoon* and *It's Always Fair Weather*, can't be all bad.
Sheridan Morley in *Theatreprint* (Vol. 5, No. 95)(May 1995)

captain(s) of industry. Mostly journalistic use, to refer to prominent figures in business and commerce. 'Captains of Industry' was a heading in Thomas Carlyle's *Past and Present* (1843). A cliché by the 1950s/60s.

A hardnosed captain of industry who wanted a pretty mannequin from tidewater aristocracy.
D. Anthony, *Long Hard Cure* (1979)

So where are the captains of industry, the entrepreneurs and knights OF YESTERYEAR – the modern equivalents of those Victorian worthies who steered the once-great civic authorities? Are local councils dying, victims of local apathy and central government emasculation?
Independent on Sunday (1 May 1994)

He has created his own brand of lobbying where prospective clients are wooed by conversation littered with the names of MPs and ministers, captains of industry and mandarins and the endless parties and lunches which they all attend.
Daily Telegraph (21 October 1994)

carbon-copy murders. Journalistic use, for killings which replicate other recent crimes and may have been inspired by them. Date of origin unknown. A cliché by the 1950s/60s. Listed by Keith Waterhouse as a cliché to be avoided in *Daily Mirror Style* (1981). But who knows what carbon paper is nowadays?

> Victim of the week-old 'carbon copy' murder.
> *Daily Telegraph* (3 April 1961)

> Detectives probing that crime revealed they are checking for possible links with the 'carbon copy' murder of housewife Wendy Speakes at Wakefield, Yorkshire, a year ago ... A spokesman for Lincolnshire police said last night: 'We have requested the file on the Wakefield case because of the similarities with our inquiry. It appears to be a carbon copy murder.'
> *Daily Mirror* (12 October 1994)

caretaker for my descendants. *See* I SEE MYSELF MORE AS ...

caring and sharing. General use, especially in the social and welfare services. Probably of American origin. The word 'caring' on its own – to describe official 'care' of the disadvantaged – was stretched almost to breaking point during the 1980s in all sorts of combinations which sought to manipulate the hearer. Marginally worse was this facile rhyme of 'caring and sharing' used, for example, to promote a Telethon-type fund-raiser in Melbourne, Australia (November 1981).

> The love I feel for our adopted children is in no way less strong than the love I feel for the three children in our family who were born to us ... It is the caring and sharing that count.
> Claudia L. Jewett, *Adopting the Older Child* (1978)

> Jeffrey, a very famous model, was walking along a sandy beach, the salt wind ruffling his hair, a small boy on his shoulders. 'Caring and sharing, you see,' murmured Geary.
> *Daily Telegraph* (11 June 1994)

case of the tail wagging the dog. General use, suggesting that the proper roles in a situation have been reversed. Known by 1907. A cliché by the mid-twentieth century. Listed as still a cliché in *The Times* (28 May 1984).

> The tail wagged the dog in this case and it still often does.
> William Hollingsworth Whyte, *The Organization Man* (1956)

> This film came with a seal of approval, from Peter Benchley, the man who wrote *Jaws*, which is a bit like Michael Crichton rubber-stamping a scientist's findings on the stegosaurus. Given that the novelist whose thrills are drawn

from the natural world is reliant on the knowledge of experts, this was a particularly implausible case of the tail wagging the dog.
Independent (15 April 1995)

cast adrift in an open boat. This is listed as a film cliché by Leslie Halliwell in *The Filmgoer's Book of Quotes* (1978 edition), though it is not one really. It cannot have been used sufficiently for it to become a worn-out phrase even though the combination of words does have a certain inevitability. The words are used in the film *Mutiny on the Bounty* (US, 1935) concerning the fate of Captain Bligh.

categorical denial. Public relations, political and journalistic use. An inevitable pairing, date of origin unknown. A cliché by the 1970s.

Mr Weisfeld said he had 'reason to believe' that Philip Green, the former chairman of Amber Day, was connected with the Pepkor bid. This is despite a categorical denial of such a link from Pepkor . . . He had asked Pepkor if Mr Green was linked with its bid. 'The reply was a categorical denial. And a categorical denial from a man like Pepkor's chairman, Christo Wiese, has to be taken seriously.'
Independent (10 May 1994)

But Price Waterhouse in London issued a categorical denial. A spokesman said the firm was 'extremely upset' about the reports.
Sunday Telegraph (12 March 1995)

caught up in a sinister maze (or **web) of plot and double-cross.** Publishing and book reviewing use (in various combinations) when promoting and discussing (usually) spy fiction and thrillers. Also in general use. A cliché by the 1970s/80s.

A sinister web of power, lust and perversion binds the psychotic killer hunting him down to the traumatic childhood murder of his mother.
The Times (19 November 1994)

Turow and Grisham are often lumped together as operators in the same territory, but separately they tend very different gardens; where Turow lures the reader into an intricate and sinister maze, with Grisham you never get beyond raking and hoeing and pulling up the weeds.
Sunday Times (22 January 1995)

Giorgio Ambrosoli, the young Milanese lawyer whose sleuthing, begun in 1974, brought down the Sicilian banking tycoon Michele Sindona. The

latter's sinister web linked the Vatican, the Mafia, the Christian Democrat Party, and the secret P2 masonic lodge.
European (7 April 1995)

Niamh went for one more session. 'They promised me the sun, moon and stars. They said I'd be put in touch with other women and that, they would pass on information as it became available.' She heard nothing. 'They left me in darkness and in fear.' By the time the results of the virus test arrived, the sense of being in a sinister maze had deepened.
Irish Times (8 April 1995)

cauldron.   *See* SEETHING/SIZZLING . . .

(causing) grave concern.   Journalistic and official use – when warning of some imminent unpleasantness, especially a person's death. Date of origin not known. A cliché by the mid-twentieth century.

While neither of the men involved in either of the Bishops Avenue deals is in any way crooked, the astonishing scale of the Eastern bloc spending spree is causing grave concern among the capital's most senior crime fighters, who fear it signals the arrival of the Russian mafia, or the Organizatsiya, as it is known and feared on the violent streets of Moscow.
Evening Standard (London) (6 May 1994)

As air traffic within Europe is predicted to rise by around 60 per cent over the next ten years, the potential for future problems is still a grave concern.
European (10 June 1994)

The Glasgow women's rights campaigner Sheena Duncan said the sheriff's remarks had caused grave concern. She added: 'It is a simplistic analysis of the problem, particularly when you think about what women suffer.'
Scotsman (24 June 1994)

A public meeting in Bansha, Co Tipperary, resolved on June 26th, 1926: 'That we the citizens desire to express our grave concern at the circulation of undesirable literature, which constitutes a grave danger to the moral and national welfare of the country, and we urge upon the Government the need for immediate legislation on the lines recommended by the Catholic Truth Society of Ireland, or on other equally adequate lines.'
Irish Times (2 January 1995)

Listen, for instance, to Father Diarmuid Connolly, chairman of the board of management of St Brigid's School (which has 930 children on the roll) and parish priest of Castleknock, who says: 'The current use of the land as

39

playing pitches has been a real safety valve and the proposal to sell them for housing is causing us grave concern.'
Irish Times (28 January 1995)

century. *See* —— OF THE CENTURY.

chain reaction. General use, especially journalistic, meaning 'a series of linked events, a self-maintaining process'. Originally scientific – 'a chemical or nuclear reaction forming intermediate products which react with the original substance and are repeatedly renewed'. Known by the 1930s. A cliché in the figurative sense by the 1940s/50s.

If you publish a candid article about any community, giving actual names of people . . . you are . . . braving a chain reaction of lawsuits, riots and civil commotion.
Saturday Evening Post (22 March 1947)

If we think they can be helped by exercise, we prescribe it. As a result, they are often encouraged to improve their diet and lifestyle and give up smoking. They can also improve their self-image. It's a chain reaction.
Independent (3 May 1994)

Scotsman John Cleland was the unluckiest man of the day after powering his Vauxhall Cavalier into the lead, passing Radisich and Soper from the standing start. Four cars were involved in a chain reaction accident which led to the red flag being brought out to halt the race.
Daily Telegraph (17 October 1994)

challenge. *See* MEET THE . . .

champagne. *See* ORGASM LIKE A CORK . . .

champagne corks will be popping. General, especially journalistic, use, to denote celebration. A cliché by the mid-twentieth century.

On Tuesday, when the industry reports on the amount of business it handled last year, the champagne corks will be popping in the City.
Observer (18 June 1995)

When Hong Kong's last British financial secretary takes his leave of the colony next week the traditional popping of Champagne corks will be missing.
Independent (1 September 1995)

After a gap of almost 100 years, the champagne corks have been popping again in the Budapest underground railway.
Independent (2 October 1995)

change our lives.   *See* THIS WIN . . .

charisma bypass (operation).   In general joke use, especially in show business and politics, to describe someone not liked or admired and who is unimpressive at self-projection. Originally rather a good joke. The earliest use of it I have found in the press is in the *Washington Post* (2 May 1986) concerning a Texas gubernatorial primary: 'When Loeffler started the campaign, his name recognition was well under 10% . . . Part of the problem, according to one Republican consultant, is his rather plodding nature. "The guy is in desperate need of a charisma bypass," said the consultant. "But if he gets into the runoff against Clements, he might get some charisma in a hurry." ' A cliché by the 1990s.

> Politicians fall victim to a quick swipe with a well-turned phrase, such as the 'charisma bypass', which the unfortunate Premier of New South Wales is said to have undergone.
> *Daily Telegraph* (14 February 1987)

> When Betty Ford slipped quietly into hospital for a heart operation, the surgeon told her he had carried out Richard Nixon's charisma bypass.
> *Today* (25 November 1987)

> [Of Steve Davis, snooker player] 'Oh yes, we say he had a charisma bypass when he was 17,' said Barry Hearn [manager] last week, without bothering to get involved in any defence of his protégé.
> *Sunday Times* (11 December 1988)

charmed life.   General use, referring to a life in which luck and ease are in full measure. 'Let fall thy blade on vulnerable crests;/I bear a charmed life' – Shakespeare, *Macbeth*, V.viii.12 (1606). *Charmed Life* – title of a book by Mary McCarthy (1956). An inevitable pairing and a cliché by the 1960s.

> 'Actually, the goaltender led a charmed life. Most of the danger was involved with the fellow who played between point and cover-point.'
> *Globe and Mail* (Toronto)(16 May 1967)

> The sport remains intensely and inherently dangerous. There have been narrow escapes in recent years. But there is little doubt that Formula One

had begun to think it led a charmed life. The trouble with the charmed life was that it coincided with the sport becoming more boring.
Guardian (2 May 1994)

They were married the following year and lived happily ever after. 'I think they had a charmed life,' says Hagerty. 'They were both passionate about photography and the landscape.'
Guardian (9 July 1994)

chequered career. General use, a working life that is full of ups and downs. Book title: *A Chequered Career, or Fifteen Years in Australia and New Zealand* by H.W. Nesfield (1881). A cliché by the mid-twentieth century.

'My career with 20th Century Fox was somewhat chequered.'
Listener (17 August 1967)

It is the latest blow to Mr Tapie's much chequered career. This year he has been prosecuted by Customs over his yacht, been accused of match rigging and seen Olympique Marseille relegated to the second division.
Daily Telegraph (21 May 1994)

Myers has spent two episodes of his chequered career with Widnes, but he rarely enjoyed the freedom in their colours that he discovered playing against their sadly depleted current line-up yesterday.
Independent (12 September 1994)

cherished belief. General use, for a belief which one holds dear. Date of origin unknown. An inevitable pairing and a cliché by the mid-twentieth century.

'I brought him up to think for himself and to challenge things if I said something was true. I wanted him to say what he felt even if it was against my most cherished belief. It has been wonderful to watch my children grow up with a sense of independence.'
Daily Telegraph (12 July 1994)

The dream is for the duvet-cover or the pillow-case to spring to life – 'I want Mark's baby,' said one girl with shocking candour. The most cherished belief is that if the object of desire could just single out her face from the crowd, then she would be the one he would choose.
Daily Telegraph (29 August 1994)

chicken and egg situation. Popular, slangy, also journalistic use, to describe a problem where cause and effect are in dispute. The construction was known by 1959. Deplored as a current cliché by Howard

Dimmock of Westcliff-on-Sea in a letter to the *Sunday Times* (31 December 1989).

> The chicken-and-egg attitude towards the home background of addicts.
> *Guardian* (24 February 1967)

> She sees no problem in finding enough readers; she sees the problem as a general lack of left-wing publishing in this country. 'If you want a good read, you don't think of buying a left magazine,' she says. 'It is a chicken-and-egg situation. *New Statesman* is the only other independent around and they have welcomed *Red Pepper*. They think we will help to open up the market.'
> *Guardian* (4 May 1994)

> The other members objected to this formula because, as a rule, UN member states will not volunteer troops unless there is a definite Security Council mandate. 'It was a chicken and egg situation,' said one diplomat.
> *Independent* (18 May 1994)

children of all ages. *See* SUITABLE FOR . . .

chips. *See* WHEN THE . . .

civilization. *See* END OF . . .

clampdown. Mostly journalistic use to describe any restriction opposed by authority. Date of origin unknown. A cliché by the 1950s/60s. Condemned by Keith Waterhouse in *Daily Mirror Style* (1981).

> The clamp-down will come at any sign of . . . hooliganism.
> *Guardian* (25 October 1968)

> UEFA have joined FIFA in their condemnation of the referee clampdown.
> *Daily Telegraph* (23 December 1982)

> Companies will hear this week how the clampdown will affect them. 'We are going to be hit badly and I am seriously concerned,' said John Hales, head of Golden Bear, a Telford-based company. He had expected to import £2m worth of teddies and other soft toys from China this year but fears that he will be limited to £300,000.
> *Sunday Times* (1 May 1994)

> Charles Wardle, the Immigration Minister, is believed to have argued that acceding to rightwing demands for a tougher clampdown on visitors could damage Britain's £25 billion a year tourist trade.
> *Guardian* (13 June 1994)

classic.   *See* MODERN ...

clear blue water.   *See* PUT CLEAR BLUE WATER ...

climate of opinion.   General use, especially journalistic and political, for the prevailing view that may dictate public decisions and actions. A phrase since 1661. A cliché since the 1950s/60s.

'To us he [Freud] is no more a person/now but a whole climate of opinion.'
W.H. Auden, poem 'In Memory of Sigmund Freud' in *Another Time* (1940)

'He likes saving causes ... he's brilliant at forming what they call now "climates of opinion." '
Angus Wilson, *Hemlock and After* (1952)

Mrs Thatcher as premier was more made by the anti-statist climate of opinion in the 1970s and 1980s than vice versa. It is a truth about her often overlooked, not least by her admirers.
Daily Telegraph (4 May 1994)

But the public can look, learn, comment, write and agitate if it feels like it, make its input as the project moves from winning entry to final design, and help create a climate of opinion that will affect future competitions.
Sunday Times (4 December 1994)

close encounter.   General, especially journalistic use, to describe any significant meeting, amorous or otherwise. Popular use derived from the title of Steven Spielberg's film *Close Encounters of the Third Kind* (US, 1977) which, in turn, is said to be taken from the categories used in the American forces to denote UFOs. A 'close encounter 1' would be a simple UFO sighting; a 'close encounter 2', evidence of an alien landing; and a 'close encounter 3', actual contact with aliens. These categories were devised by a UFO researcher called J. Allen Hynek. Used allusively to describe intimacy: 'For a close encounter of the fourth kind, ring ****'; 'Polanski's new movie – Close Encounters with the Third Grade' – graffiti, quoted 1982. A mild cliché by the 1980s.

close personal attention.   *See* MATTER IS RECEIVING ...

close proximity.   General use – a tautological phrase known by 1872. A cliché by the mid-twentieth century.

Taking advantage of Arad's close proximity to the Hungarian border, in

1990 Floria began to barter Romanian fertilisers, wood, furniture and machines for food, car batteries and agricultural machinery imported from Hungary and the west.
Financial Times (3 May 1994)

Yesterday former secret policemen and not-so-former communists sat in close proximity while around them more moderate MPs of different races back-slapped and gossiped as politicians do.
Guardian (21 September 1994)

closely knit community or **tightly knit community.** Journalistic use, invariably invoked whenever a community is hit by trouble or tragedy. Date of origin unknown. A cliché by the 1980s.

A local SDLP councillor, Ms Margaret Ritchie, also condemned the killing but said it would not shatter the community which had always been very closely knit.
Irish Times (9 August 1994)

When you have a community as closely knit as this one, what you do to one person affects everybody else. You can't threaten to evict somebody and not expect to get everybody's blood pressure up, but Schelly doesn't seem to understand that.
Herald (Glasgow) (2 November 1994)

'Everyone will be touched by this [coach crash],' said Bill McLeod, 52, owner of a local guesthouse, 'It's such a tight-knit community . . . that every-one will know someone who was killed or injured.'
Independent (25 May 1995)

Relatives and friends of the Royal Welch Fusiliers held hostage in Bosnia anxiously awaited news of their fate yesterday. The 300-year-old regiment is based in the tightly knit community of Wrexham in Clwyd.
Independent (29 May 1995)

cloud cuckoo land. *See* LIVE IN . . .

coach and horses. *See* DRIVE A . . .

coded message. *See* SEND A . . .

coffin. *See* DRIVE ANOTHER NAIL . . .

coiled spring. *See* LIKE A . . .

cold blood. *See* IN COLD . . .

cold light of day. *See* IN THE COLD LIGHT . . .

collision course. *See* ON A COLLISION . . .

come hell and/or high water. General use, meaning 'come what may'. Curiously, the *Oxford English Dictionary* (2nd edition) finds no examples earlier than the twentieth century. The phrase is mentioned as a cliché in Eric Partridge's *Dictionary of Slang and Unconventional English* (1984) but, as such phrases go, is oddly lacking in citations. *Come Hell or High Water* was used as the title of a book by yachtswoman Clare Francis in 1977. She followed it in 1978 with *Come Wind or Weather*. *Hell and High Water* was the title of a US film in 1954.

> Charged him with caring only about conquering the Valley on 13,455ft Mount Kinabalu 'come hell or high water'.
> *Daily Record* (21 September 1994)

> The shares are then held, come hell or high water, for a year. Then the process is repeated and a new portfolio is bought.
> *Independent* (1 April 1995)

come to a grinding halt, to. General use, meaning 'to come to a sudden and spectacular stop' – and not usually in a vehicular sense. Date of origin unknown. A cliché by the mid-twentieth century. Identified as a current cliché in *The Times* (17 March 1995).

> Unfortunately, things did not go quite according to plan. 'We came to a grinding halt pretty quickly,' he admitted.
> *Herald* (Glasgow) (15 December 1994)

> So this is Christmas . . . Police had a field day, towing away 14 cars. Princes Street came grinding to a halt and the city's car parks also did a roaring trade.
> *Sunday Mail* (18 December 1994)

cometh the hour, cometh the man. General use, especially journalistic sportswriters', for the timely arrival of a saviour figure. The origin of the phrase is obscure. John 4:23 has 'But the hour cometh, and now is' and there is an English proverb 'Opportunity makes the man' (though originally, in the fourteenth century, it was 'makes the *thief*'). Harriet Martineau entitled her biography of Toussaint L'Ouverture (1840), *The Hour and the Man*. An American, William Yancey, said about Jefferson Davis, President-elect of the Confederacy in 1861: 'The man and the hour have met,' which says the same thing in a different way. Earlier, at the climax of Sir Walter Scott's novel *Guy Mannering*, Chap. 54 (1815), Meg Merrilies says, 'Because the Hour's come, and the Man.' Then, in 1818, Scott used 'The hour's come, but not [*sic*] the man' as the fourth chapter heading in *The Heart of Midlothian*. Both these examples appear to be hinting at some earlier core saying that remains untraced. A cliché by the 1980s.

> Beating England may not be winning the World Cup, but, for obvious reasons, it would come a pretty close second back in Buenos Aires. Cometh the hour, cometh the man? Destiny beckons. England beware.
> *Today* (22 June 1986)

> 'Graham [Gooch] is a very special guy,' [Ted] Dexter said. 'It has been a case of "Cometh the hour, cometh the man." I do not know anyone who would have taken the tough times in Australia harder than he did.'
> *The Times* (13 August 1991)

> In the maxim of 'Cometh the hour, cometh the man,' both the Scotland [Rugby Union] manager, Duncan Paterson, and forwards coach, Richie Dixon, indicated yesterday the need to look to the future.
> *Scotsman* (29 February 1992)

coming home. *See* LIKE . . .

common decency. General use. A common pairing. 'There is one branch of learning without which learning itself cannot be railed at with common decency, namely, spelling' – S.T. Coleridge, *The Friend* (1809–10). A cliché by 1900.

> Even though he [E.M. Forster] never renounced the ideal which suffuses his novels, that of society being guided by a principle of common decency, he was undoubtedly cast adrift by the war and the end of England.
> *Scotsman* (8 May 1993)

> Now we know. How many more examples of deceit, immorality, financial impropriety and lack of common decency will have to pass before the bemused gaze of the electorate before this ragbag administration finally runs out of credit?
> Letter to the editor, *Observer* (22 May 1994)

competitive edge. General use, especially business and journalistic, meaning 'the quality that gives a product or service the ability to defeat its rivals'. Date of origin unknown. A cliché by the 1980s.

Banks and securities firms lag behind their rivals elsewhere in innovation, and have lost what competitive edge Japan's relatively low interest rates and strong currency gave them abroad a few years ago.
Economist (1 May 1993)

Over the coming months all Harris Semiconductors' employees around the world – from managers to office cleaners – will play the game to experience for themselves the tough business decisions executives must make to maintain their competitive edge.
Daily Telegraph (6 May 1995)

completely refurbished.   General use, but especially by travel writers, property writers and estate agents. Date of origin unknown. Part of the 'travel scribes' armoury' compiled from a competition in the *Guardian* (10 April 1993).

The Earl o'Moray ground floor has been completely refurbished with many period details restored in line with the property's stature as a Georgian B-listed building. It is now designated as an inn as opposed to a hotel.
Herald (Glasgow) (15 December 1994)

Renamed Bird Port to recognise its ownership by the Bird Group, the terminal has been the beneficiary of a heavy investment programme which has completely refurbished the former container terminal and drydock, which continues to be served by its 43 tonne overhead gantry which spans both the berth and the adjacent terminal.
Lloyd's List (6 January 1995)

It has five bedrooms, four bathrooms, library, laundry and a covered terrace on the north side of the house overlooking the sea. The cedar shingle roof was renewed five years ago and the interior has been completely refurbished.
Sunday Times (8 January 1995)

comprehensive review.   General, political use and especially in scientific contexts, by the 1960s. Listed in the *Independent* (24 December 1994) as a cliché of newspaper editorials.

A key argument for a comprehensive review of the system is to clarify charities' responsibilities, making it easier to set up and run a charity in an accountable and effective manner.
Scotsman (6 October 1994)

After the original plan was presented last July by a Waterfront Plan advisory board, the port's administrative and planning staffs made a comprehensive review to determine whether recommendations were consistent with the port's needs and mandated responsibilities.

Lloyd's List (10 November 1994)

concerted effort. General use, meaning 'jointly planned or arranged effort'. A pairing known by 1912. 'President Roosevelt today pledged his Administration to a "concerted effort" with other peace-loving nations to "quarantine" aggressor nations' – *New York Times* (6 October 1938). A cliché by the 1950s/60s.

> The great significance of Neddy is that it is the first time in this country that a concerted effort has been made by the Government, management and the unions to set the country moving on a course which can steadily be maintained.
>
> *The Times* (11 June 1963)

> Where there is a concerted effort coming from radiologists to advise general practitioners on more efficient use of X-ray services, there is little effort given to the education of the public in the value and hazards of routine X-rays in general practice.
>
> *The Times* (18 October 1994)

> Buxton, who believes that the unrest on the terraces at Roker Park is being exploited by visiting managers, fears that there might be a concerted effort in some quarters aimed at undermining confidence in the Sunderland camp.
>
> *Northern Echo* (14 February 1995)

concrete jungle. Journalistic use, to describe deprived urban areas where the 'law of the jungle' may apply. Known by 1969. Compare the similar 'asphalt jungle' and 'blackboard jungle' [i.e. the educational system]. The *Oxford English Dictionary* (2nd edition) finds the 'asphalt' phrase in use in 1920 though it was popularized through W.R. Burnett's novel *The Asphalt Jungle* (1949). *The Blackboard Jungle* was the title of a novel (1954; film US, 1955) by Evan Hunter. 'Concrete jungle' a cliché by the 1960s/70s.

> The May sun beats down upon the Glasgow Deccan, the hot tarmac plains that stretch to the east, to the fringe of the steaming concrete jungle.
>
> *Scotsman* (8 May 1994)

> Sir: Roy Porter's comments ('Frankly we don't give a hoot for barn owls', 19 October) might impress some fellow townies and lovers of the concrete

jungle, but this anti-rural spleen does not fool those who better understand the countryside.
Letter to the editor, *Independent* (21 October 1994)

condemned man ate a hearty breakfast.   General use, meaning that someone in apparently deep trouble managed to make a possibly ostentatious display of not worrying. Established by 1900. A book of short stories about the Royal Navy called *Naval Occasions and Some Traits of the Sailor* (1914) by 'Bartimeus', has: 'The Indiarubber Man opposite feigned breathless interest in his actions, and murmured something into his cup about condemned men partaking of hearty breakfasts.' The tone of this suggests it was, indeed, getting on for a cliché even then. The tradition seems to have been established in Britain (and/or the American West) that a condemned man could have anything he desired for a last meal. Undoubtedly a cliché by the mid-twentieth century. *The Prisoner Ate a Hearty Breakfast* is the title of a novel (1940) written by Jerome Ellison. In the film *Kind Hearts and Coronets* (1949), Louis Mazzini, on the morning of his supposed execution, disavows his intention of eating 'the traditional hearty breakfast'.

> Far from closing for ever, *Balalaika* [was merely to be] withdrawn for a fortnight during which time a revolving stage was to be installed at Her Majesty's! It was almost ridiculously like an episode from fiction, the condemned man, in the midst of eating that famous 'hearty breakfast', suddenly restored to life and liberty.
> Eric Maschwitz, *No Chip on My Shoulder* (1957)

> As tradition would have it, the condemned man ate a hearty breakfast. Lennie Lawrence, the Charlton manager, tucked into his scrambled egg and sausages before the match at Maine Road and said that to lose against fellow regulation contenders Manchester City would leave him with a 'massive, massive task'.
> *Sunday Times* (25 February 1990)

consign someone/something to the scrapheap/scrapyard, to. General use – to abandon, throw out, make redundant. Date of origin unknown. A cliché by the mid-twentieth century.

> With so much at stake, both [boxers] admit that, psychologically, defeat could consign the loser to boxing's scrapyard.
> *Sunday Express* (25 November 1984)

convenience.   *See* YOUR EARLIEST . . .

cork bursting from a bottle of champagne. *See* ORGASM LIKE A . . .

cream of the crop. General use – the very best of anything. Date of origin unknown. And which crop produces cream? A cliché by the mid-twentieth century.

> Recipe: Cream of the crop – Edward Hardy on a sauce that's so good for the sole.
> Headline, *Guardian* (16 July 1994)

> Reporting on the Lincoln Center controversy, Greg Thomas in The Guardian said that to call the jazz programme racist was 'patently ridiculous'. He also made the point that to discuss jazz musicians in this way should be unnecessary, since in jazz history, 'like post-Fifties basketball, the cream of the crop have always risen. Jazz is a music organically linked to the black American experience.'
> *The Times* (16 July 1994)

> Football: Cream Of The Crop: John Spencer Shows Off New Hairstyle.
> Headline, *People* (13 November 1994)

credibility. *See* TEST OF . . .

criminal folly. General use, especially in campaigning speeches and journalism. An inevitable pair of words meaning 'folly that has deeply serious implications or is sufficient to be likened to a criminal act'. Known in the nineteenth century. A cliché by the mid-twentieth. Listed in the *Independent* (24 December 1994) as a cliché of newspaper editorials.

> Miners' lamps . . . so convenient . . . that it would really seem to be nothing short of criminal folly to run the slightest risk with flame lamps.
> *Daily News* (10 May 1888)

> He condemned the 1982 Israeli invasion of Lebanon as a 'criminal folly' and used the same words yesterday to describe the Israeli bombardment of the villages of southern Lebanon last July.
> *Independent* (7 September 1993)

> He also warned Unionists not to entertain ideas of an independent Ulster. 'In Ulster, the greater number who may still have to contend with terrorism would be guilty of criminal folly if they opened up a second front with Britain as the other enemy.'
> *Sunday Telegraph* (16 October 1994)

critical acclaim. General, especially journalistic, use. Date of origin unknown. A cliché by the 1960s/70s.

Fassbinder . . . is about to parlay his critical acclaim into box office success as an international director.
Time Magazine (27 June 1977)

This Glasgow-based company, whose main purpose is to make art accessible to all, this year celebrates its fifth birthday and its best year ever: critical acclaim – it was awarded a Mayfest award for its innovative excellence – has been matched by commercial success.
Herald (Glasgow) (21 July 1994)

[Richard Eyre's] 'shy strength', as described by Sir Peter [Hall] in his South Bank memoirs, seemed too gentle to survive the inevitable shot directed at such an exposed position. But for most of his tenure he has reconciled the irreconcilables of box office success, critical acclaim, good publicity and the approval of his paymasters.
The Times (7 December 1994)

crowd pleaser.   General use, especially journalism, for any form of art and entertainment that contains obviously popular elements inserted simply with the intention of 'playing to the gallery'. Known by 1943 in North America. A cliché in the 1990s.

George Eliot and Charles Dickens are the giants of the Victorian novel. Eliot was an uncompromising highbrow; Dickens a shameless crowd-pleaser. In the end, only the quality matters.
Evening Standard (London) (30 June 1994)

The wish to increase the number of available third level places is a noble one and a sure fire crowd pleaser, but unless the Department of Education is willing to put its money where its mouth is by extending college facilities and employing more staff, the admission of yet more young hopefuls would be lunacy.
Irish Times (29 August 1994)

crowning glory.   General use, meaning 'whatever puts the final touches to a triumph or is the culmination of a series of triumphs or outstanding features'. Known by 1902. 'Gerty's crowning glory was her wealth of wonderful hair' – James Joyce, *Ulysses* (1922). A cliché by the mid-twentieth century.

Tennis . . . It is as though the subjects of the Queen of Eastbourne reached a collective decision at the beginning of the week to offer the 37-year-old a final crowning glory before she bids farewell to the place she has made her own.
The Times (16 June 1994)

That was the era when Coney Island was billed as The Eighth Wonder Of The World. Brooklyn was the second largest city in America, and Coney was its crowning glory.
Sunday Times (4 September 1994)

cruellest month.   *See* —— IS THE . . .

crumbling edifice.   General use, an inevitable pairing for any institution (or, even, idea) fallen on hard times. Occasionally used literally. Date of origin not known. A cliché by the late twentieth century.

Ten days ago, Geoffrey Johnston, president of Glasgow Chamber of Commerce, and one of its spokesmen at the select committee, launched a robust attack on the enterprise network, describing it as 'a crumbling edifice built on sand'. He went on to describe it as a 'shambles in need of urgent reform', using words such as 'amateur' to describe its operations.
Sunday Times (19 June 1994)

As Tony Blair proposes to deal in a summary fashion with hereditary peers, Viscounts may well be transient residents in the crumbling edifice of Marsham Street, soon thankfully to be demolished.
Lloyd's List (27 July 1994)

crushing blow.   General use – for a serious setback or defeat. Date of origin not known. A cliché by the 1970s/80s.

'We're scuppered,' said Fallon . . . It was a crushing blow.
W. Winward, *Ball Bearing Run* (1981)

Then came the crushing blow. President Oscar Luigi Scalfaro announced yesterday that it would be 'unconstitutional' for him to act as the trust committee's chief guarantor.
Sunday Times (31 July 1994)

The Foreign Office is, correctly, advising travellers from Britain not to go to Gujarat. This will be a crushing blow to the Gujarati businessmen who want to attract foreign investment. Tourism will dwindle too.
Guardian (1 October 1994)

crux of the matter/case/problem.   General use, especially in argument. The central or divisive point of interest. Date of origin unknown. A cliché by the mid-twentieth century.

The crux of the matter is that the behaviour under consideration must pass through the needle's eye of social acceptance.
Ruth Benedict, *Patterns of Culture* (1934)

'Precisely,' answered the officer, 'and that brings us to the crux of the matter. Namely, that the Eurocorps is a historical or political symbol, but remains a military nonentity.'
European (22 July 1994)

The crux of the matter is that the Europeans believe that the Bosnians are almost certain to be the losers even if the arms embargo is lifted, while the Americans profess to believe that the Bosnians could beat the Serbs if there was equality in weaponry.
Guardian (29 November 1994)

crystal-clear. General use. About as clear (in meaning) as it is possible to get. Known in connection with glass (Browning, 1845) and water (1859). Figurative use a cliché by 1900? Identified as a current cliché in *The Times* (17 March 1995).

The Administration was never crystal-clear on exactly how we would massively retaliate with nuclear weapons.
Listener (29 March 1962)

In this book we have the service itself and the crystal clear explanations of Raymond Chapman as to the meaning of various passages and who does what and why.
Advertisement for book *Draw Near With Faith* (1995)

cudgels. *See* TAKE UP THE . . .

cutting edge. Media use for what is considered to be at the centre of attention or activity. The term is derived from the ancient notion that the sharp edge is the most important part of a blade but the earliest example in the *Oxford English Dictionary* (2nd edition) is only from 1966. Before it had been watered down by overuse, Dr Jacob Bronowski used the phrase in his TV series *The Ascent of Man* (1973): 'The hand is more important than the eye . . . The hand is the cutting edge of the mind.' A cliché by the late 1980s.

Yet something has changed. Sex – except perhaps, and necessarily, for lesbians and gay men – is no longer at the cutting edge of politics, especially for women.
Guardian (14 March 1989)

Now that the cutting edge of British folk humour no longer lies with the seaside postcard, the onus has long since passed to the T-shirt . . . Much

use, however, is made of language taboos 'Same s***, different day', or the SEMINAL CLASSIC, 'Brits On The Piss Tour 90' (or whichever year).
Sunday Times (21 August 1994)

His apologists would no doubt claim Nyman as a cutting-edge post-modernist, knowingly subverting the traditional genre and exposing the hollowness within; but what is the difference?
Financial Times (19 April 1995)

Barbara Kohnstamm believes we may be at the cutting edge of mother-son relationships: The interesting question is what will happen to sons as men and women's roles continue to change? As men share parenting more, will sons begin to identify with fathers in a nurturing role? Will different family patterns be set up? We could be on the cusp of great change.
Irish Times (26 April 1995)

= D =

daggers drawn. *See* AT DAGGERS . . .

dancing in the streets. *See* THERE'LL BE . . .

dark and stormy night. *See* IT WAS A . . .

dark horse. Journalistic and political use. An inevitable pairing which refers, figuratively, to a runner about whom everyone is 'in the dark' until he comes from nowhere and wins the race – of whatever kind. It is possible that the term originated in Benjamin Disraeli's novel *The Young Duke: A Moral Tale Though Gay* (1831) in which 'a dark horse, which had never been thought of . . . rushed past the grandstand in sweeping triumph'. It is used especially in political contexts. A cliché by 1900.

> Rank dark horse in bid to run lottery . . . Brian Newman, lottery follower at Henderson Crosthwaite, says: 'Because of its low profile, Rank was unfancied at the outset. But it has emerged as the dark horse.'
> *Sunday Times* (15 May 1994)

> The biggest challenges to Britain appear likely to come from Australia and the United States, with South Africa, back in both events for the first time since 1976, emerging as a possible dark horse.
> *The Times* (30 December 1994)

dark night of the soul. General use, denoting mental and spiritual suffering prior to some big step. The phrase *La Nóche oscura del alma* was used as the title of a work in Spanish by St John of the Cross. This was a treatise based on his poem 'Songs of the Soul Which Rejoices at Having Reached Union with God by the Road of Spiritual Negation' (*c.*1578). In *The Crack-up* (1936), F. Scott Fitzgerald wrote: 'In a real dark night of the soul it is always three o'clock in the morning, day after day.' Douglas Adams wrote *The Long Dark Tea-time of the Soul* (1988), a novel. A semi-cliché by the mid-twentieth century.

Governor Nelson Rockefeller ... has emerged from the dark night of the soul that afflicts all politicians pondering the SUPREME SACRIFICE.
Guardian (22 December 1970)

Mahler's last movement, his 'dark night of the soul', is full of terrifying apparitions: reptilian bass woodwinds, the shrill, demented sound of panic, craggy climaxes bravely wrought only to disintegrate.
Independent (27 August 1994)

But comedy is a serious business, forged from long dark nights of the soul, wrestling with manic ideas as the dawn comes up on another sleepless night.
Today (26 January 1995)

I ask Terry Pratchett if he ever has any dark nights of the soul, any doubts about freezing up as a writer ...
Independent (12 June 1995)

darkness. *See* FORCES OF ...

dash than cash. *See* MORE ...

daunting prospect/task. General use. A very difficult task in prospect. Date of origin unknown. A cliché by the mid-twentieth century.

Reclaiming prostitutes was a daunting prospect for charitable women however tough-minded.
F.K. Prochaska, *Women and Philanthropy in Nineteenth Century England* (1980)

She's always been honest with me. When I was about 21 I cooked dinner for her, which was a daunting prospect. I made a salmon souffle which I thought was rather good, but she said: 'This is disgusting.'
Daily Mail (24 January 1995)

Owning a second home is an attractive, but daunting, prospect. However, a Scottish property firm believes that it has the answer at its holiday cottages in St Andrews in Fife and Drummore, near Portpatrick.
Herald (Glasgow) (22 February 1995)

Jane Forder rings to see whether I will still produce 'HBR' diary entries to run alongside those of James Lees-Milne ... It's a very daunting task.
National Trust Magazine (Summer 1995)

day and age. *See* IN THIS ...

day of destiny. *See* RENDEZVOUS WITH DESTINY.

Day One. *See* ON . . .

deadly earnest. General use, meaning 'with very real seriousness'. Known by 1880. A cliché by the mid-twentieth century.

A recital which had more of the air of friendly music-making at home than the deadly earnest aspiration usually encountered on this platform.
The Times (1963)

The Getaway is in deadly earnest about its deadly games. Without a trace of irony, it often looks crude and cruel. A sub-plot in which Madsen (less certain of his depravity here than in *Reservoir Dogs*) kidnaps a doctor and seduces his wife in front of him, is distastefully revelled in.
Independent on Sunday (3 July 1994)

All good knockabout stuff, but Elvis is in deadly earnest about his new venture. Okay, so he has more important priorities in life now like setting up a new wine bar with a partner, and the Dump Truck and his fellow young professional monsters will never have to worry about a 36-year-old BATTLE-SCARRED dad-of-three from England, but he reckons he could make a sizeable mark in the amateur ranks for a couple of years.
Sunday Times (27 November 1994)

deafening silence. General use, to mean 'a silence which by being so noticeable is significant'. Known by 1968. A cliché soon after this date.

Conservative and Labour MPs have complained of a 'deafening silence' over the affair.
The Times (28 August 1985)

Many in the Rosyth area would like to know why he has maintained a deafening silence on the issue since it was first mooted in 1986.
Letter to the editor, *Scotsman* (19 August 1994)

As the internationals begin to multiply in the run up to the World Cup, it is deflating to realise that in too many aspects, the game in Britain is in a mess. The deafening silence which has greeted a sequence of discreditable events in recent months is shaming enough.
Daily Telegraph (5 November 1994)

death diminishes. *See* HIS DEATH . . .

death knell. General use, meaning 'an event that signals the end or destruction of something'. Originally, the tolling of a bell that signals a person's death. The figurative use has been known since the nineteenth century. 'A slogan cry which would . . . sound the death-knell of ascendancy and West Britishism in this country' – *Dundalk Examiner* (1895). A cliché by the mid-twentieth century.

> Boston's union longshoremen have sounded the death knell of their traditional but unwieldy dock shape-up.
> *Boston Sunday Herald* (30 April 1967)

> The Polish Parliament . . . yesterday voted . . . for a new trade union law that sounds the death knell of Solidarity.
> *The Times* (9 October 1982)

> 'This announcement will almost certainly be the death-knell to the 25-square-mile site,' he said before asking: 'What will the Scottish Office do, given that it has done nothing about help in the past for that area?'
> *Scotsman* (9 February 1995)

> The European Union and Canada yesterday ended their six-week fishing dispute with a deal hailed in Ottawa as a 'victory for conservation' but condemned in Spain as the 'death knell for the fishing industry'.
> *The Times* (17 April 1995)

deathless prose.   General use. An often ironical description of writing, sometimes used self-deprecatingly about one's own poor stuff. A borderline cliché by the late twentieth century.

> Robert Burns once expressed in deathless verse a Great Wish. His wish, translated into my far from deathless prose, was to the effect . . .
> Collie Knox, *For Ever England* (1943)

> No piece of prose, however deathless, is worth a human life.
> Kenneth Tynan, *Observer* (13 March 1966)

> [From an actor's diary:] 'The writer . . . concentrates his most vicious verbal gymnastics [in these scenes]. After we've mangled the deathless prose we have another cup of tea.'
> *Independent on Sunday* (13 May 1990)

declaration of principle.   *See* RINGING . . .

—— deeply regret(s) any embarrassment/inconvenience caused.
A cliché of apology. The standard form is something like: 'British Rail apologizes for the late running of this train and for any inconvenience that may have been caused' (never mind the pain of having to listen to the apology being trotted routinely out). A cliché by the 1980s. Lieut. Col.

Sitiveni Rabuka, leader of a coup in Fiji (May 1987) was quoted as saying: 'We apologize for any inconvenience caused.'

defining (moment).   General use, especially in British politics, though probably of American origin. Meaning 'a time when the nature or purpose of something is made clear'. A coinage and a cliché by the 1980s. Identified as a current cliché in *The Times* (17 March 1995).

> The political advisers of Vice-President George Bush claim that his confrontation on Monday with Mr Dan Rather, the CBS Television news anchorman, was a 'defining moment' which has galvanized his campaign for the Republican Party's presidential nomination.
> *Financial Times* (28 January 1988)

> While investment from unions in the £2.7bn project is only likely to be counted in hundreds of thousands of pounds, it could mark a defining moment for the movement. Other unions approached are the Transport and General; the RMT transport union; Aslef, the train drivers' union; and TSSA, the rail white collar union.
> *Independent* (9 September 1994)

> But Mr Skinner was wrong to dismiss the proposals as an irrelevant distraction from Labour's battle against the divided Conservative government. As Mr Blair told the world after Monday's vote, the change was a defining moment in the party's history.
> *Financial Times* (15 March 1995)

> The defining moment of mid-life crisis for me was Tony Blair's election. I felt quite safe with dear old John Smith. Now they are coming from behind, a younger man has got there before you.
> Tony Banks, Labour MP, quoted in *Independent* (6 May 1995)

> The Daily Mail believes the Conservatives face 'a defining moment' in their history.
> *Independent* (23 June 1995)

> [Bob Geldof] has never once watched a video of the [Live Aid] concert that was, in its way, a defining moment for a generation.
> *Independent* (15 July 1995)

In fact, any use of the word 'defining' now borders on the cliché:

> Today we bear witness to an extraordinary act in one of history's defining dramas, a drama that began in a time of our ancestors when the word went

forth from a sliver of land between the River Jordan and the Mediterranean Sea.
President Clinton, speech at signing of Middle East peace accord (13 September 1993)

Bosnian Serb television yesterday showed dramatic footage, likely to be remembered among the defining images of the war, of UN military observers chained to poles beside ammunition dumps and key bridges.
Independent (27 May 1995)

But Marlowe's *Edward II*, the defining role in McKellen's career 26 years ago, makes spiritual and technical demands beyond this performer's capacity.
Observer (28 May 1995)

descendants. *See* I SEE MYSELF MORE AS A CARETAKER FOR MY . . .

deserving of serious consideration. Pompous public affairs and journalistic use. Date of origin not known. A cliché by 1900. Cited as a 'resounding commonplace' by George Orwell in 'Politics and the English Language' (*Horizon*, April 1946).

If three newspapers read by nearly 20m readers present politics in such simplistic terms, is it any wonder that serious issues deserving serious consideration do not get a serious hearing?
Sunday Times (2 February 1992)

diametrically opposed/opposite/antagonistic. General use. Completely opposed with no overlapping of views. Known by 1645. A cliché by the late twentieth century.

A sense of determinism that is diametrically opposed to the ruler-class 'LAW-AND-ORDER and individualism'.
Black World (December 1973)

Confusion surrounding the US action in Haiti has not destroyed optimism . . . but the existence of two diametrically opposed political camps did not dampen the euphoria in Port-au-Prince last week.
Financial Times (24 September 1994)

Economists undeniably have a bad name. Blamed for the nation's economic ills . . . they are regarded as reliable only for the capacity to come up with diametrically opposed views on any question put to them.
Observer (15 January 1995)

die is cast. General use. The fateful decision has been made, there is no turning back now. Here 'die' is the singular of 'dice' and the expression has been known in English since at least 1634. When Julius Caesar crossed the Rubicon, he is supposed to have said *Jacta alea est* – 'the dice have been thrown' (although he actually said it in Greek). A cliché by 1900. Identified as a current cliché by Howard Dimmock of Westcliff-on-Sea in a letter to the *Sunday Times* (31 December 1989).

> Making reality take over in takeovers ... Whatever finance directors may argue, the die is cast and they will have to comply from next year.
> *The Times* (22 September 1994)

> Ardiles might still be at Tottenham – in one capacity or another – had he buried his pride and accepted a sideways shift after the 3–0 Coca-Cola Cup humiliation at Notts County last Wednesday that, he conceded, ended his Spurs career; 'the die was cast' even before Saturday's home win over West Ham.
> *Guardian* (2 November 1994)

difference. *See* —— WITH A ...

dignity in destiny. *See* RENDEZVOUS WITH DESTINY.

dire straits. General use. Meaning 'desperate trouble, circumstances'. Date of origin not known. A cliché by the early 1980s when this was compounded by the name Dire Straits being taken by a hugely successful British pop group.

> In fact, as a Mori survey in one of the Sunday newspapers pointed out, the middle classes in Britain have seldom been in such dire straits.
> *Daily Telegraph* (29 June 1994)

> War heroes' rents soar ... In Staffordshire, another St Dunstaner blinded by shell fire at Normandy in 1944, said: 'I can't understand how they have got into such dire straits.'
> *Mail on Sunday* (2 April 1995)

dirty work at the crossroads. General use, meaning 'despicable behaviour, foul play' (in any location). Mostly a Hollywood idiom, but perhaps not quite a full cliché. The earliest film citation found is from *Flying Down to Rio* (1933), although P.G. Wodehouse had it in the book *Man Upstairs* in 1914 and Walter Melville, a nineteenth-century melodramatist, is said to have had it in *The Girl Who Took the Wrong Turning, or, No Wedding Bells for Him* (no date). A *Notes and Queries* discussion of the phrase in 1917 threw up the view that it might have occurred in a music-hall sketch of the 1880s and that the chief allusion was to the activities of highwaymen.

> Why couch it in arcane, ridiculous questions? If you think there is dirty work at the crossroads, say so. Don't shilly shally, don't ask the minister concerned what information he possesses about what may have occurred at the crossroads on such and such a date.
> Peter McKay, *Evening Standard* (London) (13 July 1994)

> Miss Downs's withdrawal upset the congregation. 'This was dirty work at the crossroads and gross discrimination of the worst kind,' a man who attended the service, but refused to take communion, said yesterday.
> *Independent* (5 August 1994)

divorce. *See* WE'LL GET MARRIED . . .

dizzy heights. General use – meaning 'a position of success' (while hinting at its dangers). Date of origin unknown. A cliché by the mid-twentieth century. Sometimes used non-figuratively, as in the first citation:

> Steel-erectors . . . walk along girders at dizzy heights as though they were strolling along Piccadilly.
> *Radio Times* (25 July 1958)

> But with Saints on a roll, Ball dearly wants to climb even further from their dizzy heights of eighth spot, Everton will find it tough.
> *Daily Mirror* (8 October 1994)

> Poor Kylie's having a tough time. Her new single entered the charts at the dizzy heights of number 17, the Virgin 1215 poster campaign screaming 'We've done something to improve Kylie's songs. Banned them' started, and now she's being sued over her last single 'Confide In Me'.
> *Daily Record* (26 November 1994)

> If the comparisons are extreme it is because England's cricket has had so little to commend it, or to truly excite its audience, that the dizzy heights of Gough's daring retaliation deserved exaggeration.
> *Daily Telegraph* (3 January 1995)

dog. *See* CASE OF THE TAIL WAGGING THE . . .

dogged determination. General use – an alliterative inevitable, meaning 'grimly tenacious' (like a dog holding on to something). Known by 1902. A cliché by the mid-twentieth century.

Before Boycott's appointment can be confirmed, the problem of recon-
ciling his media role with the coaching job needs to be resolved. Given his
dogged determination, no one should be surprised if he manages to juggle
both roles – unlike his future boss, Illingworth, who had to give up his
column in the *Daily Express*.
Sunday Telegraph (30 April 1995)

As opinion polls provided the relentless message of a ruling party up to
30 points behind Labour, a dogged determination reigned at Conservative
Central Office.
Financial Times (4 May 1995)

doom and gloom or **gloom and doom (merchants).**   General use. A
rhyming phrase (sometimes reversed) that became especially popular in
the 1970s/80s and a cliché almost simultaneously. 'Doom and gloom
merchants' was part of the 'travel scribes' armoury' compiled from a
competition in the *Guardian* (10 April 1993). An early appearance was in
the musical *Finian's Rainbow* (1947, film 1968) in which Og, a pessimistic
leprechaun, uses it repeatedly, as in: 'I told you that gold could only bring
you doom and gloom, gloom and doom.'

It was only last month that Mr Alex Park, chief executive of British Leyland,
was attacking the news media for 'pouring out gloom and doom about the
car industry'.
BBC Radio 4, *Between the Lines* (9 October 1976)

Amongst all the recent talk of doom and gloom one thing has been largely
overlooked . . .
Daily Telegraph (7 November 1987)

The doom-and-gloom merchants would have us convinced that only an
idiot would ever invest another hard-earned penny in property.
Daily Record (7 March 1995)

Yet athletics usually gets its own back on the doom-and-gloom merchants,
and can do so here when people such as Privalova and Johnson take the
stage.
Guardian (10 March 1995)

down memory lane.   Journalistic cliché, though once a pleasant phrase
referring to where you go, figuratively, for a reminiscent, nostalgic trip. It
seems have developed from 'Memory Lane', the title of a popular waltz
(1924) written by Buddy De Sylva, Larry Spier and Con Conrad – not
to be confused with 'Down Forget-Me-Not Lane' by Horatio Nicholls,

Charlie Chester and Reg Morgan (1941). *Down Memory Lane* was the title of a compilation of Mack Sennett comedy shorts (US, 1949). The *Oxford English Dictionary* (2nd edition) gives 'Down Memory Lane' as a 'title by Dannett and Rachel' (1954). A cliché by the 1960s/70s.

> Our opponents began this campaign hoping that America has a poor memory. Well, let's take them on a little stroll down memory lane. Let's remind them of how a 4.8 percent inflation rate in 1976 became back-to-back years of double-digit inflation.
> Ronald Reagan, speech accepting the GOP Presidential Nomination, Dallas, Texas (23 August 1984)

> NWPC: Hear Them Roar . . . The women last night sure thought so. Everything was wonderful. Whoops, cheers and standing ovations were politically correct and enthusiastically bestowed for even the bumpiest ride down memory lane.
> *Washington Post* (12 July 1991)

draconian powers. General use – especially journalistic, for SWEEPING POWERS, DRASTIC POWERS or very harsh or severe powers, chiefly legal ones. Named after Draco, the seventh century BC Athenian legislator. Date of origin for this use unknown. A cliché by the mid-twentieth century.

> Dean Marsh, solicitor (advises on music licences): 'It's a further infringement of civil liberties. It gives the police draconian powers to seize equipment they consider to be involved and there seems to be no provision for these to be returned.'
> *Independent* (3 November 1994)

> In a speech yesterday, Mr Mandela made an apparently veiled threat that he might be forced to use draconian powers to clamp down on violence in the troubled province of KwaZulu/Natal.
> *The Times* (25 February 1995)

drag. *See* WILD HORSES WOULDN'T . . .

drastic measures. General use. Known by 1915. A cliché shortly after this.

> Drastic measures should be taken to complete whatever trade negotiations and shipping are necessary to hasten receipt of raw sugars and off-shore refined sugars.
> *Sun* (Baltimore) (30 January 1946)

'There were four horses around him and he did not see the fence. He's one of those animals who, if they cannot see, won't bother to jump.' Master Oats weighs nearly half-a-ton. At 30 mph every pound of it whacked the obstacle but somehow he stayed upright. Drastic measures were now demanded.
Sunday Telegraph (2 April 1995)

Far more drastic measures were being discussed. As the death toll rose in Oklahoma, senior figures in the administration privately conceded that some of the cherished freedoms Americans take for granted would have to go.
Daily Mail (21 April 1995)

drastic powers. *As for* DRASTIC MEASURES.

The central government has no authority in law for doing that, and, whatever might happen in the house of commons, new legislation for any such drastic powers would face stiff opposition in the lords.
Economist (21 September 1985)

Caracas attacked over drastic powers.
Headline, *Financial Times* (29 June 1994)

dream come true. *See* LIKE A DREAM . . .

dream turned to nightmare. Journalistic use – employed when any happy situation turns to bad. Date of origin unknown. A cliché by the 1960s.

He said yesterday: 'It was supposed be a dream holiday but it turned into a nightmare and I lost three months of my life.'
Today (16 March 1995)

Continue the process with a tram or taxi to a communist industrial dream-turned-nightmare: the Nowa Huta suburb, in which more than 200,000 people live and work, producing over half of Poland's steel – a living relic of Stalinist town planning.
European (7 April 1995)

Compare ANGUISH TURNED TO JOY.

dreams. *See* STUFF THAT . . .

dreams of avarice. *See* RICH BEYOND THE . . .

drink this – it'll do you good. Drama use. After bad news has been delivered, this succour is invariably provided. Observed by Fritz Spiegl in an article on drama cliché lines in the *Listener* (7 February 1985).

(drinking in the) last-chance saloon.   Mostly media use – to indicate that the person who is so associated with this place and activity has run out of options and is making some desperate move or one that could prove terminal. It is not clear where precisely this metaphor comes from except from a vague view of film Westerns and the second citation may be the coinage. The Last Chance Saloon was the location of a famous Marlene Dietrich song in *Destry Rides Again* (film US, 1939) and in Eugene O'Neill's play *The Iceman Cometh* (1946), there is the similar line, 'It's the No Chance Saloon.' A cliché from the late 1980s.

> The authority of the Takeover Panel and its shadowy status within our legal system are once again under threat. But this time the battle resembles a shoot-out at the last-chance saloon.
> *The Times* (19 January 1988)

> I do believe the popular press is drinking in the last-chance saloon.
> David Mellor, quoted in *The Times* (22 December 1989) (The Home Office minister responsible for the press, warning that Britain's popular papers had their last chance of avoiding legislation.)

> John Major's last-chance saloon.
> Headline, *Independent* (23 June 1995) (When the British Prime Minister gambled over his re-election as party leader in order to silence his critics.)

drive a coach and horses through something, to.   General idiomatic use. Meaning 'to overturn something wantonly, and to render it useless'. Sir Stephen Rice (1637–1715), a Roman Catholic Chief Baron of the Exchequer, is quoted as saying in 1672: 'I will drive a coach and six horses through the Act of Settlement.' In 1843 Charles Dickens wrote in *A Christmas Carol*: 'You may talk vaguely about driving a coach-and-six up a good old flight of stairs, or through a bad young Act of Parliament' (which might seem to allude to the first example). A cliché by the 1960s/70s.

> [Jubilation which was] to drive a number of coaches and horses through the contempt laws: the popular press seems to have decided that this was such a fantastic story that they would publish what they wanted and let the lawyers pick up the pieces later.
> Leading article, *The Times* (January 1981)

> 'Labour lawyers argued that Mr Justice Mervyn Davies had "driven a coach and horses" through Conservative legislation designed to limit the scope of

trade disputes and outlaw political strikes, by refusing to ban the "blacking" of Mercury.'
The Times (22 October 1983)

drive another nail into the coffin, to. General, slangy use – to bring something even nearer to its end if not actual death. Known by 1824. A cliché by the 1880s. Included in the parody of sportswriters' clichés by David Frost and Peter Cook in the book *That Was The Week That Was* (1963) was: 'This British soccerbluesday – there is no other word for it – drove another nail into the tottering coffin of Britain's BARONS OF BALL AND CALIPHS OF KICK.'

'The Candidate'. . . is one more nail in the coffin of slow acting.
Illustrated London News (29 November 1884)

An aesthete? One of those scruffy long-haired fellows in peculiar garb, lisping about art for art's sake? . . . Old Oscar screwed the last nail in the aesthete's coffin.
Harold Acton, *Memoirs of an Aesthete* (1948)

And this is another nail in the Tory coffin.
Daily Record (5 April 1995)

To gag the Press would be another nail in the coffin of democracy. We have every moral right to know what people we have elected into power are up to. They should live with dignity.
Letter to the editor, *Today* (15 April 1995)

drunken stupor. General use – to describe a person's helpless state brought about by alcohol consumption. Date of origin unknown. A cliché by the mid-twentieth century.

A policeman who had mistaken an Insulin coma for a drunken stupor.
Monica Dickens, *One Pair of Feet* (1942)

The episode is significant: first, because a fire in these circumstances is notoriously associated with drunken stupor, and – secondly – because Ronnie Welsh, whose role in McRae's death is significant and strange, has since vanished.
Herald (Glasgow) (27 March 1995)

He fell into a drunken stupor, but before he did, one of the old prophecies of Nostradamus floated through his head. '. . . A pearled isle will give birth to a leader, a man of the circus, and he shall destroy a nation.'
Short story in *Herald* (Glasgow) (25 April 1995)

dulcet tones. General use, to describe a person's voice. Sometimes used ironically. Known by 1800. A cliché by 1900.

> I suspect I will not have been alone in watching Sky's pictures but occasionally turning down the sound in favour of the Test Match Special team on Radio 5 Live and the dulcet tones of Christopher Martin-Jenkins, Jonathan Agnew and Neville Oliver and the rather less dulcet views of Geoffrey Boycott.
>
> *The Times* (28 November 1994)

> 'Guess what I've just done,' said my friend Jane one Sunday morning over the phone. We'd been gossiping, and this came out of the blue. 'What?' I said, expecting to hear about some new illicit sex romp. 'Cindy,' she said sheepishly. She'd just spent the morning on her living room floor toiling away to Cindy Crawford's dulcet tones.
>
> *Independent* (8 December 1994)

dynamite. *See* POLITICAL . . . ; THESE ARE . . .

= E =

each and every (one of you). General use, near-tautological and particularly American. 'Each and every' on its own was known by the seventeenth century; the longer form is a mostly American and especially political periphrastic use – dating from the Nixon era at least. Eric Partridge, *A Dictionary of Clichés* (5th edition, 1978), lists 'each and every one' as late nineteenth to twentieth century; the longer form, I would say, was a cliché almost as soon as it was started in, say, 1970.

> Each and every of the said Articles ... and all and singular matters ... therein contained.
> *Articles of Confederation of the U.S.* (1781)

> There are people who strictly deprive themselves of each and every eatable.
> Mark Twain, *Autobiography* (1897)

> I'm a peacemaker who reaches out to each and every one of you.
> Harold Washington, on becoming Mayor of Chicago (May 1983)

earliest convenience. *See* YOUR EARLIEST ...

earth shattering. General use. Date of origin unknown. A cliché by the mid-twentieth century.

> According to their style guru Veronica Manussis, these rings can be casual on the beach, eye-catching at a rave or 'incredibly dressy for playing bridge'. That's the other earth-shattering thing about plastic: it will go out with anyone.
> *Guardian* (22 April 1995)

> Today will probably not be as earth-shattering for Hiroshi Nakajima, controversial head of the World Health Organization, as some Geneva-watchers make out. For despite calls from African members of the WHO

for his resignation – over allegedly racist remarks – Nakajima looks set to live to fight another day.
Financial Times (11 May 1995)

echo these fears. General use, especially in opinion writing. Date of origin unknown. A cliché by the 1970s/80s. Listed in the *Independent* (24 December 1994) as a cliché of newspaper editorials.

To many outside observers these allegations will appear ridiculous, but they echo the fears of many Asian families in the East End that their traditional way of life is threatened by the 'Western disease'.
Observer (1 March 1992)

A Shanghai newspaper, Wenhuibao, last week expressed its fears about the consequences of these changes, in words that will echo eerily in other parts of the world.
Economist (12 June 1993)

elder statesman. General use, meaning a 'person of ripe years and experience whose counsel is sought and valued', especially a retired former leading politician. An expression derived from the Japanese *Genro*. Known in English by 1921. A cliché by the 1950s/60s.

Balfour, the Elder Statesman.
Heading, *Illustrated London News* (15 January 1937)

The Elder Statesman
Title of play by T.S. Eliot (1958)

Nixon, whom Bill Rogers ... referred to as the world's youngest elder statesman, had acquired enormous stature in world affairs.
Billings Gazette (Montana) (20 June 1976)

Chingford's Elder Statesman [Lord Tebbit] repeatedly urged his party to campaign on their traditional – and popular – strengths: United Kingdom sovereignty, strict immigration control, adequate defence and police forces.
Letter to the editor, *Sunday Telegraph* (19 April 1992)

elegant sufficiency. *See* EXCELLENT ...

eloquent testimony. *See* BEARS ...

end of civilization as we know it. Hollywood use, now only in parody. The kind of thing said when people are under threat from invaders from

Mars or wherever: 'This could mean the end of civilization as we know it.' Known by the 1930s, a cliché soon after this. *See also* — AS WE KNOW IT.

> 'I've talked with the responsible leaders of the Great Powers – England, France, Germany, and Italy. They're too intelligent to embark on a project which would mean the end of civilization as we now know it. You can take my word for it: there'll be no war!'
> *Citizen Kane* (US, 1941) (Orson Welles as the newspaper magnate Kane is heard saying this at a pre-war press conference.)

> *The End of Civilization As We Know It*
> Title of an announced but unreleased film (US, 1977)

> [A second Danish television channel] was about to take to the air, with the certain result that culture would be relegated to the dustbin . . . In short, it will be for Danes the end of civilisation as they know it.
> *Independent* Magazine (4 February 1989)

end of the day. *See* AT THE . . .

enjoying a well-deserved/earned break/rest. General use, especially journalistic. 'The statesman is now enjoying a well-earned rest' was dated 'ca. 1880' by Eric Partridge in *A Dictionary of Clichés* (5th edition, 1978), and who am I to disagree?

> Meanwhile, although enjoying a well-earned rest before being geared up for her autumn campaign, Balanchine was still very much in the limelight after Cezanne, who led her in all her work before the Oaks and Irish Derby, had come to the rescue of beleaguered York bookies by outgalloping the heavily-backed favourite, Midnight Legend, in the Magnet Cup.
> *Sunday Times* (10 July 1994)

> The Courtyard also has a soft play area which is ideal for the tiny tots. They can romp safely while Mum and Dad take a well-earned rest!
> *Daily Mirror* (21 March 1995)

> Savouring the moment: Normandy veterans in Hyde Park take a well-earned break yesterday.
> Photo caption, *Observer* (7 May 1995)

> Sophie Grigson is taking a well-deserved holiday.
> *Sunday Times* Magazine (10 September 1995)

everybody has one book in them. Publishing and literary proverbial saying – or perhaps not, for it advances a popular belief with which publishers might well disagree. Presumably, the idea behind the saying is that all people have one story that they alone can tell – namely, the story of their life. Known by the 1940s. A cliché by the 1960s.

> It is commonly said that every human being has in him the material for one good book, which is true in the same sense as it is true that every block of stone contains a statue.
> George Orwell in *New Statesman and Nation* (7 December 1940)

> 'Every one, it is said, has one good book inside him, and, if this be so, it would be unkind to suggest that Mr James Agate is the exception that proves the rule. All one can in fairness say is that his good book is not among the thirty-six he has so far produced.'
> *Punch* book review, quoted in James Agate, *Ego 6* (entry for 12 November 1942)

everything you always wanted to know about —— but were afraid to ask. Journalistic and publishing use. A format phrase inspired by the title *Everything You Always Wanted to Know About Sex But Were Afraid to Ask*, a book (published in 1970) by David Reuben MD (b.1933). The use was popularized even further when Woody Allen entitled a film *Everything You Always Wanted To Know About Sex, But Were Afraid To Ask* (US, 1972) – though, in fact, he simply bought the title of the book and none of its contents. A cliché soon after.

> All you ever wanted to know about video but were afraid to ask.
> Advertisement for *Video Today* magazine (December 1981)

> *Everything That Linguists Have Always Wanted to Know About Logic But Were Ashamed to Ask*

> *Everything You Always Wanted to Know About Drinking Problems And Then a Few Things You Didn't Want to Know*

> *Everything You Always Wanted to Know About Elementary Statistics But Were Afraid to Ask*

> *Everything You Always Wanted to Know About Mergers, Acquisitions and Divestitures But Didn't Know Whom to Ask*

> *Everything You Wanted to Know About Stars But Didn't Know Where to Ask*

> *Everything You Wanted to Know About the Catholic Church But Were Too Pious to Ask*

> *Everything You Wanted to Know About the Catholic Church But Were Too Weak to Ask* . . .
> List of book titles, up to 1984

Everything You Ever Wanted to Know About Sex – But Never Dared Ask.
Title of book by Robert Goldenson and Kenneth Anderson (1988)

evil in our midst. *See* WE MUST STAMP OUT . . .

excellent sufficiency. Conversational use. When declining an offer of more food, my father (1910–89) would say, 'No, thank you, I have had an excellent sufficiency'. Paul Beale's *Concise Dictionary of Slang* . . . (1989) has this, rather, as 'an **elegant sufficiency** . . . Jocular indication, mocking lower-middle-class gentility, that one has had enough to eat or drink, as "I've had an elegant sufficiency, ta!" since *c.*1950.' Compare: 'An elegant sufficiency, content,/Retirement, rural quiet' – James Thomson, *Spring* (1728–46). A borderline cliché.

(exchange) sardonic grin(s), to. General use. Date of origin unknown, but one of the clichés cited by Ted Morgan in *Somerset Maugham* (1980) as having been used by the writer in his efforts to achieve a 'casual style'.

> The idea that by the end of the century it could regularly be turning out large-scale films for the international market, and even drawing talent away from the West Coast . . . this is almost enough to remove that sardonic grin from the Hollywood mogul.
> *The Times* (25 March 1995)

exclusive. Journalistic, promotional use. Newspapers love to splash 'exclusive' labels all over their copy, believing that this will impress readers. Readers know, however, that any 'exclusive' worthy of the hype is soon replicated in all other papers and is thus, except for a period of about an hour on publication, a meaningless boast. Journalists also like to emphasize the supposed 'exclusiveness' of certain areas where people live or the clubs and restaurants they visit. Here 'exclusive' usually means no more than 'expensive'. In both senses, a cliché by the 1950s.

> IN LONDON'S exclusive Park Lane.
> ITN news (28 May 1994)

> But from the start it was widely accepted in Reed's comfortable head office, off Curzon Street in London's exclusive Mayfair, that Elsevier was a high-risk partner.
> *Independent on Sunday* (3 July 1994)

The chain-smoking viscount gave the exclusive interview in the darkened lounge of his elegant Mayfair home.
Daily Mirror (20 September 1994)

Ince, who played in Wednesday's match against Arsenal at Old Trafford, arrived later after jumping on the first available flight. First the pair dropped in at the exclusive Brown's nightclub in Mayfair.
Today (24 March 1995)

Sir Nicholas was arrested . . . a short distance from the scene of the accident in exclusive Sydney Street.
Observer (4 June 1995)

existing conditions. General use, especially political. An inevitable pairing. Known in the US by 1858. It occurs along with other rhetorical clichés during the 'Party Political Speech' (written by Max Schreiner) on the Peter Sellers comedy album *The Best of Sellers* (1958): 'MY FRIENDS, in the light of present-day developments, let me say right away that I do not regard existing conditions likely.' A cliché by the mid-twentieth century.

Among the national claims are increasing pay equity between men and women, the regulation of fixed-term and casual contracts, codification of existing conditions where these are not already covered under an industrial award, and greater flexibility in working hours for staff with families.
Times Higher Education Supplement (25 November 1994)

—— experience. Marketing, promotional use. A cliché of the 1980s, particularly with regard to 'heritage' material. It suggests that by going to some historical site or theme park the visitor will have a life-enhancing visit and not just an ordinary day out. Date of origin, probably in the 1960s/70s. A cliché almost instantaneously. Could the popularity of this usage somehow lie with the Jimi Hendrix Experience, the name given to the 1960s rock musician's group?

At Land's End, for instance, there's the Land's End Experience, a multi-media retelling of our island story, in which visions of Excalibur gleam through dry ice, waves crash and – for that extra tang of actuality – visitors are lightly-moistened with simulated sea-spray. A curious thing: to go to the sea-side to get wet indoors.
Independent on Sunday (25 April 1993) (A few miles away it was possible, in the same year, to have the Minack Experience – a rather unnecessary indoor display attached to a wonderful open-air theatre, which truly is an experience.)

The Dracula Experience exhibition in Whitby, North Yorkshire, is for sale

. . . The exhibit, in the town that inspired Bram Stoker, author of the legend, attracts 80,000 visitors a year.
Independent (20 August 1992)

The Definitive Perlman Experience.
Title of series of concerts by Itzhak Perlman at the Royal Festival Hall, London, June 1995

Leave your worries and the traffic behind and enjoy the Cotswold Experience . . . For your Cotswold Experience leaflet and booking details, just give us a call.
Advertisement in the *Observer* (27 August 1995)

[expert's] [expert].   The *Observer* Magazine ran a series for many years in the 1980s wherein specialists in many fields nominated the person whose expertise they respected most. A borderline cliché since about that time.

[Jeffrey] Archer might be 'the extrovert's extrovert' in Margaret Thatcher's phrase, but even with the details fleshed out his life remains a far from open book.
Independent (29 May 1995), quoting Margaret Thatcher, *The Downing Street Years* (1993)

He was every boy's ideal elder brother. 'The adolescent's adolescent,' Hascy Tarbox . . . later said.
Simon Callow, *Orson Welles: The Road to Xanadu* (1995)

explore every avenue.   Political, rhetorical use. Known by 1922. A cliché soon after. Cited as a 'silly expression' that had recently been 'killed by the jeers of a few journalists' by George Orwell in 'Politics and the English Language' (*Horizon*, April 1946). Earlier, A.P. Herbert in *What a Word!* (1935) had thought it was disappearing. In *Usage and Abusage* (last revised 1957) Eric Partridge called this a 'fly-blown phrase'. Still with us.

Fancy picture of an eminent politician in search of a formula, LEAVING NO STONE UNTURNED while exploring every avenue.
Caption to cartoon, *Punch* (2 December 1931)

'In war-time we are bound to explore every avenue, whether it's likely to be productive or not.'
Nancy Mitford, *Pigeon Pie* (1940)

To achieve our ultimate aim of Grand Slam and World Cup victories we must explore every avenue, not least in the mind. Far from being an

admission of weakness, talking to a psychologist is simply striving for the best in oneself and for the team.
Independent (18 February 1995)

There was, however, a 'moral obligation to explore every avenue to reduce the numbers out of work', she added. Work-sharing should aim to secure 'a fairer distribution of the income which a job brings, and as a corollary, reduce the unequal burden of unemployment'.
Irish Times (29 March 1995)

exposed to the ravages of ——. General use, mostly journalistic. Date of origin unknown. A cliché by the 1950s/60s?

Mr Derek Hodgson, deputy general secretary of the UCW postalworkers' union, attacked Post Office management for promoting privatisation. 'They are a disgrace,' he said. 'The Post Office does not need to be exposed to the ravages of money-grabbing speculators.'
Financial Times (6 October 1994)

The mermaid, originally believed to be a siren who enticed seamen to their doom, has been exposed as the harmless, placid and less than seductive manatee, a species of sea cow increasingly vulnerable to the ravages of the powerboat propeller.
Sunday Telegraph (26 February 1995)

'The [Churchill] graves are exposed to the ravages of thousands of tourists every year'.
ITN news (28 April 1995)

—— extraordinaire! Journalistic, promotional use. A format phrase, current by 1940 and a cliché since the 1960s.

[Culture Club's] flexible eight-piece includes Steve Grainger's sax, Terry Bailey's trumpet, Phil Pickett's keyboards, and their secret weapon, Helen Terry, a backing singer extraordinaire.
Max Bell, *The Times* (27 September 1983)

'If not Ivan the Terrible, then a Terrible Ivan,' in the catchy phrase coined by US defence lawyer extraordinaire, Alan Dershowitz.
Financial Times (28 May 1994)

Even the peacemaker extraordinaire, former president Jimmy Carter, has offered his services – yet while Haiti, the Middle East and Bosnia were soothed by his touch, baseball would not budge.
Guardian (29 March 1995)

= F =

fact of the matter is . . . Journalistic and rhetorical use. Date of origin unknown. A cliché by the mid-twentieth century. Identified as a current cliché in *The Times* (17 March 1995).

> Pressed as to how farmers could produce leaner carcasses, Prof James said: 'It's a complex inter-play between breeding, earlier slaughter and feeding. The fact of the matter is that successive support measures have persuaded farmers to keep cattle longer than they should just to gain extra weight and therefore a seemingly greater reward.
> *Scotsman* (8 November 1994)

> Anyone who willingly jumps from an aeroplane at 3000 feet might be accused of having a death wish. Or perhaps it might be because two successive defeats have undermined his club's dream of promotion. Jim Duffy would argue differently. The fact of the matter is that the Dundee manager is neither a vicarious thrill-seeker nor a crackpot in urgent need of medical assistance.
> *Daily Mail* (3 May 1995)

—— factor. Journalistic use and also a cliché of book titles. Since the early 1980s, when the alliterative lure of the 'Falklands Factor' gave rise to numerous other inventions. This 'factor' was the apparent reason for the supposed improvement in Margaret Thatcher's fortunes in the 1983 British General Election following her 'victory' in the previous year's conflict with Argentina over the Falklands. A cliché soon after this initial flourish. Indeed, in the 1980s, almost any phenomenon was liable to be dignified by the '-factor' suffix. It gave a spurious sense of science – or at least journalistic weight – to almost any theory or tendency that had been spotted.

> '[Geraldine] Ferraro's "sleaze factor" . . . Anything questionable which emerges subsequently about their background becomes known as the "sleaze factor".'
> *Observer* (19 August 1984)

The Chernobyl factor appears to have cast its shadow over not just British lamb, but the homes of those unfortunate to live near the four areas shortlisted for the NIREX nuclear dumping site.
Daily Telegraph (3 July 1986)

Liz Howell, the woman behind GMTV, admits that when Fiona Armstrong was employed she was asked to have an image makeover – shorter skirts, shorter hair and a big flirtatious smile that could give her the F-Factor (F for fanciability) rating they wanted.
Today (6 January 1993)

Fiona Armstrong, Good Morning TV's new presenter, has it. Her co-host, Michael Wilson, is on the way to having it. GMTV swears by it. 'It' is the F-Factor, where 'F' stands, officially at least, for 'fanciability'.
The Times (6 January 1993)

To be greeted by Paul Johnson as a Christian gentleman who has no time for class politics and understands that public spending must be controlled contributes nicely to the ripple effect Blair seeks to spread across the surface of politics, dispelling the fear factor which lurks in the stagnant depths. The fear factor was a killer in 1992. Anything that accelerates the party's move out of the time-warp is a contribution.
Guardian (11 April 1995)

[Joan Littlewood] scorns the 'elocution' of Edith Evans but is a sucker for the Gielgud factor.
Independent (18 June 1995)

fair. *See* NEITHER FAIR TO YOU . . .

fair sex. General use, for the female sex. Known by 1688. A cliché by 1900, and a phrase only to be used with caution following the rise of feminism in the 1970s and the politically correct movement in the 1990s. Compare GENTLE SEX.

The aspirin age needed its drugs largely because the fair sex tried so hard to look anything but.
News Chronicle (27 July 1960)

Since Dale Reid and Corinne Dibnah won the [golf] title in crushing style in 1990, the fair sex have seen their handicap allowance cut. 'We keep telling them but they won't listen,' Ms Moon complained. 'It was just too long for us.'
Independent (23 March 1995)

fairy tale. *See* LIKE A . . .

faith in British justice. *See* THIS HAS RESTORED . . .

false security. *See* LULLED INTO A SENSE OF . . .

family. *See* I WOULD LIKE TO SPEND MORE TIME . . .

fast lane. *See* LIVING LIFE IN THE . . .

fatal attraction. General use, for any leaning or obsession which involves a person in trouble. Date of origin unknown. A cliché particularly since 1987 when the American film *Fatal Attraction* described a man's adulterous affair with a woman who took terrible revenge when he tried to drop her. The phrase became irresistible to journalists.

> Peter Brooke, the former Northern Ireland Secretary, has never quite thrown off his fatal attraction for the stage . . . yesterday, he was looking at ease among the theatrical folk gathered in Soho for the unveiling of a plaque to musical star, Jessie Matthews.
> *Evening Standard* (London) (4 May 1995)

> At 16, her [Courtney Love's] fatal attraction to rock stars took effect: she flew to Dublin, where she worked as a music photographer, then to Liverpool, where she . . . lost her virginity listening, with terrible irony, to Joy Division.
> *Evening Standard* (London) (4 May 1995)

fate worse than death. General use, originally referring to rape or loss of virginity, this is an expression dating from the days when such dishonour for a woman would, indeed, have seemed so. In John Cleland's *Memoirs of a Woman of Pleasure* (1748–9), Fanny Hill talks of a 'dread of worse than death'. The *Oxford English Dictionary* (2nd edition) has the phrase in its original sense by 1810. In *The Trumpet-Major* (1882), Thomas Hardy reproduces what purports to be a document headed 'Address to All Ranks and Descriptions of Englishmen' dating from the time of Napoleonic invasion scares: 'You will find your best Recompense,' it concludes, '. . . in having protected your Wives and Children from death, or worse than Death, which will follow the Success of such Inveterate Foes.' Now used semi-jokingly of any situation one might wish to avoid and, as such, a cliché since the 1950s.

> And it was an unimaginably awful week for the two young princes, William and Harry, who missed out on being 'blooded' at their first real hunt.

Though at least the fox, which got away, was spared a fate worse than death.
Guardian (24 February 1995)

The two-hour film had all the familiar Sharpe elements. He and his smelly squad of crack marksmen are still invulnerable ("'Tis but a scratch, ma'am'); the love interest (Wellington's niece, in this case) is still destined to face a fate worse than death at the hands of some swarthy psychopath in the last 15 minutes.
Herald (Glasgow) (15 April 1995)

fear.   *See* FLIGHT FROM . . . ; PALL OF . . .

fears.   *See* ECHO THESE . . .

feel.   *See* HOW DID YOU . . .

feel cheap.   *See* I COULDN'T, BILL, . . .

feel-good factor.   Mostly political use to describe a type of feeling in the electorate whose presence may inhibit it from voting for change or whose absence encourages dissatisfaction with the *status quo*. As an example of the first type, it was advanced by Neil Kinnock, British Labour Party leader, as a reason why he was unable to defeat the long-running Conservative government in the election of 1987. As an example of the latter type, it was frequently evoked in 1994–5 to explain the continuing lack of popularity of the Conservative government. Identified as a current cliché in *The Times* (17 March 1995).

As for the element 'feel good', this had been established earlier and was already something of a cliché before it was added to the 'factor'. Coined in the US, the phrase for the idea of 'feeling good with yourself' was a way of describing your 'quality of life' which, in due course, became a very politically correct thing to have. Was the name of the British vocal and instrumental group 'Dr Feelgood' (late 1970s) some influence on this or was it, in turn, derived from the earlier use of the phrase?

Then there are the 'Mr Feel Good' labels. These assure you a position in lefty heaven because you have bought yogurt from Fred, 'made with loving care and pure Jersey milk from a nearby farm' or politically-correct coffee beans made by workers in Nicaragua who will never use Hair Salad on contras.
Washington Post (27 December 1987)

Even economic failure by a Government which bases its entire appeal on economic success isn't going to do Labour much good. The economic 'feel good factor' on which Mr Kinnock blamed his 1987 election defeat apparently works one way only.
Guardian (12 December 1988)

[A] way to get patients under control without bullying them . . . Invented by the hippy generation in the Sixties and developed later by the advertising industry, 'feel good' techniques such as assertiveness training and counselling are designed to reassure customers such as airline passengers and patients that they are in control of situations over which patently they have not the slightest influence.
Daily Telegraph (21 April 1992)

Kohl beams from on high: 'Feelgood' chancellor radiates poll confidence . . . In this heartland of West German prosperity, where the tennis stadium itself has been built merely to satisfy the whim of a local industrialist who wanted a Wimbledon in his home town, his top theme goes down well.
Headline and text, *Financial Times* (26 September 1994)

These ignorant new Tories are puzzled by the lack of a 'feel-good factor' . . . They have never felt better in their lives.
Auberon Waugh, quoted in the *Independent* (3 December 1994)

Shadow Scottish Secretary George Robertson disagreed. 'Ian Lang must be living on another planet to everyone else. The Secretary of State may think everything in the garden is rosy, but for the thousands of ordinary Scots the "feel good factor" is nothing but a cruel joke.'
Herald (Glasgow) (13 December 1994)

feet under the table. *See* GET ONE'S . . .

—— *File.* Book, film and television programme title, used to give a spurious sense of fact-gathering and investigativeness. Possibly inspired by the title of Len Deighton's espionage novel *The Ipcress File* (1962; film UK, 1965), the cliché was well-established by the 1970s. In 1976 TV reporters Anthony Summers and Tom Mangold published *The File on the Tsar*. In 1978 two BBC reporters, Barrie Penrose and Roger Courtior, published a book about plots involving leading British politicians and gave it the curious title *The Pencourt File*.

filming for television. General, but particularly journalistic, use. Not only a cliché but nowadays increasingly inaccurate. TV cameras do not use film. Only film cameras use film. TV cameras either televise (electronically) or are used to record (electronically). There was a time when events *were* filmed for screening on television but this is rare nowadays. Only the occasional drama series is filmed. Accordingly, it is also incorrect to apply talk of film 'footage' with regard to video recording where length or duration is measured in terms of minutes and seconds rather than the length of the material upon which the images are stored.

> Follett's staff feel unable to explain Ken's change of gear, but I gather that he may have tired of the Bentley after it broke down while he was filming a television programme.
> *Evening Standard* (London) (27 March 1995)

> I spied a BBC cameraman filming the concert. I was stationed a few metres behind him but, even at that distance, something on his monitor did not look quite right.
> Vicky Ward, *Independent* (15 August 1995)

> ITN is experimenting with new equipment supplied by Sony which will enable journalists to edit their stories on film from a desk-top terminal.
> *Observer* (24 September 1995)

films. *See* I COULD HELP GET YOU INTO . . .

final/last/ultimate analysis. *See* IN THE FINAL/LAST/ULTIMATE . . .

finest swordsman in all France. *See* BEST SWORDSMAN . . .

finger. *See* HAVE MORE GOODNESS IN . . .

finish off that dress. *See* WHEN ARE YOU GOING TO . . .

fish out of water. *See* LIKE A FISH . . .

fishing in troubled/muddy waters. General idiomatic use, meaning 'prepared to try and extract advantage from difficult circumstances' or, simply, 'to concern oneself with unpleasant or confused matters' (often used by journalists in a literal sense when writing about fisheries disputes, etc.) Known by 1625. 'Fishing in trouble waters' was cited as a 'dying metaphor' by George Orwell in 'Politics and the English Language' (*Horizon*, April 1946). Also the phrase **troubled waters** on its own. A cliché by the mid-twentieth century.

He was fishing in the muddy waters of race . . . 'Racism,' he began, 'destroys those it touches.'
Listener (25 September 1975)

The Arts: More troubled waters? – Interview / Charles Laurence talks to singer Paul Simon about his first visit to South Africa since the stormy days of Graceland. [The Simon and Garfunkel song 'Bridge Over Troubled Waters' was published in 1965.]
Daily Telegraph (2 January 1992)

Troubled Waters – Victoria Griffith examines growing concerns about the ecological impact of fish farming.
By-line, *Financial Times* (27 July 1994)

'What all this shows is that Iran is prepared to fish in troubled waters where it can,' a senior United States administration official said.
Guardian (28 December 1994)

Canadian Fisheries Minister Brian Tobin is unrepentant and unyielding. He made it quite clear that the answer to any further attempts to fish in these troubled Newfoundland waters was more gunboats.
Evening Standard (London) (10 March 1995)

fit.   *See* LOOKING BRONZED . . .

flags are out.   General slangy use, especially in downmarket journalism or in parody thereof. Meaning 'the celebrations have already begun'. Date of origin unknown. A cliché by the 1960s.

The flags are out for the link-up we've waited so long to see; the inauguration of the Channel Tunnel is a real splash of colour for a grey 'fin de siècle'.
Guardian (6 May 1994)

The flags are out for tomorrow's start of the 1994 French Open, and with them comes the Roland Garros magic. It is a quality less easy to grasp than the garden-party aura of Wimbledon, though no less real. It is perhaps just a component of that illogical but romantic phenomenon known as 'Paris in the spring'.
Independent on Sunday (22 May 1994)

Compare, from the *Sunday Express* (25 November 1984): 'If [boxer] Sibson, weaving and bobbing, can find his former big-punch savagery – and Kaylor's chin – the requiems will be in full swing down West Ham way on Tuesday night.'

flight from/of/to fear. A cliché of journalism, demonstrating the lure of alliteration yet again. Date of origin unknown. A cliché by the mid-twentieth century.

> To Britain on flight from fear. A flight from fear ended at Heathrow Airport yesterday for passengers on the first plane to arrive from Poland since martial law was proclaimed at the weekend.
> Jon Ryan, *Daily Mail* (18 December 1981)

> Flight of fear as families pray for rain.
> Headline, *Sunday Telegraph* (9 January 1994)

> Flight To Fear: Pato Tells Of His Israeli Asylum Hell.
> Headline, *Daily Mirror* (27 October 1994)

flights of fancy. In the basic sense of 'something extravagantly imagined' (in which it has been known since 1687) probably only a borderline cliché. However, when applied to air travel it becomes a part of the 'travel scribes' armoury' compiled from a competition in the *Guardian* (10 April 1993).

> Platt, a most practical man, does not often indulge in flights of fancy. A millionaire already, he needs only to be a winner to fulfil every ambition he has set for himself.
> *Daily Mirror* (27 March 1995)

fly on the wall. Media use, to describe a type of documentary in which the participants are observed going about their normal lives or work without too much awareness that a camera crew is following them. Probably in use by 1974 when BBC TV produced *The Family* about a working-class family in Reading (in imitation of the previous year's PBS show *An American Family*). A cliché by the 1980s but not too bad a one – a useful term and there does not appear to be an alternative.

> The 'fly-on-the-wall' technique, so successful elsewhere, would not overcome this problem.
> *Listener* (10 February 1983)

follow that cab/taxi/van! A cliché of the cinema, said to a taxi driver by the hero/policeman in pursuit of a villain. Few people can ever have said it in real life. (It is as much of a cliché as the ability film actors have, on getting *out* of taxis, to tender exactly the right change to the driver.) In *Top Hat* (US, 1935) Eric Blore as a butler says 'Follow that cab' when he is shadowing Ginger Rogers. In *Let's Dance* (US, 1950) Fred Astaire says 'Follow that cab' in order to chase Betty Hutton. The film *Amsterdamned* (1989), a cop thriller set amid the canals of the Dutch capital, includes the memorable injunction, 'Follow those bubbles!' A cliché by the 1950s.

fond farewell. General use, wherever alliteration rules. Date of origin unknown. A cliché by the 1950s, particularly in connection with funerals and memorial services.

> It might have been a day of double farewells; goodbye to Brian Moore, and perhaps goodbye to the First Division. Fond farewell and laughing-stock demotion. Highly charged stuff.
> *Observer* (30 April 1995)

> Four legs and a fond farewell – Liz Hurley.
> Headline, *Today* (1 May 1995)

> And his [Dudley Moore's] jokey performance hit the right note with more than 500 [Peter] Cook admirers who gathered for the fond farewell in a London church.
> *Daily Mirror* (2 May 1995)

fool's paradise. *See* LIVE IN A . . .

football. *See* IT'S A FUNNY GAME . . .

for the best mum in the world. In disc jockey-speak, usually when quoting from a record request letter from a listener. Since the 1950s/60s? – and very rapidly thereafter a cliché.

> Pamela has continued to fight. When she was awarded a car for being Best Mum In The World by Esther Rantzen's *Hearts Of Gold* TV programme in 1991, she sold it to fund her work.
> *Daily Mail* (13 August 1994)

forces of darkness. Mostly journalistic use, a consciously purple phrase to describe opponents, whether evil or not. Date of origin unknown. A parallel phrase to 'the forces of evil', which was known by 1862. A cliché by the time the phrase was mocked by Tom Stoppard in his play *Night and Day* (1978): 'Commandeered it as the NERVE CENTRE of Mageeba's victorious drive against the forces of darkness, otherwise known as the Adoma Liberation Front.'

I've stood by and watched as the Gaelic language is regularly savaged by a prominent Harris-based columnist, by the name of John Macleod. I've listened as the forces of darkness snigger in pubs that more Scots speak Urdu than Gaelic.
Scotsman (20 January 1995)

Mr Blair's challenge is to push his party in a radical but non-socialist direction when its heart remains wedded to the old tunes, and to keep these forces of darkness at bay when in power.
Sunday Times (19 March 1995)

foregone conclusion. General use, an inevitable pairing for 'predictable outcome'. Known by 1856. A cliché by 1900.

The privatization of the BBC and the race down-market of ITV would then be a foregone conclusion.
Listener (2 February 1984)

Investors were looking decidedly punch-drunk after finding themselves on the receiving end of the Government's double whammy. It was a foregone conclusion that the Conservatives would take a beating in the local government elections, but the extent of the rout shocked both brokers and investors alike.
The Times (6 May 1995)

'If Celtic Swing doesn't win by eight lengths your reputation is smashed forever,' bellowed McCririck, having taken the gravest exception to Timeform (with which McGrath is closely involved) rating Celtic Swing 15lb ahead of Pennekamp and famously describing the race's outcome as a 'foregone conclusion.'
The Times (8 May 1995)

Forth Bridge. *See* LIKE (PAINTING) THE ...

fountains. *See* MURMURING ...

fray. *See* RETURN TO THE ...

free, gratis and for nothing. General slangy use – a double tautology on the word 'free'. Eric Partridge's *Dictionary of Slang and Unconventional English* (1985 edition) quotes Thomas Bridges as saying in 1770 that 'the common people' always put 'free' and 'gratis' together; and notes that the longer version occurs in an 1841 book. In fact, 'free, gratis' was current by 1682 and the longer version occurs a little earlier than 1841. Charles Dickens in *The Pickwick Papers*, Chap. 26 (1836–7) has Sam Weller's father say 'free gratis for nothin' '. In *Usage and Abusage* (1947) Partridge decides that it is a cliché, only excusable as a jocularity.

> Another part was the advice of Paul Russell, a Welsh cricketing nut at Andersen Consulting, who persuaded his firm that it would win the goodwill of Welsh businessmen, and so lots of new work, if it could – free, gratis and for nothing – come up with a plan to turn the club from chump into champ.
> *Economist* (14 May 1994)

> It's all tosh, and I can prove it. Did you know (not a lot of people know this) that there are 153 free shows or exhibitions on the fringe? Yes, that's free, gratis, for nothing, zilch, not a bean.
> *Herald* (Glasgow) (10 August 1994)

free the ——. Protest group use. This all-purpose slogan came into its own in the 1960s – usually in conjunction with a place name and a number. Hence: 'Free the Chicago 7' (charged with creating disorder during the Democratic Convention in 1968), 'Free the Wilmington 10' and so on. Dignifying protesters with a group name incorporating place and number may have begun with the 'Hollywood 10' (protesters against McCarthyite investigations) in 1947.

The format has now become a cliché of sloganeering. Various joke slogans from the late 1970s demanded: 'Free the Beethoven 9/the Heinz 57/the Intercity 125/the Chiltern Hundreds/the Indianapolis 500/the Grecian 2000.'

friendly persuasion. General use. Popularized by *Friendly Persuasion* as the title of a film (US, 1956), based on a novel by Jessamyn West, and by the accompanying song. A cliché, too, since then.

> In business his most obvious talent is salesmanship. 'I'm not a foot-in-the-door person, but I believe in persuasion, and friendly persuasion at that,' he says. He has also become a good delegator.
> *Sunday Telegraph* (19 June 1994)

> Even without the scandals, selling in the UK had begun a mini-revolution. The time when an irrepressible confidence plus friendly persuasion were the way to earn a fortune in sales is fast fading.
> *The Times* (19 October 1994)

friends. *See* JUST GOOD . . . ; MY FRIENDS . . .

friends thought I was mad. General use, also journalistic, when describing some activity or adventure. Date of origin unknown. Part of the 'travel scribes' armoury' compiled from a competition in the *Guardian* (10 April 1993), and used particularly in describing unusual holidays, property purchases and so on.

> After that we started seeing each other, initially quite casually. Some friends thought we were mad to get back together; many were surprised Duncan would even contemplate seeing me again. One friend said we were perfectly matched, we just acted too fast.
> *Daily Mail* (10 May 1994)

> Friends thought they were mad. Family shook their heads as they surveyed the mildew-spotted wall, peeling plaster, rusty radiators, and the gull droppings on the parquet floor. Amazingly, all is now restored to its former art deco glory.
> *Daily Mail* (28 May 1994)

> His friends apparently thought him mad to even think about it, but the atmosphere and the surrounding 34 acres of park and woodland not surprisingly appealed to Mackenzie.
> *Herald* (Glasgow) (6 July 1994)

> A 17th-century convent on the edge of the Tuscan Maremma, with wheat plains rolling down to the sea, provided his retreat. When Pollock found the convent, it was a shelter for sheep and goats. There was no electricity, no running water. His friends thought him mad to sink his cash into this enormous pile of crumbling stone but it was a Bohemian idyll.
> *European* (12 August 1994)

—— from hell. General slangy and especially journalistic use, meaning 'ghastly' or 'hellish' or, simply, emphasizing the negative qualities of the species or type being described. The origin would seem to lie in the neighbouring fields of horror movies and rock albums. A writer in the *Independent* (24 September 1988) joked about videos with titles like *Mutant Hollywood Chainsaw Hookers From Hell!* Pantera recorded 'Cowboys from Hell' in 1990, and Original Sin recorded 'Bitches from Hell' in 1986. A cliché from 1992.

> [US figure-skating champion Christopher Bowman] – the Hans Brinker from Hell.
> *Hartford Courant* (Connecticut) (7 February 1992)

> Lisa Samalin's painting of grandma from hell.
> *New York Times* (9 May 1993)

[Hillary Clinton:] 'She is alternately deified and vilified as nun or Lady Macbeth, Florence Nightingale or Yuppie From Hell.'
New York Times (13 June 1993)

The chief executive of Cunard walked the plank yesterday, taking responsibility for the QE2's Christmas 'cruise from hell' which has cost the liner's owner, Trafalgar House, at least £7.5m in compensation payments.
Independent (19 May 1995)

from the grassroots.   *See* AT/FROM THE . . .

fulfil a long-felt want, to.   Inevitable phrasing. Known by the 1910s. 'I would suggest the following as likely to fulfil a long-felt want of the weekend visitor' – *Punch* (24 February 1915). A cliché by the 1950s/60s.

Casanova (Frank Finlay): I'll be perfectly frank with you – I have a long felt want.

Eric Morecambe: There's no answer to that.
Eddie Braben, *The Best of Morecambe and Wise* (1974)

Shots rained in on the Dutch area, but the long felt want of a great international class finisher was once again the team's failing.
Irish Times (5 July 1994)

full of memories.   General use, in connection with elderly people or the recently departed. Date of origin unknown. Listed in the *Independent* 'DIY travel writers' cliché kit' (31 December 1988): ' "Before the tourists came," said Old —— , his sad, wet eyes full of memories, "things were different." '

I happened to be in the speaker's chair presiding over one debate in the union in 1963 when the news of Hugh Gaitskell's premature death came through. Now John himself has gone before his time, perhaps equally cheated of the highest office. The past few days have been full of memories and echoes.
Sunday Times (15 May 1994)

The sleeves of records like Dylan's Blood on the Tracks, the first two Roxy Music albums, the first Clash album, Bowie's Ziggy Stardust and Diamond Dogs, anything by the Beatles and the Stones, The Best of the Doors with Joel Brodsky's portrait of Jim Morrison as a crucified Adonis are aesthetically beautiful and full of memories in a way that a CD could never be.
Daily Telegraph (16 June 1994)

funny game, football.   *See* IT'S A . . .

further ado.   *See* WITHOUT . . .

= G =

——gate. Journalistic suffix, used especially to help in the naming of any political and Royal scandal in the US and UK. 'Watergate' was the name given to the scandal in US politics that led to the resignation of President Richard Nixon in 1974. It came from the Watergate apartment block in Washington DC where a bungled burglary by those seeking to re-elect the president led to a cover-up and then the scandal. Among the scores there have been subsequently are: Koreagate, Lancegate, Billygate, Liffeygate, Westlandgate, Contragate, Irangate, Thatchergate, Camillagate and Squidgygate. A cliché really from the second or third such coinage.

Genghis Khan. *See* SOMEWHERE TO THE RIGHT OF . . .

gentle giant. General use, but especially media and obituary. The alliteration is important and the application to any tall, big, strong person has become a journalistic cliché. A policeman killed by an IRA bomb outside Harrods store in London (December 1983) was so dubbed. Terry Wogan used the expression allusively in the early 1980s to describe the BBC Radio 2 network. Larry Holmes (b.1950), world heavyweight boxing champion, is another to whom the label has been affixed, as also James Randel Matson (b.1945), the US track and field champion.

In 1967 there was an American film entitled *The Gentle Giant*. This was about a small boy in Florida who befriends a bear which later saves the life of the boy's disapproving father. In the 1930s Pickfords Removals were promoted with the rhyme:

> A note from you, a call from us,
> The date is fixed, with no worry or fuss,
> A Pickfords van, a gentle giant,
> The work is done – a satisfied client.

Going back even further, the journalist William Howard Russell wrote of

Dr Thomas Alexander, a surgeon who served in the Crimean War, as a 'gentle giant of a Scotchman'. A cliché by the 1960s/70s.

> Rugby: Gentle giant Munro keen to kick the losing habit.
> Headline, *Scotsman* (10 June 1994)

> Controversy has stalked the 35-year-old gentle giant nicknamed 'Piggy' every step of his dual-international career, resulting in numerous brushes with authority.
> *Today* (26 August 1994)

> I speeded up as I left the canal and into the open waters of Coot Bay, a stiff breeze whipping up the surface, only to slow down again on the other side for Tarpon Creek, a habitat of the Florida manatee, or sea-cow, a gentle giant whose numbers have been decimated by weekend boaters.
> *Daily Mail* (15 April 1995)

gentle sex.   General, non-PC use, to describe the female sex. Known by 1583. A cliché by the 1960s.

> So while fashions may change and student starter packs come and go, no self-respecting young lady need ever find herself unarmed. Parasol or rape alarm, the gentle sex are not what they seem. Let the unsuspecting fresher beware!
> *The Times* (13 March 1995)

get along like a house on fire, to.   General idiomatic use, meaning to get on together extremely well. One of the clichés cited by Ted Morgan in *Somerset Maugham* (1980) as having been used by the writer in his efforts to achieve a 'casual style'.

> The two parties express shock, embarrassment, excitement etc, but are soon getting on (or off) like a house on fire. This is all very jolly, but after a short while becomes, like most sex films, unbearably repetitive.
> *Sunday Telegraph* (30 April 1995)

get away from it all, to.   Cliché of travel journalism/advertising, and meaning 'to have a rest, holiday'. Date of origin unknown. A cliché by the 1960s/70s.

> Somebody who wants to get away from it all is likely to wind up in a chalet in a Heidi-like village on a mountain.
> *National Observer* (US) (13 March 1976)

> In 1943 where did Churchill go to get away from it all?
> Headline to an advertisement for the Moroccan National Tourist Office (February 1989)

get one's feet under the table, to.   General use, especially in trades unions and business, to suggest the point at which real work ('substantive negotiations') starts to be done. Date of origin unknown. Identified as a current cliché by Howard Dimmock of Westcliff-on-Sea in a letter to the *Sunday Times* (31 December 1989).

> The Social Affairs Unit has performed a public service by drawing attention, in a pamphlet published today, to the fact that counselling has been allowed to get its feet under the national table without serious examination of its medical or philosophical credentials.
> *Daily Telegraph* (2 May 1994)

> The IRA cessation of violence was announced on 31 August; the historic handshake between Mr Reynolds and Gerry Adams took place on 6 September; and yesterday Sinn Fein got its feet under the political table in Dublin.
> *Independent* (29 October 1994)

> Private sector's feet 'under the operating table': MP lists contracts going outside NHS.
> Headline, *Herald* (Glasgow) (9 March 1995)

giant among men.   *See* HE WAS A . . .

giant stride (forward).   General use, some journalistic. Date of origin unknown. A cliché by the 1970s.

> Britain took a giant stride towards becoming self-supporting in oil yesterday.
> *Guardian* (1 September 1972)

> The Government's rate-capping plan was 'yet another giant stride along the path of tight Whitehall control over life in Britain.'
> *Daily Telegraph* (28 September 1983)

> Giant stride forward for a mint Murray.
> Headline [about athlete], *Observer* (21 May 1995)

give something one's best shot, to.   Business use, mainly – but also in politics, especially in the US, where the phrase originated. Meaning 'to try as hard as possible' and known by 1984. Presumably this comes from the sporting sense of 'shot' (as in golf) rather than the gun sense. The US film *Hoosiers* (1986), about a basketball team, was also known as *Best Shot*. A cliché soon after.

'We're not able to adequately counsel the farmer with the present plan,' he said. 'With this, we'll be able to give him our best shot.'
Washington Post (13 February 1984)

The editor must keep his powder dry. He is there to sell newspapers and his best shot is to find and project material denied to his rivals.
Guardian (14 May 1984)

For Clinton and the Democrats, the issue his candidacy continues to pose is electability. His primary claim to the nomination lies not in ideology and political correctness but in being the Democrat who has the best shot at winning in November.
Washington Post (31 January 1992)

[Imran Khan] had prepared for marriage like a cricket match. He had no guarantees it would work but he would give it his 'best shot'.
Independent (21 June 1995)

glare of television lights. *See* UNDER THE GLARE OF . . .

gloom and doom. *See* DOOM AND GLOOM . . .

gloves are off. General use, mostly journalistic, to describe when a dispute becomes serious. By allusion to boxing in which, when the gloves are taken off, one is left with a bare-knuckle fight. Date of origin unknown. A cliché by the 1970s/80s.

We've got to take the gloves off and we're in a bare knuckle fight on some of the things we've got to do. Because we've got to have an effective and a prosperous industry, and it matters to the people of this country.
Sir Terence Beckett, speech, Confederation of British Industry conference (November 1980)

Billington describes well but his tone is more conscientious than enthusiastic, and one feels that the gloves are still on.
Independent (25 October 1988)

Tottenham chairman Alan Sugar warned his manager Ossie Ardiles today that the gloves are off. The crucial, battling 2–0 win at Oldham has kept Spurs in the Premiership but it is clear that the tough talking is only just beginning.
Evening Standard (London) (6 May 1994)

The European Elections: Gloves are off for main parties as posters paint divisions on Europe with the zeal of an advertising campaign.
Headline, *Independent* (26 May 1994)

If Murdoch can offer big bucks and get them, then so can we. The gloves are off now. We don't like some of the amounts we are having to offer but, if that is what is necessary, that is what will happen. We are fighting for survival here.
Guardian (29 April 1995)

Probably this has grown out of the expression **with the gloves off.** General use, meaning (figuratively) bare-fisted, ready for a fight, setting to without mercy, in earnest. Known by 1827 in the US. A cliché by the mid-twentieth century.

There were now eighteen days left to the campaign, and Mr Nixon was free to take the gloves off and 'peak' in his own manner.
Theodore H. White, *The Making of the President 1960* (1961)

Indications that this latest radio wannabe is ready to take off the gloves in the fight for listeners came this week . . .
Independent (10 June 1995)

gnarled old fishermen. Travel writing use. Date of origin unknown. Listed in the *Independent* 'DIY travel writers' cliché kit' (31 December 1988).

A few miles south of Barfleur is St-Vaast-la-Hougue which has the sort of fishing harbour which guidebooks describe as 'picturesque' and being full of 'gnarled old fishermen'.
Independent (1 October 1988)

Its members were indeed fishermen and 'beach boys', who were not what one might expect at Bondi Beach or Malibu, but entrusted with the task of hauling the fishing-boats on to the shingle, and were often as gnarled and weather-beaten as the old, tarred lugger on view in the town's maritime museum.
The Times (18 March 1989)

The traditional view is instantly recognizable on entering Penlee Art Gallery in Penzance, a brief journey away across a windswept moor. Here are the Gnarled Fishwives of Walter Langley, Percy Craft's weary Fishermen and Garstin's evocative The Rain it Raineth Every Day.
Independent (27 November 1990)

go the whole hog, to. Meaning 'to go all the way'. Known in the US by 1828. In a *Beyond the Fringe* revue sketch in 1961, when Alan Bennett pointed out that Jonathan Miller was 'a Jew', Miller replied by saying that, rather, he was 'not really a Jew, but Jew*ish* – not the whole hog'. A cliché by the mid-twentieth century.

> I suggest we go the whole hog and shove them up 1%. No use being namby pamby about it and going for itsy bitsy fractions.
> *Herald* (Glasgow) (6 June 1994)

> Sebastian Coe, as clean-cut and as mother-in-law-friendly as Andrew, has gone the whole hog and become a Conservative MP. How far does this reflect a trend? Have the moral leaders become young fogeys; or pillars of the Establishment; or SUPPORTERS OF THE STATUS QUO?
> *The Times* (28 September 1994)

goes without saying. *See* IT GOES . . .

golden age of ——. General use. The original golden age was that in which, according to Greek and Roman poets, men lived in an ideal state of happiness. It was also applied to the period of Latin literature from Cicero to Ovid (which was followed by the lesser, silver age). Now the phrase is widely used in such clichés as 'the Golden Age of Hollywood' to describe periods when a country or a creative field is considered to have been at the height of its excellence or prosperity. Kenneth Grahame's story *The Golden Age* (1895) refers to childhood. A cliché by the mid-twentieth century.

> The 'eighties and 'nineties were the Golden Age [of music-hall]; and in 1905 the writing was ON THE WALL . . . Musical comedy, the cinema, television all hastened its decline.
> *Listener* (2 December 1965)

> The Golden Age detective story is ALIVE AND WELL.
> Review in *The Times* of Ruth Rendell's *Put On By Cunning* (1981)

> My generation, the twentysomethings, were fortunate enough to catch the golden age of American TV detectives.
> *Guardian* (3 May 1991)

> Explorers hail 1990s as 'golden age of discovery'.
> Headline, *Independent on Sunday* (30 April 1995)

golden opportunity. General use. Known by 1703. A cliché by 1900.

> With try-scoring so difficult, Wales missed a golden opportunity of taking a decisive lead midway through the first half.
> *The Times* (4 February 1974)

Oxford had thrown away a golden opportunity to finish the day at least on level terms, but they had already done enough to show that they will be a force to be reckoned with in matches to come this season.
The Times (15 April 1995)

One of her tasks is to organise the annual British ABBA day in Bristol – a golden opportunity for hundreds of fanatics who, like Muriel in the film, can forget their real lives, come out of the closet and live out their fantasies as Dancing Queens.
Daily Mirror (21 April 1995)

golden sand. *See* MILES OF ...

gone before. *See* NOT LOST BUT ...

gone but not forgotten. Gravestone and memorial use. The earliest example found (in a far from exhaustive search) is on the headstone to John Worth (died 7 June 1879 aged 71) in Princeton churchyard, Devon. Ludovic Kennedy in his autobiography *On My Way to the Club* (1989) suggests that it is an epitaph much found in the English graveyard at Poona, India. The precise origin of the phrase is not known but it may have been used as the title of a Victorian print showing children at a grave. A cliché by 1900.

Good —— Guide. Commonly used in the titles of books and broadcast programmes. A format which is obviously helped by the alliteration. The first in the field was *The Good Food Guide*, edited by Raymond Postgate (1951). Subsequently, there have been Good – Book, Cheese, Hotel, Museums, Pub, Reading, Sex, Skiing, Software, Word – Guides, and many others.

good news. *See* IT'S GOOD NEWS ...

goodnight. *See* IT'S GOODNIGHT ...

got away. *See* —— THAT ALMOST ...

grasp the nettle, to. General idiomatic use, meaning 'to summon up the courage to deal with a difficult problem'. Known by 1884, possibly earlier. Compare from Shakespeare, *1 Henry IV*, II.iii.9 (1597): 'I tell you, my lord fool, out of this nettle, danger, we pluck this flower, safety.' A cliché by the mid-twentieth century.

The difficulty which the EU and Canada are having in coming to an agreement highlights the scale of the task, however, since no nation appears willing to grasp the nettle and act on what everyone knows – namely that there are too many fishermen chasing too few fish.
Scotsman (13 April 1995)

The fact that individual party membership has now passed the 300,000 mark, the level at which the 1993 constitutional resolution suggested the union's share of conference votes might drop from 70% to 50%, should speed the process. But Mr Blair is unlikely to grasp this particular nettle before the general election.
Economist (29 April 1995)

grasp —— with both hands, to.   General use. Date of origin unknown. A cliché by the mid-twentieth century. It occurs along with other rhetorical clichés during the 'Party Political Speech' (written by Max Schreiner) on the Peter Sellers comedy album *The Best of Sellers* (1958): 'Grasp, I beseech you, with both hands – oh, I'm sorry, I beg your pardon, Madam – the opportunities that are offered. Let us assume a bold front.' Identified as a current cliché in *The Times* (17 March 1995).

If there was to be anything resembling a normal childhood ahead of her, Laura Davies demonstrated she was the sort of girl who would grasp it with both hands.
Daily Telegraph (12 November 1993)

grassroots.   *See* AT/FROM THE . . .

grave concern.   *See* (CAUSING) GRAVE . . .

greatly to be desired.   Rhetorical use. Known by 1603. A cliché by 1900. Cited as a 'resounding commonplace' by George Orwell in 'Politics and the English Language' (*Horizon*, April 1946).

If we are to update the world's fleet, a consummation greatly to be desired in the interests of efficiency and environmental protection, there is no alternative but to accelerate the scrapping of older tonnage.
Lloyd's List (13 September 1994)

The fact that consumption is now growing more slowly than the economy as a whole means that Britain is at last starting to reverse the 1980s trend, when consumption rose sharply as a percentage of GDP, resulting in

rapid de industrialization and a gaping current account deficit. In macro-economic terms, all this is greatly to be desired.
Guardian (21 November 1994)

green and pleasant land. *See* THIS GREEN AND . . .

grinding halt. *See* COME TO A . . .

grist to/for the mill. General use. Capable of being turned to profit or advantage, made use of. Known by 1583 and referring to the saying 'All is grist that comes to his mill', i.e. 'the miller makes profits from any corn that comes to his mill'. Cited as a 'dying metaphor' by George Orwell in 'Politics and the English Language' (*Horizon*, April 1946).

Local artists often are grist for the critic's malevolent word mill. This isn't fair because area performers are competing with world-class companies that tour here. Good, bad and indifferent, local artists are the heart of a town. It's important for them to perform, but not always pleasant to see.
Washington Post (4 April 1995)

On the 1992 tribute album 'Sweet Relief: A Benefit for Victoria Williams,' Williams's songs were interpreted by a wide variety of bands and musicians, including Pearl Jam and Soul Asylum. 'Loose' boasts a similarly convivial atmosphere. Folk, country, pop and rock are all grist for the mill.
Washington Post (11 December 1994)

ground-breaking. Mostly media use for any activity that 'breaks new ground'. At the start of building operations there is often a ground-breaking ceremony performed. In the figurative sense, the phrase was known by 1907. A cliché from about 1985.

Such suspicions are, at present, almost completely without foundation, according to Professor Carl McMillan of Carleton University in Ottawa who presented a ground-breaking study to a Nato economic seminar last month.
Financial Times (18 May 1983)

The judge, who made his order under section 4 (2) of the 1981 Contempt of Court Act, said that he did not doubt a sincere attempt would be made to present a balanced picture in what Channel 4 had described as 'ground-breaking coverage' of a trial.
Guardian (29 January 1985)

Ingram's legal battle to stay alive, defeated in the US Supreme Court last

month and again minutes before his death, led to a ground-breaking ruling that jurors' beliefs on whether a death penalty will be imposed or not is legally irrelevant.
Press Association report (8 April 1995)

Delivering the James MacTaggart Memorial Lecture ... the creator of ground-breaking shows such as *Network 7, The Vampyr* and the *Def II* youth strand said that British television had been pushed to crisis point.
Independent (26 August 1995)

growing experience. *See* IT'S A ...

guilty men. *See* WE NAME THE ...

gymslip mums. Journalistic use, for teenage girls who become pregnant while still attending school (hence the, by now dated, reference to the traditional sleeveless tunic worn by British schoolgirls – the gymslip). Listed (and deplored) by Keith Waterhouse in *Daily Mirror Style* (1981) who wrote that the gymslip: 'Must have given way to jeans and T-shirt mums by now.' No, it hasn't. Not in the minds of out-of-touch journalists, at any rate.

Other vintage episodes being re-run for the first time include the October 1985 teaser which revealed the identity of gymslip mum Michelle's seducer – Dirty Den again.
Herald (Glasgow) (30 January 1995)

Today, Clare, Chris and Linda open their hearts exclusively to *The People* to reveal how they coped from the moment Linda discovered her daughter was about to become a gymslip mum.
People (30 April 1995)

= H =

hair.   *See* AFTER I'VE SHAMPOOED MY . . .

hair's breadth.   *See* WITHIN A . . .

***Hamlet* without the Prince.**   General use, meaning an event without
the leading participant. Byron wrote in a letter on 26 August 1818: 'My
autobiographical essay would resemble the tragedy of Hamlet . . . recited
"with the part of Hamlet left out by particular desire".' This and other
early uses of the phrase may possibly hark back to the theatrical anecdote
(as told in the *Morning Post*, 21 September 1775): 'Lee Lewes diverts them
with the manner of their performing Hamlet in a company that he
belonged to, when the hero who was to play the principal character had
absconded with an inn-keeper's daughter; and that when he came forward
to give out the play, he added, "the part of Hamlet to be left out, for that
night".' A cliché by the 1920s/30s. In 1938 James Agate headed his review
of a Ralph Richardson performance: 'Othello Without the Moor.' Note
also the title of Philip King's play *Without the Prince* (1946).

> For a performance of Hamlet without the prince, prime minister's question
> time on March 15th was surprisingly well-attended. This owed nothing to
> the attractions of John Major's understudy, Tony Newton, who filled in for
> the prime minister while Mr Major toured the Middle East.
> *Economist* (18 March 1995)

> Without skill, football is a meaningless expenditure of energy. Like Hamlet
> without the Prince. Significantly the best talent in our game today, by a light
> year or two, is also a Dane.
> *Herald* (Glasgow) (20 April 1995)

hand in glove.   General idiomatic use, meaning 'going together
extremely well or closely, as snugly as a hand in a glove, in close association
or partnership'. Sometimes with a suggestion of connivance. Originally

101

'hand *and* glove', by 1680. A cliché by 1900. Listed in the *Independent* (24 December 1994) as a cliché of newspaper editorials.

> Architects and builders seldom work hand-in-glove on the kind of housing people can afford to buy.
> *Guardian* (22 February 1975)

> It is a much more smoothly organized system now, almost seamless, and it makes us much more effective in getting our jobs done. Because they have improved their organization, [our customers] are also going to get an improvement, because the two go hand in glove.
> *Lloyd's List* (18 October 1994)

> 'Oh Ireland, my first and only love/Where Christ and Caesar are hand in glove.' Those lines by James Joyce seem at first sight, to encapsulate poetically the dramatic developments which have unfolded in Dublin over the last few days.
> *Scotland on Sunday* (20 November 1994)

hanging by a slender thread.　General idiomatic use. Known by 1707: 'Great God! on what a slender Thread Hang everlasting Things!' – from a hymn by Isaac Watts. A cliché by the mid-twentieth century. Identified as a current cliché in *The Times* (17 March 1995).

> Yet the narrow margin also emphasises the slender thread on which the EU's constitutional arrangements are hung. Having won 'co-decision' rights with the Council of Ministers, the parliament has much more say over European legislation.
> *Financial Times* (22 July 1994)

happiness is ——.　General use, especially in advertising. Samuel Johnson declared in 1766: 'Happiness consists in the multiplicity of agreeable consciousness.' In 1942 along came E.Y. Harburg with the lyrics to his song 'Happiness is a Thing Called Joe'. However, it was Charles M. Schultz (b.1922) creator of the Peanuts comic strip, who really launched the 'Happiness is – ' format. In *c.*1957 he had drawn a strip 'centring around some kid hugging Snoopy and saying in the fourth panel that "Happiness is a warm puppy".' This became the title of a best-selling book in 1962 and let loose a stream of promotional phrases using the format, including (mostly from the mid- to late 1960s): 'Happiness is egg-shaped' (UK, selling eggs); 'Happiness is a quick-starting car' (US, Esso); 'Happiness is a cigar called Hamlet' (UK, since 1964); 'Happiness is a warm ear-piece' (UK); 'Happiness is being elected team captain – and getting a Bulova watch' (US); 'Happiness is a $49 table' (US, Brancusi furniture); 'Happiness is giving Dad a Terry Shave Coat for Christmas' (US, Cone Sporterry); 'Happiness is the Sands' (US, Las Vegas hotel); 'Happiness is a bathroom by Marion Wieder' (US, decorator); 'Happiness can be the color of her hair' (US, Miss Clairol); 'Happiness is being single' (US bumper sticker, seen in NYC, 1981); 'Happiness is seeing Lubbock, Texas, in the rear view mirror' (line from a Country and Western song); 'Happiness is Slough in my rear-view mirror' (car sticker, seen in London, 1981); 'Happiness is a Warm Gun' (song title, 1968); 'Happiness is Wren-shaped' and many, many more.

By which time one might conclude that 'Happiness is ... a worn cliché'.

happy couple. General use, referring to a pair about to be or just joined in matrimony. Known by 1753. A cliché by 1900.

> 'There were cards and good luck messages for the happy couple,' said the insider. 'But now things don't look too good, we're getting phone calls blaming Des for everything again.'
> *Daily Mirror* (14 January 1995)

> About 40 friends and family joined the happy couple at the church.
> *Daily Record* (28 January 1995)

Similarly, **happy pair.** This phrase was known by 1633 and, in the specifically marital sense, by 1697. Also a cliché by 1900.

hate. *See* I'M GONNA . . .

have more goodness in one's little finger than another has in his/her whole body, to. General use. 'She has more goodness in her little finger than he has in his whole body' – cited by Jonathan Swift in *Polite Conversation* (1738). A cliché thereafter.

> Hendry was quick to praise O'Sullivan, saying: 'He's the most talented young player I've ever seen, with more talent in his little finger than 99 per cent of players have in their entire body.'
> *Daily Record* (26 April 1995)

have no/an axe to grind, to. General idiomatic use, meaning 'whether or not there is an ulterior motive, a private end to serve'. This would appear to have originated in an anecdote related by Benjamin Franklin in his essay 'Too Much for Your Whistle'. A man showed interest in young Franklin's grindstone and asked how it worked. In the process of explaining, Franklin – using much energy – sharpened up the visitor's axe for him. This was clearly what the visitor had had in mind all along. Subsequently, Franklin (1706–90) had to ask himself whether other people he encountered had 'another axe to grind'. A cliché by 1900. Cited as a 'dying metaphor' by George Orwell in 'Politics and the English Language' (*Horizon*, April 1946).

> Manhattan Cable showed that some of the most ordinary people are very good on TV. In Britain, where the idea of access is a familiar one, it's still a very mediated and restricted thing where you have to have a politically correct axe to grind.
> *Guardian* (24 October 1991)

have only himself/herself/itself to blame, to.   General use format cliché. Date of origin unknown. A cliché by the 1940s/50s? Listed in the *Independent* (24 December 1994) as a cliché of newspaper editorials.

> Novel reviewers who complain about the mongrel genre of 'faction' have only themselves to blame.
> *The Times* (13 December 1969)

> Mr Byatt thinks that the companies are being silly but he has only himself to blame. He argues that the debate is over, although few outside the industry noticed. There have been strong hints that K may equal zero in some cases, since shareholders have done excessively well since flotation.
> *Daily Telegraph* (7 May 1994)

> Her remark that her husband had only himself to blame for bedding people 'of below-stairs class' is probably the most revealing of all. That a judge and his family should be regarded in modern Britain as having mere servant status is sadly indicative of a society stuck firmly in the past.
> *The Times* (31 May 1994)

having a wonderful time.   *See* WISH YOU WERE HERE!

having said that ...   General use in speech, particularly by politicians and other people when being interviewed by the media. Some written use. A cliché by the 1970s/80s. Identified as a current cliché in *The Times* (17 March 1995).

Having said that, there are of course neg/pos experts who will tell you how to produce a 20 × 16 print . . .
SLR Camera Magazine (March 1979)

I concede that our match fitness and sharpness has been affected by the lengthy period between the end of the Five Nations and the start of the World Cup but, having said that, we will become fresher and stronger the longer the tournament goes on.
Daily Mail (3 June 1995)

he was a big man/a giant among men/larger than life/in every sense of the word/in every way. Clichés of obituary and tribute, especially but not exclusively. Dates of origin not known. Clichés by the 1970s/80s.

Roddy was an excellent stockbroker and wonderful friend. His memorial service . . . was a marvellous tribute to a man who was larger than life in every way.
Money-Brief issued by stockbrokers Gerrard Vivian Gray (April 1989)

Michael Swann, a big man in every way, was a RENAISSANCE figure, scholar, scientist, soldier . . .
Marmaduke Hussey, appreciation of Sir Michael Swann, in the *Independent* (24 September 1990)

John Drummond, a big man in every sense of the word, has protected his fiefdom well. Not one for committee meetings, he has been around the musical world, and the BBC, for decades. He seems to have been allowed a long leash as he approaches retirement after the 1995 season.
Financial Times (11 July 1994)

Sean Bean is many things; former welder, giant among men, supporter of Sheffield United and a lovely little thespian when he is in the mood. But above all, Sean Bean is sexy.
Sunday Times (19 February 1995)

'Absolutely magnificent, a giant among men,' was Alan Hansen's verdict on his fellow Scot.
Herald (Glasgow) (3 April 1995)

Judge Hugh Morton was a big man in every sense of the word. His imposing physical stature was matched by his courage and constant concern for the ordinary people that the law is meant to serve.
Herald (Glasgow) (28 April 1995)

Arnold Goodman, who has died in London after a long illness at the age of 81, was – in both senses of the phrase – larger than life.
Roy Hattersley, *Mail on Sunday* (14 May 1995)

Former prime minister Lord Callaghan described Robert Maxwell as 'a very big man'. He praised Maxwell's 'remarkable gift of leadership.'
Independent (3 June 1995)

head and shoulders. *See* STAND . . .

heading for the rocks. Journalistic and political use. Date of origin unknown. A cliché by the 1980s.

[On being sacked as Deputy Foreign Secretary by Margaret Thatcher] 'It does no harm to throw the occasional man overboard, but it does not do much good if you are steering full speed ahead for the rocks.'
Sir Ian Gilmour, quoted in *Time* Magazine (September 1981)

New Leader's bid to steer Labour off rocks. Captain Kinnock sets sail for No 10.
Headline, *Sunday People* (2 October 1983)

The Tory party is split from stem to stern. The captain of the ship has lost his rudder. And now the mate [Mr Clarke] is steering us towards the rocks again.
Leading article, *Sun* (about 9 December 1994)

To resign now, six months into a new job at Trade, would seem and would be quixotic if this was still an administration heading for victory at the polls. But it isn't. It's an administration heading for the European rocks. Increasingly it's beginning to be every man for himself in the rush for the lifeboats.
Guardian (13 February 1995)

Another Tory political career looked to be heading for the rocks last night after five pages of allegations in the *News of the World* about the sex life of Conservative MP Richard Spring, writes Andy McSmith.
Observer (9 April 1995)

heads must/will roll. General, especially journalistic, use – meaning 'some people will be ousted from their positions of authority for their mistakes or as scapegoats (as if they were being guillotined)'. 'If our movement is victorious there will be a revolutionary tribunal which will punish the crimes of November 1918. Then decapitated heads will roll in the sand' – Adolf Hitler, quoted in *Daily Herald* (26 September 1930). A cliché by the 1960s/70s. 'Heads must roll' listed in the *Independent* (24 December 1994) as a cliché of newspaper editorials.

> Wales lost, and heads rolled.
> *Rugby World* (April 1978)

> Heads are rolling at Warner Music, the world's most successful record company ... Gerald Levin, Time Warner's embattled boss, is out to bring the music makers to heel.
> *Economist* (1 July 1995)

heady mixture. General use, a potent mixture liable to go to the head (like liquor). Date of origin unknown. A cliché by the mid-twentieth century.

> The inquiry last week of the origins of the word 'balderdash' has taken many an intriguing turn, as word inquiries often do. Says Robert Dalgliesh of Cumbria: 'The word is obscure in origin and once meant a heady mixture of alcoholic liquids, thereby resulting in slurred speech and unsound opinions.'
> *Herald* (Glasgow) (13 August 1994)

> Artists from the west travelled into the Moslem and Arab world ... They were drawn inevitably by those living civilizations, no less ancient, through which they had to pass. There they tasted that heady mixture of the exotic and the refined, the cultured and the barbaric, the sympathetic and the alien, that altogether was irresistible.
> *Financial Times* (12 November 1994)

heard in the news. *See* AS YOU MAY HAVE ...

heart. *See* IN THE HEART OF ...

heart(s) of gold. General use, especially journalistic, as in the concept of the 'tart with the heart of gold' (a prostitute with a generous nature). 'There are hearts of gold among those Broadbrims' – G.A. Sala, *The Strange Adventures of Captain Dangerous* (1863). A cliché by the mid-twentieth century. In the early 1990s a sentimental BBC TV series *Hearts of Gold* (hosted by Esther Rantzen) rewarded members of the public who had been nominated for their good deeds.

> Rescued by heart-of-gold Rosie and endeavouring to rehabilitate herself,

Lorraine realises that she is the only witness who can recognize the serial killer.
Irish Times (9 September 1994)

David James of the Hilliard Ensemble, the group responsible for performing most of Pärt's music, explains: 'Arvo's the most lovable guy with a heart of gold and a wonderful, zany sense of humour.'
Independent (21 April 1995)

As Bessie Burgess, a truly rough-voiced, hard-looking Aideen O'Kelly valuably restricts the number of glimpses we get of the heart of gold beating beneath the battle-axe exterior.
Independent (4 May 1995)

heat. *See* IT'S NOT THE HEAT . . .

heave a sigh of relief, to. General use. Date of origin unknown. A cliché by 1900? Listed in the *Independent* (24 December 1994) as a cliché of newspaper editorials.

There were plenty [of women] still to heave a sigh of relief (if their waspies would let them).
The Times (27 May 1976)

Is she his mistress? We certainly presume so until we realise that their arrival at a country hotel is not an indicator of where they'll be spending the night but the setting for a surprise party for his wife. Just as we heave a sigh of relief and begin to think he's a really nice guy he leaves the party and hits the road again.
Sunday Times (22 May 1994)

With the Booker Bingo over for another year, you might have thought that television would heave a sigh of relief and wave cheerio to all that book-chat.
Independent (28 October 1994)

hectic —— (usually **schedule).** An inevitable pairing, especially in journalistic use. Date of origin unknown. A cliché by the 1980s.

Earlier this year Princess Diana took time out of her hectic schedule to sit for this new photographic portrait.
Hello! (13 May 1995)

The acting couple show us the dream farm that's allowed them to put down their roots and provides a break from their hectic film careers.
Hello! (13 May 1995).

With his hectic lifestyle, I asked [Donald] Trump if he found the house relaxing.
British TV programme, *Selina Scott Meets Donald Trump* (18 June1995)

heinous crime.   Inevitable pairing, meaning an utterly odious or wicked crime, but now mostly used figuratively. Known by 1594. A cliché by 1900.

In their feeble discussion of the controversy at Brown University and the so-called PC movement, columnists Jonathan Yardley (Style, Feb. 18) and Nat Hentoff (op-ed, Feb. 26) committed perhaps the most heinous crime of all: labeling justice politically correct.
Washington Post (16 March 1991)

It is lamentable that you ... find you need to portray the crimes as more heinous than they already are, with conjecture rather than the facts contained in the trial transcripts.
Myra Hindley, quoted in the *Independent* (23 September 1995)

hell.   *See* —— FROM . . .

hell and/or high water.   *See* COME . . .

helping the police with their inquiries.   A journalistic stock phrase, now a cliché (mostly British use). When a suspect is being interviewed by the police but has not yet been charged with any offence, this rather quaint euphemism is trotted out and eagerly passed on by the media. It is quite possible, of course, that the suspect in question is, in fact, being quite unhelpful to the police in their inquiries and they are being impolite to him in equal measure. Current by 1957. A cliché shortly thereafter.

A 17-year-old girl ... was found battered to death ... Later, a man was helping police with their inquiries.
Sunday Times (14 October 1973)

Woman knifed to death in garden. A man was arrested close to the scene and was later helping police with their inquiries.
Evening Standard (London) (23 November 1994)

Several hurt in North beatings ... After a brief chase, three men, were arrested and are now helping police with their inquiries.
Irish Times (13 February 1995)

Herod.   *See* OUT-HEROD . . .

highly acclaimed.   Promotional use, especially in theatre, broadcasting and publishing. As with AWARD-WINNING, this adjective, while not being laden with meaning, is often self-serving and thus depressing. The reason for its use is not hard to discover. During the course of the first series of my BBC Radio show *Quote . . . Unquote* (in 1976), I connived with the producer to have it billed in *Radio Times* as 'the highly acclaimed quiz', even though at that stage it was too early for it to be such a thing (compare publishers' use of 'best-selling' on the jackets of books even before they have been put on sale). In no time at all, the servile print media took to describing *Quote . . . Unquote* as 'highly acclaimed' in preview columns.

> Anthony Page directed the acclaimed BBC TV production of *Absolute Hell . . . Richard II* reunited the highly-acclaimed director/actor/designer team . . .
> Royal National Theatre brochure (26 June – 28 August 1995)

his death diminishes us all.   A cliché of obituaries, this derives from John Donne's *Devotions*, XVII (1624): 'Any man's death diminishes me, because I am involved in Mankind: and therefore never send to know for whom the bell tolls; it tolls for thee.' If one can make the distinction, the cliché resides not so much in the words themselves as in the inevitable use of the quotation.

> In some respects, he was a beardless Patrick Geddes. His death diminishes us.
> *Scotsman* (19 July 1993)

> If one person's death diminishes us all, as John Donne believed, the year's crop of celebrated demises has shrunk us to an immoderate degree. Nowhere did the reaper's scythe cut a wider swath than through the arts.
> *Sunday Times* (26 December 1993)

> In our sorrow at his loss we are all united. Our parliamentary life is the poorer; and so is our national life. 'No man is an island,' said the poet, 'each man's death diminishes me.'
> *Scotsman* (13 May 1994)

> 'Any man's death diminishes me, because I am involved in Mankind', wrote John Donne. The latest death to diminish sport was Simon Prior, a 40-year-old Briton who had been racing as a passenger in motorcycle sidecars for two decades.
> *Sunday Times* (19 June 1994)

The word the lawyer, and Ingram's mother, kept using was 'barbaric'. It fitted, twice over. A man had been sentenced not just to death but to 12 years on a knife-edge. 'Any man's death diminishes me,' Donne wrote. But some more than others; and this one more than most.
Independent on Sunday (9 April 1995)

hit the —— for six. General, especially journalistic use, meaning 'to destroy an opponent or demolish an argument completely'. From cricket, where knocking or hitting a ball over the boundary results in six points (or runs) being won. A cliché by the mid-twentieth century. Identified as a current cliché in *The Times* (17 March 1995).

> I began to wonder if my massive and inexpert administration of chloroform had hit his liver – perhaps not inappropriately – for six.
> *Lancet* (1 July 1967)

> Conscious of the rightness of our cause, let us knock the enemy for six.
> *Punch* (23 October 1974)

hog. *See* GO THE WHOLE . . .

hog the limelight. General use, meaning 'to keep the focus of attention upon oneself'. From theatrical use where a spotlight singles out the most prominent performer. Known by 1959 and a cliché shortly thereafter. Listed as a cliché in *The Times* (28 May 1984).

> A back injury had compelled him to return from Pakistan's recent tour of New Zealand after the first Test, leaving Shane Warne to hog the limelight in the new world of the wristy men.
> *Independent* (10 May 1994)

> After several seasons when the Italians, the French and even the Americans seemed to hog the limelight, and several of London's top designers (Vivenne Westwood, John Galliano and Rifat Ozbek) had decamped to join them to show in Milan or Paris, the pendulum has swung back as a new generation of talent has grown up to make London swing again.
> *European* (14 October 1994)

holiday of a lifetime. Mostly promotional and travel-writing use. Date of origin unknown. A cliché by the mid-twentieth century – the most prevalent example of —— of a lifetime phrases.

> Travel: Win the holiday of a lifetime – A week for two in the Philippines by indulging in travel writers' favourite phrases.
> Headline, *Guardian* (23 January 1993)

Building societies change the habits of a lifetime.
Headline, *Daily Telegraph* (19 May 1995)

In December 1995 the Marco Polo is going to take passengers on the Christmas holiday of a lifetime.
Mailshot, Orient Lines (Europe) Ltd (September 1995)

home. *See* LIKE COMING . . .

honeymoon is over for ——. Especially journalistic use, indicating that the period when goodwill is shown to a newly arrived person or plan has finished. Known in a literal sense since Walter Scott, *The Bride of Lammermoor*, Chap. xxi (1818): 'The women could never bear me and always contrived to trundle me out of favour before the honeymoon was over.' A cliché by the 1970s/80s.

'Rise and shine, lovebirds!' he shouted. 'The honeymoon is over!'
H. Nielsen, *The Severed Key* (1973)

The split opposition vote has helped the Tories win the last four general elections; when Blair's honeymoon is over, it could help them win a fifth.
Sunday Times (19 June 1994)

Five years on, Romania's honeymoon is over and the unresolved affairs of the past have returned, like old lovers, to threaten the future.
Daily Telegraph (4 March 1995)

hook or by crook. *See* BY HOOK . . .

hostage to fortune. General idiomatic use – what one establishes by delivering one's future into the hands of fate, usually by making some specific move or decision. 'He that hath wife and children, hath given hostages to fortune; for they are impediments to great enterprizes, either of vertue, or of mischief' – Francis Bacon, *Essay* (Marriage) (1607–12). A cliché by 1900. Listed in the *Independent* (24 December 1994) as a cliché of newspaper editorials.

Every manager who indulges in advertising is giving a hostage to fortune in that he is inviting public confidence in his goods and service, and he will rapidly go out of business if he cannot live up to his claims.
Listener (4 November 1965)

To let a 3–0 lead slip into a narrow 3–2 success as Newcastle had done at St James' Park was always creating a hostage to fortune and the true cost of

their slipping concentration became apparent with Ciganda's strike. It was a desperately disappointing conclusion to a European adventure.
Independent (2 November 1994)

The Budget: The anger has been fuelled: is revenge on the cards? The Political Outlook – Simon Heffer sees the Budget as opportunities missed – with Major giving a hostage to fortune.
By-line, *Daily Telegraph* (30 November 1994)

hotbed of ——. Journalistic use, for anywhere that appears to be a hive of connivance. Date of origin not known. A cliché by the mid-twentieth century. Cited as a 'dying metaphor' by George Orwell in 'Politics and the English Language' (*Horizon*, April 1946).

The University of the Philippines, a hotbed of student activism before Mr Marcos declared martial law in September 1972.
Hongkong Standard (14 April 1977)

It is as though Britain had gone off football or France had tired of haute cuisine. California, that hotbed of new-age political correctness, is beginning to balk at the burden of keeping the globe green.
Sunday Times (26 April 1992)

Backed by News International and enjoying 60,000 gates back home, they have trod a similar precarious path. Brisbane, rugby league-wise once the London of Australia and isolated from the game's hotbed of New South Wales, was barren ground for league colonists.
Observer (22 May 1994)

hotly contested. Inevitable pairing. Known by 1895 and a cliché by 1900.

Swiss Bank has come in for stinging criticism in some quarters for building up a stake in Northern Electricity which is subject to a hotly contested £1200m bid from Trafalgar House.
Herald (Glasgow) (19 January 1995)

They have played in some of the most hotly-contested matches to grace the table-top.
Daily Mail (31 January 1995)

Ever since the establishment of the university acts in the mid-1970s which banned political activity on Malaysian campuses, academic freedom has been a hotly contested issue.
Times Higher Education Supplement (17 March 1995)

house on fire. *See* GET ALONG LIKE A . . .

how did you feel when ——? An appallingly clichéd question from TV newsgathering, especially in the UK: 'How did you feel when your daughter was raped before your eyes/your house was blown up/you'd forgotten to post the pools coupon and lost your next-door neighbour a million pounds?' It may be necessary for the question to be asked in order to elicit a response, but the nearest any of the newsgatherers has come to doing anything about it is to suggest that, while asking the question is a legitimate activity, the question itself shouldn't actually be broadcast – only the answer. Noticed since the mid-1970s. Condemned in *The Times* (31 December 1981) as: 'One of those questions, specialities of television reporting, to which there seems to be no answer that is both rational and polite . . . It was firmly in the category of public interest interrogations which requires Miss Worlds, dismissed football managers and shot policemen to say how they feel about it.'

When Thurgood Marshall was retiring from the US Supreme Court in 1992, he was asked at a press conference, 'How do you feel?' He replied, 'With my hands.'

human dynamo. General idiomatic use, for a person who is tireless in performing any activity. Date of origin probably early 1900s. A cliché by the mid-twentieth century.

A human dynamo of enormous kilowattage.
Daily Express (5 April 1935)

So badly was the Spaniard being mauled that she received an ovation whenever she won a point, but after recovering another break to level at 2–2 in the second set, the human dynamo finally hummed into action and competed in some fierce baseline rallies.
Mail on Sunday (11 September 1994)

A pensioner, known as the Human Dynamo to her friends, has celebrated her 101st birthday.
Northern Echo (14 October 1994)

Moon in . . . Aries: You're the original human dynamo. Nothing stops you from getting what you want, apart from your occasional lack of foresight or self-restraint.
Horoscope, *Daily Mail* (7 December 1994)

humble abode. An inevitable pairing. Date of origin unknown. A cliché by the mid-twentieth century.

A mangy pi-dog shared his humble abode.
The Times (12 June 1959)

Only much later, when the price of whatever humble abode they have managed to secure starts to look like telephone numbers, will they, too, begin with calculating eye to look on their home as a property and contemplate the prospects of trading up.
Irish Times (23 July 1993)

His life revolves around a humble abode on an estate 'at the tap o' the hill' in the ancient Scottish border town of Jedburgh.
Daily Mail (4 February 1994)

= I =

I could help get you into films.   Cliché of seduction, presumably since the 1930s/40s.

I couldn't, Bill, I'd only feel cheap.   Film script use, rejecting a pass. Probably from the 1940s/50s – could Doris Day have said it? Cited in the song 'I Love a Film Cliché' by Dick Vosburgh and Trevor Lyttelton from the show *A Day in Hollywood, A Night in the Ukraine* (1980). *See also* I'M GONNA HATE MYSELF . . .

I don't know much about art but I know what I like.   In *Are You a Bromide?* (1907), the American writer Gelett Burgess castigated people who spoke in clichés. Among the 'Bromidioms' he listed was: 'I don't know much about Art, but I know what I like.' In his novel *Zuleika Dobson* (1911), Max Beerbohm says of the heroine when she is at a college concert: 'She was one of the people who say, "I don't know anything about music really, but I know what I like".'

> [Keith Floyd says: 'My] house is full of daft articles I've picked up from all over the place . . . I don't know anything about art or music; I just know what I like.'
> *Irish Times* (11 August 1994)

I found that if I made people laugh they left me alone.   What all comics say about the origins of their success. It all started with having to deal with bullies at school. First noticed in the 1970s/80s.

I love it but it doesn't love me.   A cliché of conversation – what people say to soften the refusal of what they have been offered in the way of food or drink. Jonathan Swift lists it in *Polite Conversation* (1738):

> *Lady Smart*: Madam, do you love bohea tea?
> *Lady Answerall*: Why, madam, I must confess I do love it; but it does not love me . . .

116

I see myself more as a caretaker for my descendants. What aristocrats tend to say when challenged with the fact that they have inherited vast wealth, estates, stately homes, etc.: 'Of course, all this doesn't really belong to me, I see myself more as a caretaker for my descendants . . .' Used by Gerald Grosvenor, 6th Duke of Westminster, when interviewed on BBC TV's *Aristocrats* (November 1983).

I think that shows we're getting it about right. A cliché of argument. For example, when defending itself in the 1980s, the BBC was in the habit of pointing out that half the letters of complaint it received about a particular programme were critical, the other half supportive. 'I think that shows we're getting it about right . . .', a spokesman or mandarin would say.

> Top TV dramatist Andrew Davies is the latest figure to pour scorn on Alan Yentob, embattled head of BBC1 . . . Indeed, so contradictory are the complaints that Mr Yentob probably feels he's getting it about right.
> John Naughton, *Evening Standard* (London) (4 January 1995)

> For a man caught in such vitriolic crossfire, the Scottish National Heritage chairman is remarkably sanguine . . . 'We get opposition from both sides, which pleases me very much, because it means we're getting it about right. We are going along the line of mediation between them, of the practical, the possible, not just the ideal. We are working towards what we can achieve.'
> *Herald* (Glasgow) (3 May 1995)

I want to make it perfectly clear. Politicians' cliché, often said when doing quite the opposite. Much used by William Whitelaw, British Conservative politician – especially when Home Secretary in the early 1980s.

> Is it too much to ask the Conservative government here to make it perfectly clear that we do consider Mussolini to be a notorious mass murderer and we hold with contempt all those in Italy who consider him some sort of hero?
> *Independent* (5 May 1994)

> I want to make it perfectly clear that he was under no pressure from the Argyle board to resign due to the club's poor start.
> *Today* (14 September 1994)

> Mr Hamilton said last night: 'I entirely refute the allegations and the writ will make that perfectly clear.' When asked if there was any grain of truth in the Guardian report Mr Hamilton said: 'My writ I think is eloquent testimony to

the view that I have as to their veracity. Nobody issues a writ to launch a libel action for fun.'
The Times (21 October 1994)

I want to make it perfectly clear that Lough Derg Yacht Club didn't cancel the regatta, it was cancelled by the ISA.
Irish Times (31 March 1995)

See also BEARS ELOQUENT TESTIMONY.

I would like to spend more time with my (wife and) family. A cliché of (mostly British) political resignations. In March 1990, two of Prime Minister Thatcher's ministers – Norman Fowler and Peter Walker – withdrew from the Cabinet, both giving as their reason for going that they wished to 'spend more time with their families'. Fowler, in his resignation letter, wrote: 'I have a young family and for the next few years I should like to devote more time to them while they are still so young.' Prime Minister Thatcher replied: 'I am naturally very sorry to see you go, but understand your reasons for doing this, particularly your wish to be able to spend more time with your family.'

Subsequently, Gordon Brown, the Labour MP, suggested in the House of Commons that Nicholas Ridley might care to follow suit. But the Secretary of State for Industry was having none of it. 'The last thing I want to do,' he said, 'is spend more time with my family' (quoted in the *Independent*, 14 July 1990).

I would not touch it with a barge-pole. General, slangy use, to indicate that the speaker will not have anything to do with something, will keep his or her distance, avoid at all costs. From the *length* of the barge-pole used to propel a barge. Known by 1893. Eric Partridge, *A Dictionary of Clichés* (5th edition, 1978), dates it as late nineteenth to twentieth century. Yes, a cliché almost since its inception.

'Hideous little beast! I wouldn't touch him with the end of a barge pole.'
A.H. Gibbs, *Persistent Lovers* (1915)

She has begun to campaign on behalf of other badly hit Names concentrated on the so-called 'spiral' syndicates – those which provided reinsurance against large-scale losses for other Lloyd's syndicates. 'If I knew then what I know now I wouldn't touch (Lloyd's) with a bargepole,' she says.
Financial Times (1 May 1993)

'Frankly, I wouldn't touch any of the men I have met in nightclubs with a bargepole,' says Jane, 23, who lives in Surrey.
Today (24 August 1993)

I'll be going back. Journalistic use. Travel writers' and restaurant critics' recommendation phrase. Listed as part of the 'travel scribes' armoury' compiled from a competition in the *Guardian* (10 April 1993).

Neither of us liked the sound of any of five puddings which included a fig and cinnamon tartlet – probably very good, if you liked figs – a rice pudding and a praline and chestnut meringue with vanilla ice-cream. I've since been told that the Cantina's puds have been known to prop up smart London dinner-party conversation, so I'll be going back to try them.
Independent (10 July 1994)

Mr Smart said Americans were very friendly. 'They could teach us a few lessons in manners and on the roads as well. I'll be going back next year.'
Scotsman (18 September 1993)

I'll see myself out. Drama use. What the visiting policeman invariably say after having come to break some bad news. It enables the other participants to continue the scene without a break. Observed by Fritz Spiegl in an article on drama cliché lines in the *Listener* (7 February 1985).

I'm gonna hate myself for this in the morning. Drama use. Observed by Fritz Spiegl in an article on drama cliché lines in the *Listener* (7 February 1985). *See also* I COULDN'T, BILL, . . .

I'm sorry, I'll read that again. The BBC radio newsreader's traditional apology for a stumble was registered as a cliché when the phrase was taken as the title of a long-running radio comedy show (1964–73) featuring ex-Cambridge Footlights performers.

I've never believed in anything so much/been so serious in all my life. Something of a cliché of film scriptwriting, though perhaps not too painful as clichés go. An example occurs in Noël Coward's play *Design for Living* (1932) in the form: 'I've never been so serious in my life.' There is a 'believed' version in the film *Dangerous Moonlight* (UK, 1941). Compare what Mickey Rooney says to Judy Garland in *Strike Up the Band* (US, 1940): 'Mary, I was never more sure of anything in my life'; and what Fred Astaire says to Rita Hayworth in *You'll Never Get Rich* (US, 1941): 'I was never so sure of anything in my life.'

But it is an old format. In Henry Fielding's *Tom Jones* (1749) there is: 'D–n me if ever I was more in earnest in my life'. In Conan Doyle's 'The Priory School' (1905): 'I was never more earnest in my life'; and in 'The Cardboard Box' (1917): 'I was never more serious in my life.'

iceberg.   *See* TIP OF THE . . .

icon/ikon.   *See* — IS AN . . .

icy grip.   *See* WINTER HOLDS . . .

if they/we can put a man on the moon, why can't they/we . . .?   'The Apollo program . . . inspired the most seductive, the most overused, and the just plain silliest cliché of our time. You've all heard it a million times. It's the one that begins, "Well, if we can put a man on the moon, why can't we . . ." and here you fill in the blank. Why can't we cure cancer . . . feed the hungry . . . end poverty' – Robert Eaton, chairman and chief executive officer of Chrysler Corporation, quoted in *The Executive Speaker* (April 1995). The cliché – if it is indeed one – soon took shape. From BBC TV *Monty Python's Flying Circus* (29 September 1970): 'It is incredible, isn't it, that in these days when man can walk on the moon and work out the most complicated hire purchase agreements, I still get these terrible headaches.'

if you'll excuse the pun!   Arch use by the humourless, when they have just committed one. So ghastly, I feel like calling it a cliché, which it isn't really. Alternatives are **pardon the pun** and **no pun intended**. Nothing new about it: in *Pictures from Italy* (1846), Charles Dickens wrote, 'The ten fingers, which are always – I intend no pun – at hand.'

> I begin to think that perhaps there is a point in keeping a foot in both camps [theatre and films]. No pun intended.
> Kenneth Williams, letter of 11 January 1973, in *The Kenneth Williams Letters* (1994)

> But these have to be dry cleaned! Apart from the expense, can you imagine men remembering to drop off their underwear (excuse the pun!) at the cleaners – not to mention all those red faces as their knickers are spread out on the counter to be labelled.
> *Northern Echo* (25 July 1994)

> You could refer to it as a case of cheap sex – just under £1m was used to

set up the campaign using the advertising world's favourite tool (no pun intended) i.e. sex.
Today (10 August 1994)

But other headlines suggest that what we have here is an offshoot of *Farmer's Weekly*. There are lots of pictures of golden ears of wheat and the happy slogan 'It's Harvestime!' . . . The magazine is, in fact, a product of 'Covenant Ministries International'. Alongside the key words 'Toronto' and 'blessing', all the words and pictures which I have mentioned fall (no pun intended) into place.
Independent (25 February 1995)

ill-gotten gains. General use. An inevitable coupling, referring to money or other benefit gained illegally or in any underhand way. Macaulay used it in his *History of England* (1859). A cliché by 1900.

The resorts seemed to be full of elderly English derelicts . . . all . . . anxiously searching the Times ordinary share index for news of their ill-gotten gains.
Kenneth Williams (letter of 12 March 1972) in *The Kenneth Williams Letters* (1994)

Undercover Britain claims to be a 'hard-hitting documentary series which exposes injustices', but who is it ultimately aimed at? Not the exploiters, who are far too busy enjoying their ill-gotten gains to watch TV; nor the exploited, who have probably never pressed the CH4 button on their handsets.
Evening Standard (London) (28 March 1995)

Businesses up and down the land are receiving faxes from Lagos sent by one Mr Nko Ezeh, the chairman of the contract award and implementation committee and chief accountant of the corporation who is offering $10 million to anyone prepared to let him use their bank account to transfer ill-gotten gains of 35 million out of Nigeria.
Irish Times (21 April 1995)

illustrious dead. General use. Known by 1809 and a cliché by the 1920s/30s.

Goethe is in danger of turning into a Nobodaddy – a booming, boring member of that depressed class, the illustrious dead.
Listener (29 November 1962)

Such illustrious dead as Orpheus and Eurydice, Vermeer and his pearl girl, a swami and an American millionaire couple are repetitively enacting key

moments of their lives at the command of the jackal Anubis who feeds off their desires.
Sunday Times (30 October 1994)

Marie Curie, who discovered radium, was yesterday chosen to be the first woman for burial in the Paris Pantheon, resting place of France's illustrious dead.
Herald (Glasgow) (15 March 1995)

immemorial elms. Cliché of quotation – from Alfred Tennyson, *The Princess*, Canto vii, 206 (1847): 'The moan of doves in immemorial elms'. A cliché by 1900.

The PM . . . dreams of a Britain where we all drink warm beer in the shadow of immemorial elms, and nuns bicycle to church through the mist, and Denis Compton is still at the crease on the final day of the Oval test match.
Observer (19 February 1995)

I have driven for hours around those winding lagoon-like car parks, lovingly landscaped between clumps of immemorial elms, trying to find the exit.
Times Higher Education Supplement (31 March 1995)

impish grin. General use. An inevitable pairing. Used by George Eliot in *Romona* (1863). A cliché by 1900.

The Roux brothers, who have not changed their name or, as far we know, their religion, but simply become more discernibly Albert and Michel, would doubtless agree with that lyric – although an impish grin is a valuable part of their public personae.
Evening Standard (London) (26 July 1994)

'Sully in *Nobody's Fool* is about that stubborn, wilful and foolish part of my father that I love so deeply. I guess I may have inherited too many of those qualities,' he says with an impish grin.
Scotland on Sunday (9 April 1995)

in a nutshell. General idiomatic use. Meaning 'compactly, in brief'. Known by 1693. Book title: *The Franco-Prussian War in a Nutshell* by E. Perkins (1871). A cliché shortly thereafter.

Muddling Through, or Britain in a Nutshell
Title of book by Betty Askwith and Theodora Benson (1936)

That, in a nutshell, is the mysterious art of switch trading.
Economist (14 January 1967)

Management (The Growing Business): British businesses on the rise – in a nutshell.
Headline, *Financial Times* (24 January 1995)

My highest scorer has netted five goals, the next best four. Le Tissier has scored 29. That's the difference in a nutshell.
Evening Standard (London) (4 May 1995)

in a time warp. *See* TIME HAS PASSED BY . . .

in a very real sense. Mostly rhetorical use and flannel of the worst sort. Date of origin unknown. In 1970 I wrote a sketch called 'Yes, Folks, It's Obituary Time' which parodied the obituary clichés spoken at a memorial meeting for a recently dead author. This phrase was intoned ritually in turn by about six speakers: 'The death of A.B. Porter has plucked from our midst, in a very real sense, one of the greatest and most significant figures in twentieth-century English literature . . .'

> What I think is clear is that what Lawrence is trying to do is to portray the sex relationship as something essentially sacred . . . as in a real sense an act of holy communion.
> Rt. Rev. John Robinson on *Lady Chatterley's Lover* (evidence in Regina *v.* Penguin Books Ltd, 27 October 1960)

> You know, when I was preparing this Thought for the Day my glance fell on a painting of The Last Supper, and I couldn't help feeling, in a very real sense, that Jesus and the twelve disciples were much like a prime minister and his cabinet.
> Miles Kington, *Independent* (12 June 1995)

in anybody's list of the ten most . . . Journalistic use, mostly. The compiling of lists became in itself a journalistic and publishing cliché in the 1980s – see *Hunter Davies's Book of British Lists* (1980) – and shows no sign of dying out in the 1990s. This particular phrase was listed as part of the 'travel scribes' armoury' compiled from a competition in the *Guardian* (10 April 1993). Heralding the announcement of 'crowded beaches/unlikely holiday resorts/hazardous safari holidays' it harks back to the original traveller's list of lists: the Seven Wonders of the World.

> A top ten hit list of the most complained about goods has been published by trading standards officers.
> *Northern Echo* (7 July 1993)

In the process he has overtaken Mr Reagan in the polls and has featured

seven years running in Good Housekeeping magazine's list of the ten most-admired Americans.
The Times (16 June 1994)

The offer, and the inclusion of the two men on the FBI's Ten Most Wanted Fugitives List, had 'the ring of banditry', said Lord Macaulay.
Herald (Glasgow) (19 May 1995)

in cold blood. General use, meaning 'with cool deliberateness', especially as in 'murdered in cold blood'. Known by 1711. *In Cold Blood* was the title of Truman Capote's 'non-fiction novel' (1965). A cliché by that time.

'The obvious motive was payment of money and the act was carried out in cold blood,' the Recorder of London, Sir Lawrence Verney, told Te Rangimaria Ngarimu.
Guardian (23 December 1994)

It wasn't akin to the actions of a street brawler at pub throwing-out time, it was a case of a highly trained athlete attacking someone in cold blood.
Today (26 January 1995)

in London's ——. Journalistic use. Unnecessary and failed attempt at avoiding saying that somewhere is '... in London'. Noticed by the 1960s/70s.

In London's EXCLUSIVE Park Lane.
ITN news (28 May 1994)

But from the start it was widely accepted in Reed's comfortable head office, off Curzon Street in London's exclusive Mayfair, that Elsevier was a high-risk partner.
Independent on Sunday (3 July 1994)

The Sports Cafe in London's bustling Haymarket makes no apologies for being a bloke-ish sort of place.
Observer (4 June 1995)

in no uncertain terms. General use as waffle filler. Known by 1958. A cliché possibly before this.

Let me forecast in no uncertain terms that this policy can lead only to a severe shortage of high quality reds in five years' time.
Age (Melbourne) (18 January 1977)

When I asked her to calm down, she informed me, in no uncertain terms, of my place in the scheme of things.
Today (15 February 1995)

I told him in no uncertain terms to go to bed. He just would not listen to reason. He would not listen to the fact he should not do it.
Herald (Glasgow) (4 March 1995)

in pole position, to be.   General use, but especially journalistic. Derived from motor racing: it is the grid position which is on the front row and on the inside of the first bend. Hence taken to mean any advantageous position. Previously 'to have the pole' meant the same thing in horse racing. Known by 1953. A cliché from the 1970s/80s onwards.

Ipswich relinquished their hold on the pole position to champions Liverpool.
News of the World (17 April 1977)

Eurovision Song Contest 1995 ... with Love City Groove's Euro-rap in pole position, Dublin can finally be rid of the whole affair.
Independent Metro (12 May 1995)

In Question.   *See* QUESTION OF ...

in the cold light of day.   General use, to describe how things look realistically, as compared to the feverish perceptions of night-time or just after the event has taken place. Date of origin unknown. A cliché by the mid-twentieth century.

And always in the cold light of the Falklands dawn, the ... Marines ... have always been ready to 'yomp on'.
Daily Telegraph (3 June 1982)

The bag follows her everywhere and gets bigger as she asks a number of people for advice, but gets no help. Finally, her grandmother steps in and, slowly and with great care, she pulls out the worries, which seem small in the cold light of day.
Scotsman (21 September 1994)

'In the cold light of day you could not say yesterday was strictly Gold Cup form,' Henderson said. 'But it was a great race, a good step up for him and I thought he was very brave to answer all the questions. He's getting there quite quickly.'
Independent (19 December 1994)

in the final/last/ultimate analysis. General *horrendous* use. A venerable construction. 'Ultimate analysis' was known by 1791. 'Last analysis' by 1844. 'Final analysis' by 1944: 'In the final analysis, there are two types of program music . . .' – Willi Apel, *The Harvard Dictionary of Music* (1944). 'In the final analysis, all girls aspire to be beauties' – Vladimir Nabokov, *The Gift* (1963). 'Poetry . . . is in the last analysis an endeavour to condense . . .' – W.B. Yeats, Preface to *Poems* (1906). *H.L. Mencken's Dictionary of Quotations* (1942) contains this translation of a passage from J.M. Charcot, *De l'Expectation en Médecine* (1857): 'In the last analysis, we see only what we are ready to see, what we have been taught to see.'

All clichés by the mid-twentieth century. 'Final analysis' was listed in the *Independent* (24 December 1994) as a cliché of newspaper editorials. *Fowler's Modern English Usage* (2nd edition, 1965) had earlier concentrated its fire specifically on 'in the ultimate analysis'.

> Fenella Fielding has rushed into print saying 'I feel outraged on behalf of the entire profession' . . . But really – in the last analysis – who cares?
> Kenneth Williams, letter of 19 June 1967, in *The Kenneth Williams Letters* (1994)

> Which is more 'barbaric' in the final analysis? A highly controlled society which deters crime by punitive retribution, or a society where innocent people are subjected to daily torment by vandalism and crime – much of which goes unpunished?
> *Daily Mail* (6 May 1994)

> In Europe, British Airways occupied middle rankings for much of the final analysis, despite having one of the most profitable first-class cabin operations. BA's staff service was commended for its consistency, but the finer 'service delivery quality' lacks finesse, with too many staff adopting a take-it-or-leave-it attitude.
> *European* (24 March 1995)

> Mr Taylor's solo dash may have been intended to gain political brownie points for the Labour Party. It was not an exercise in open, accountable and transparent politics. But in the last analysis a slightly less individualist and slightly more inclusive approach might win greater support within the Government, within the Oireachtas, and among the electorate.
> *Irish Times* (4 May 1995)

> The same kind of audit behaviour that is permissible within the institution and its own staff and students is often totally inappropriate when used upon an external clientele who, in the last analysis, are the university's customers.
> *Times Higher Education Supplement* (5 May 1995)

in the heart of ——. Show business, journalistic use. A cliché by the mid-twentieth century. I recall writing in a 1966 sketch: 'The well-known male impersonator, Miss Deirdre de la Zouche, has just opened a new cabaret club in the heart of London's theatreland'.

> All Carlton's UK companies were required to use VIP, which operates out of EXCLUSIVE premises in the heart of London's Mayfair.
> *Mail on Sunday* (12 June 1994)

See also IN LONDON'S ——.

in the land of the living. General slangy use, meaning 'alive'. From Jeremiah 11:19: 'Let us cut him off from the land of the living, that his name may be no more remembered.' A cliché by the mid-twentieth century. One might say of a person referred to: 'Oh, is he still in the land of the living?'

in the lap of luxury. General use, where (usually) the luxury is being envied. Known by 1802. A cliché by 1900.

> If you just want to be pampered, try . . . the Lap of the Minch in the lap of luxury (£900–£3000 per person).
> *Herald* (Glasgow) (16 July 1994)

> Shock for our man in the lap of luxury.
> Headline, *Daily Mail* (21 September 1994)

> Even though judges are living in the lap of luxury, they can still claim £40 a day for meals.
> *Daily Mirror* (22 September 1994)

in the pipeline. Mostly media use, meaning 'in train, on the way'. Known by 1955. A cliché by the 1970s.

> We have several more [test-tube] babies in the pipeline.
> A doctor speaking on BBC Radio in 1985

> Evidence of the bulge of higher prices working along the inflation pipeline is shown in Dun & Bradstreet's finding that the proportion of retailers expecting to raise prices climbed from 66.5 to 69.5 per cent.
> *Independent* (19 April 1995)

> The drive in the Mondeo was a tantalizing glimpse of the near future. Renault, Volvo, Volkswagen and other manufacturers have similar systems in the pipeline.
> *Independent* (6 May 1995)

in the tradition of ——. Mostly promotional use in publishing. Possibly since the 1970s and always an obnoxious habit if not quite a cliché. At its worst, this device is used to get the name of a better or more famous author on to the cover of a (usually) paperback edition of a lesser one. So, the new authors are said to be writing 'in the tradition of Catherine Cookson/Dick Francis' or whoever – when what they are really doing is hoping that some of the established authors' gold dust will descend upon them. At its least offensive, as in the first citation, it is just rather pompously self-serving (even if that is what blurbs are supposed to be . . .)

> In the tradition of his best-selling books *'Quote . . . Unquote'* and *Graffiti Lives, OK* and his popular radio and television shows, Nigel Rees presents another galaxy of quotes and quizzes.
> Blurb, *The 'Quote . . . Unquote' Book of Love, Death and the Universe* (1980)

> A nostalgic Cockney novel in the Lena Kennedy tradition.
> Paperback blurb on Harry Bowling, *Conner Street's War* (1987)

> In the grand tradition of Catherine Cookson.
> Paperback blurb for Josephine Cox, *Alley Urchin* (1992) and other books of hers published by Headline

in this day and age. General use, another piece of verbal padding. Date of origin unknown, though there was a film with the title *This Day and Age* (US, 1933). Identified as a still current cliché by Eric Partridge in the preface to the 5th edition of his *A Dictionary of Clichés* (1978). Dating it since 1960, he says the phrase, 'originally possessing sonority and dignity, now implies mental decrepitude and marks a man for the rest of his life'. Also condemned by Howard Dimmock of Westcliff-on-Sea in a letter to the *Sunday Times* (31 December 1989).

> What a comfort it was in this day and age to meet someone obliging.
> *New Yorker* (17 October 1970)

> Given the wonderful, or supposedly so, communications that we have these days, surely this could all have been avoided, or am I the one who needs his head examined for expecting people in this day and age to have some simple, old-fashioned ethics.
> *Herald* (Glasgow) (22 July 1994)

> We knew drug-dealing was going on in one part of it but I thought that, in this day and age, you just had to learn to accept that sort of thing.
> *People* (4 December 1994)

inch war. Journalistic tag for dieting. Date of origin unknown. Listed as a phrase to be avoided by Keith Waterhouse in *Daily Mirror Style* (1981).

> Business Travel: Battle of the inch war is hotting up – Airlines are fighting hard to offer more space by dropping First class, reports Trevor Webster.
> By-line, *Evening Standard* (London) (8 June 1994)

> As part of a two-day investigation into why our bodies are shaped the way they are, *Today* talks to some former champion slimmers . . . and discovers that, in the inch war, one battle doesn't always make a victory.
> *Today* (7 November 1994)

inconvenience. *See* — DEEPLY REGRET(S) ANY . . .

industrial action. Used in British journalism for a strike or stoppage, and thus something of a cliché denoting, rather, 'inaction'. An odd coinage, which was established by 1970. There even used to be the occasional 'Day of Action' on which no one did any work – for example, the TUC's on 14 May 1980.

> Labour also pointed out that the proposal . . . was a response to two important changes: the tight restrictions, including ballots, on lawful industrial action – which Labour will not reverse – and the relatively new industrial practice of sacking workers en masse.
> *Independent* (2 May 1995)

> Strikes or 'days of action' are planned for later this month by workers in social-security offices, France Telecom, the state gas and electricity monopolies, the postal service and Air Inter. Renault, Bull, and Thomson CSF are also threatened with further industrial action.
> *Independent* (10 May 1995)

inquiries. *See* HELPING THE POLICE WITH . . .

***Insight* style.** *See* AT FIVE MINUTES PAST EIGHT . . .

integrity. *See* IT'S ABSOLUTELY VITAL . . .

introduction. *See* NEEDS NO . . .

iron fist/hand. *See* (WITH AN) IRON . . .

iron resolution. General idiomatic use. An inevitable pairing. Date of origin unknown. A cliché by the mid-twentieth century. Cited as a 'dying metaphor' by George Orwell in 'Politics and the English Language' (*Horizon*, April 1946).

> There is one overriding concern in today's Labour Party. Indeed it is part of John Smith's legacy: an iron resolution not to allow anyone to know what it is thinking.
> *Daily Mail* (26 May 1994)

> Cricket: Hick gives England heart . . . Instead, he proceeded to play one of iron resolution, which was equally impressive.
> *The Times* (29 November 1994)

—— *is* ——. A cliché of sloganeering, in which actors or singers are promoted as if they are indistinguishable from the characters they are portraying. The film *You Only Live Twice* (1967) was promoted with the slogan, 'Sean Connery *is* James Bond' – surely, a debatable proposition at the best of times and only likely to encourage a regrettable tendency, particularly among journalists, to confuse actors with their roles. Other examples:

> Michael Caine is Alfie is wicked!
> (1966)

> Paul Hogan *is* Crocodile Dundee.
> (1987)

> *Phil Collins* is *Buster*.
> Title of video about the making of the film *Buster* (UK, 1988)

> Domingo *is* Otello.
> [*sic*] advertisement in *Los Angeles* Magazine (March 1989)

> Jessye Norman *is* Carmen.
> Advertisement on LBC radio, London (August 1989)

—— **is a long time in** ——. *See* WEEK IS A LONG TIME . . .

—— **is an icon/ikon.** General use, especially journalistic, often meaning no more than that something or somebody is a popular idol of the moment. A cliché in the early 1990s.

> The Icon and the Dambuster – From the Birth of Venus to bouncing beachballs, the legendary Pamela Green spent two shaven decades taking her clothes off in the cause of art. Byron Rogers met her and her husband in retirement on the Isle of Wight.
> By-line, *Sunday Telegraph* (15 May 1994)

130

If Cobain quite literally found himself unable to live with the pressures of being a rock star, will Love survive the increasing intensity of the spotlight over the next year or so? ONLY TIME WILL TELL, but Cobain was insular, shy and convinced he should have been not a rock icon but an anonymous painter, whereas Love is a party animal driven by her determination to be a star.
Guardian (10 May 1995)

With ambivalent implications, Queen Elizabeth contrived to appropriate that tradition for her own purposes, making a blazon of herself and turning her own body, with a pinch of poetic licence, into a symbol of nationhood (Gloriana, Astraea) and a quasi-religious erotic icon.
Times Higher Education Supplement (26 May 1995)

His best remembered design (his favourite) may well be Lunar Rocket, produced for Warner's centenary year in 1970 when space exploration was topical. Commercially unsuccessful at the time, it has become a period icon.
Guardian (29 May 1995)

It is as an icon of single-minded, coherent, unsinkable, passionate sensibility that [Oscar Wilde] survives in the public mind.
Independent Magazine (3 June 1995)

—— **is the cruellest month.** Journalistic use – or rather misuse – of a quotation. 'April is the cruellest month, breeding/Lilacs out of the dead land' – the first five words of T.S. Eliot's *The Waste Land* (1922) are frequently misquoted. Often 'August' is substituted for 'April', possibly out of confusion with *August is a Wicked Month*, the title of a novel (1965) by Edna O'Brien. But, really, almost any month can be inserted into the format:

After the highs and lows of Christmas and the winter holidays, February always seems to me the cruellest month.
Daily Telegraph (15 February 1992)

Sometimes March can be the cruellest month.
Northern Echo (18 February 1992)

August used to be the cruellest month.
The Times (25 August 1992)

June is the cruellest month in politics.
The Times (5 June 1993)

August has always been the cruellest month.
The Times (25 August 1993)

—— **is the name of the game.** General use, meaning '... is what it's all about' or '... is the essence of the whole thing'. Of American origin and a cliché since its inception. Eric Partridge's *Dictionary of Catch Phrases* finds an example in 1961. US National Security Adviser McGeorge Bundy talking about foreign policy goals in Europe in 1966 said: 'Settlement is the name of the game.' In time, almost everything was, following the title of an American TV movie called *Fame Is the Name of the Game* (1966). Then followed several series of American TV's *The Name of the Game* (1968–71).

> The name of the game this week is survival.
> *The Times* (29 September 1972)

—— **is the new rock 'n' roll.** Journalistic use, mainly. A buzz phrase of the early 1990s, open to adaptation, was to the effect that 'comedy is the new rock 'n' roll'. In Britain at that time, such was the attention paid to comedy performers and writers in the 'alternative' and 'improvisational' fields, and such was the wealth and fame accrued by other young comedy practitioners in the media generally, that the parallel was drawn with the exciting, fashionable phenomenon of an earlier time. The phrase made an early appearance in the *Guardian* (19 October 1991): 'In this age of CDs, Discmasters, videos, prototype virtual reality, handheld computer games, all-night raves, and stand-up comedy as the new rock 'n' roll, the gig has become a tedious anachronism.' A cliché shortly thereafter.

> This year's award recognizes the way the arts can reach out and extend into new areas and to a new audience. For many who have seen it, the Citizens' Theatre production of *Trainspotting* is a reminder of how powerful drama can be. *Trainspotting* proves that theatre can be the new rock 'n' roll.
> *Herald* (Glasgow) (21 May 1994)

is there life after ——? Media use and generally. Presumably derived from the question of life after death, there seems no end to the variations on this theme. The original question was posed, for example, in BBC TV *Monty Python's Flying Circus* (21 December 1972): 'Tonight on "Is There" we examine the question, "Is there a life after death?" And here to discuss it are three dead people.' The cliché use followed very quickly. There were films (US, 1971 and 1973) with the titles *Is There Sex After Death?* and *Is There Sex After Marriage?*

The variant 'Is there life *before* death?' was recorded as a graffito in

Ballymurphy, Ireland, *c.*1971 and is confirmed by Seamus Heaney's poem 'Whatever You Say Say Nothing' from *North* (1975) which has:

> Is there a life before death? That's chalked up
> In Ballymurphy . . .

But as if this underlines the saying's Irish origins too well, bear in mind that 'Is there life before death?' had earlier been the epigraph to Chapter 9 of Stephen Vizinczey's novel *In Praise of Older Women* (1966). There, it is credited to 'Anon. Hungarian'.

Is There Life After Housework?
Title of book (1981) by Don A. Aslett

Is there life after redundancy?
Headline, *Sunday Times* Magazine (14 October 1984)

Is there life after Wogan?
Headline, *Sunday People* (14 October 1984)

island paradise.   Travel journalism and promotional use. Date of origin unknown. A cliché by the 1960s/70s.

For the opening programme, Jill reports from the island paradise of Mauritius.
Daily Record (1 November 1994)

As a blood red sun settled across the Pacific Ocean, Brando learned that he had failed his daughter for the last time. She had hanged herself in her bedroom on the South Pacific island paradise of Tahiti.
Daily Mail (18 April 1995)

Even on their wedding day they were to be found exchanging sacred vows on the paradise isle of Fiji.
Hello! (13 May 1995)

issue.   *See* BREAD AND BUTTER . . .

it does help in a crowded restaurant when you're trying to get a table.   What British aristocrats invariably reply when asked if there is any advantage to having a title. 'No, I don't think it helps me at all, but . . .' Used by Gerald Grosvenor, 6th Duke of Westminster, when interviewed on BBC TV's *Aristocrats* (November 1983).

it goes without saying.   General rhetorical use, always risking the rejoinder, 'Well, don't bother then.' Translated from the French *cela va sans dire* and found in American English by 1878. A cliché by 1900.

> To hold the public's confidence, and take another step towards finding a team that can recapture the Ashes from Australia next winter, it goes without saying that England have to win the series, and ought to win the match.
> *Evening Standard* (London) (1 June 1994)

> In our view, the American and French positions can be modified by just listening to the UN demands. It goes without saying that if all the UN member states act consistently and fairly when dealing with world problems, the UN will accordingly succeed as a peace broker worldwide.
> *Guardian* (13 June 1994)

it pays to advertise. General use, but only a borderline cliché. We are probably looking for an origin in the 1870s to 1890s when advertising really took off in America (as in Britain). Indeed, *Benham's Book of Quotations* (1960) lists an 'American saying *c.*1870' – 'The man who on his trade relies must either bust or advertise' – and notes that 'Sir Thomas Lipton [1850–1931] is said to have derived inspiration and success through seeing this couplet in New York about 1875'. Ezra Pound wrote in a letter to his father in 1908 about the launch of his poems: 'Sound trumpet. Let rip the drum & swatt the big bassoon. It pays to advertise.' A cliché by the 1920s/30s.

it was a dark and stormy night . . . A story-teller's clichéd opening. As a scene-setting phrase, this appears to have been irresistible to more than one story-teller over the years and has now become a joke. It was used in all seriousness by the English novelist Edward Bulwer-Lytton at the start of *Paul Clifford* (1830). At some stage, the phrase also became part of a jokey children's 'circular' story-telling game, 'The tale without an end'. Iona and Peter Opie in *The Lore and Language of Schoolchildren* (1959) describe the workings thus: 'The tale usually begins: "It was a dark and stormy night, and the Captain said to the Bo'sun, 'Bo'sun, tell us a story,' so the Bo'sun began . . ." And such is any child's readiness to hear a good story that the tale may be told three times round before the listeners appreciate that they are being diddled.'

Used as the title of one of Charles Schultz's 'Snoopy' books (1960s), the line is also given to Snoopy in his doomed attempts to write the Great American Novel.

it was going to be a long night. Catchphrase that becomes a cliché when used by would-be creative writers. Date of origin not known. A cliché by the 1960s/70s.

> He was doing the crossword from *The Washington Star*. He had finished three clues; it was going to be a long night.
> Jeffrey Archer, *Shall We Tell the President* (1977)

> Paul told his mother how he managed to clamber on to a raft and crouched wet and shivering until he saw the lights of a helicopter overhead. As Paul waited to be rescued – he later told his mother – he sighed: 'It's going to be a long night.'
> *Daily Mirror* (29 September 1994)

it was just like a fairy tale. *See* LIKE A FAIRY TALE (PRINCESS).

it was like an Aladdin's cave (in there). Journalistic description of any treasure trove or collection of rare and valuable objects (especially if they have been missing or been recovered after a robbery). Alluding to 'Aladdin and the Wonderful Lamp' in *Tales from the Arabian Nights*, in which the hero has a palace built for him by the 'genie in the lamp'. Curiously, however, there is no mention of a cave in the original story. As a journalistic allusion (in, for example, the full headword sentence above), a cliché by the mid-twentieth century.

> With the vivid sunlight streaming in upon thousands of rainbow-coloured glass drops . . . it seemed as unreal as Alladin's [*sic*] Cave.
> Rudyard Kipling, in *Civil and Military Gazette* (1884)

> There has, after all, been a tantalising, semi-official figure quoted by the Russo-German Commission which sits on this problem of 134,000 paintings and works of art – a fabled Aladdin's cave allegedly kept since 1945 at Zagorsk . . .
> *Daily Telegraph* (8 April 1995)

> The planning consent envisages the restoration of a working grist-mill. Inside the mill house is an Aladdin's cave of dogs and implements but the only remnants of the mill-wheel outside are a few rusted paddles.
> *Daily Telegraph* (29 April 1995)

> The National Lottery was to have been an Aladdin's cave overflowing with treasures for all.
> Leading article, *Independent* (2 May 1995)

Sybarite's is a VERITABLE Aladdin's Cave of possible gifts!
Advertisement in *Kensington & Chelsea Times* (7 July 1995)

it was worse than the Blitz/World War Two all over again.
Journalistic use – or, rather, the way members of the public talk when
reported in the press. Since the 1950s/60s and an instant cliché.

Mr David Steele ... in a Volkswagen van which was behind the Mini
carrying Mr Waldorf [was asked about the number of police officers he
saw]: 'I saw one, then two, then it was World War Two all over again.'
Daily Telegraph (14 October 1983)

Another dewy-eyed heroine hits the screen in an all-guns-blazing wartime
weepie. But this one bombs worse than the blitz over Dresden.
Today (28 October 1988)

Palestinian gunmen wilfully killed several of Mann's horses. Twenty-two
more died in an Israeli air raid during the 1982 invasion, which Sunnie Mann
always described as being worse than the blitz.
The Times (1 December 1992)

What they say: 'It's worse than the blitz' – police officer at blast scene.
Evening Standard (London) (26 April 1993)

it's a funny game, football. Journalistic use, also by players. Date of
origin unknown. A cliché by the 1980s. Listed as a cliché in *The Times* (28
May 1984).

Funny old game football, as Greavsie might have said ... even when it's
TV's fantasy kind.
Today (30 August 1994)

Almost as darkly comic as they are deeply sinister, Grobbelaar's wasted
efforts show that football, to quote one of the game's hoariest clichés, really
is a funny old game.
Scotland on Sunday (13 November 1994)

All of which proved once again that football is indeed a funny game because
it was Grobbelaar, perhaps inevitably, who did most to bring about the
misfiring Gunners second defeat in 15 games.
Irish Times (21 November 1994)

it's a growing experience. What people inspired by Californian
psycho-babble say to turn misfortune into something more constructive.
The American show business couple David and Talia Shire were quoted in

1984 as having said of their 'very loving separation' in Hollywood: 'We're going to rotate the house and we even rotate the cars. We've been separated for four months and it's a growing experience' – quoted by William Safire in the *New York Times* Magazine (20 January 1980).

it's absolutely vital both to the character and to the integrity of the script. What actresses (and, I suppose, occasionally actors) invariably answer when asked whether there is any nudity in the play or film they are about to appear in and whether there is any justification for taking their clothes off. When I consulted Glenda Jackson about it in 1983, she suggested that the remark was usually made in reply to a reporter's question, 'Is there any nudity in this film?' – 'Yes, but it is absolutely vital to the character and the part.' *The Naff Sex Guide* (1984) gave as one of the 'naff things starlets say': 'Yes, I would appear nude, as long as I trusted the director and the integrity of the script demanded it.'

BBC TV *Monty Python's Flying Circus* was already guying the answer on 7 February 1969. A policeman stated: 'I would not appear in a frontal nude scene unless it was valid'; and a woman: 'Oh, no, no, no . . . unless it was artistically valid.' Other responses to the nudity question include, 'I don't mind if it's *relevant* to the script' or '. . . if it's done in a meaningful way'. Lord Delfont, the impresario, is quoted by Hunter Davies in *The Grades* (1981) as saying: 'I do allow four-letter words and nudity in my films, if they are in the right context, if it has integrity.'

it's good news for —— and it's good news for ——. A cliché of politicians when their strings are being pulled by PR people in the age of the soundbite. Unfortunately reminiscent of the 'good news/bad news' jokes of the 1960s/70s, this format was much used by Norman Lamont, the British Chancellor of the Exchequer (1990–3) when announcing interest rate reductions.

it's goodnight from me/and it's goodnight from him! A cliché of TV presentation was gently sent up when it became the basis for this stock exchange at the end of the BBC TV comedy series *The Two Ronnies* (1971–88). Ronnie Corbett would feed Ronnie Barker with, 'It's goodnight from me . . .' And Ronnie B. would sabotage this with, 'And it's goodnight from him.'

it's got to get worse before it gets better. General use, mainly journalistic. Date of origin unknown. A cliché by the 1970s/80s. Given as an example of a cliché in the *Collins English Dictionary* (1979).

> Encouraging the kind of dynamic economy in which lots of jobs are created will mean hacking away at policies that have long operated in favour of rigid work rules, high social costs, subsidies and protectionism; and that may mean things getting worse for the poor before they can get better.
> *Economist* (30 July 1994)

> Divisional Commander Mike Currie appealed yesterday for more help in ensnaring the criminals and condemned those who were withholding information. 'The situation could get worse before it gets better,' he said.
> *Daily Mail* (31 March 1995)

it's not the heat, it's the humidity. In his booklet *Are You a Bromide?* (1907), the American author Gelett Burgess lists 'it isn't so much the heat (or the cold), as the humidity in the air' as the sort of thing a 'bromide' (someone addicted to clichés and platitudes) would say. In the first paragraph of P.G. Wodehouse's novel *Sam the Sudden* (1925), he describes the inhabitants of New York on a late August afternoon: '[One half] crawling about and asking those they met if this was hot enough for them, the other maintaining that what they minded was not so much the heat as the humidity.' The expression was extremely popular among British servicemen in the Middle East and Far East during the Second World War. Now probably no more than a quaint catchphrase.

it's nothing. Drama. What the wounded say, invariably, to the question, '(Are) you hurt?' Observed by Fritz Spiegl in an article on drama cliché lines in the *Listener* (7 February 1985).

jewel in the crown. General use, meaning 'the bright feature, outstanding part of something'. An old phrase. In the poem 'O Went Thou in the Cauld Blast', Robert Burns has: 'The brightest jewel in my crown/Wad be my queen.' Charles Dickens in *The Pickwick Papers*, Chap. 24 (1836–7), has (of Magna Carta): 'One of the brightest jewels in the British crown.' A thumping cliché since 1984 when a British television adaptation of Paul Scott's 'Raj Quartet' of novels was given the title of the first in the series, *The Jewel in the Crown* (1966). Listed as a cliché in *The Times* (28 May 1984).

> Sir Thomas Beecham, Bart., conducting the 'Ballet of the Red Shoes' would be the final jewel in our crown.
> Michael Powell, *A Life in Movies* (1986)

> Poor David Steel. He's bound for Southport on Saturday for a regional conference in what ought to be one of the precious few jewels in the Liberals' dented crown.
> *Guardian* (2 March 1988)

> Annecy is considered to be the jewel in the Savoyard crown.
> *Harpers & Queen* (March 1988)

journey into the unknown. Journalistic cliché. Date of origin unknown, but *Journey To the Unknown* was the title of a TV suspense series (US, produced in England, 1968–9).

> To the strains of 'We are Sailing', the ropes were slipped and *Canberra* was off into the unknown.
> J. Hands & R. McGowan, *Don't Cry for Me, Sergeant-Major* (1983)

joy. *See* ANGUISH TURNED TO . . .

joy of ——. A cliché, mostly of book-titling. First on the scene were I.S. Rombauer and M.R. Becker, American cookery experts, with *The Joy of*

Cooking (1931). A US film was entitled *Joy of Living* in 1938. Then, in 1972, along came Alex Comfort with *The Joy of Sex* and even *More Joy of Sex*. Then everyone joined in, so that we have had books about the 'joys' of computers, chickens, cheesecake, breastfeeding and geraniums, among many others. So a cliché from this point. In 1984, I published *The Joy of Clichés* – which I thought would be seen to be ironical – though Gyles Brandreth seems to have had no compunction in naming a book *The Joy of Lex* (1980) or Fritz Spiegl *The Joy of Words* (1986).

jury is (still) out on ——. A mostly journalistic cliché, noticeable from the late 1980s, meaning that no final conclusion can be drawn, minds are not yet made up. Compare QUESTION-MARK STILL HANGS OVER.

> The royal family now face an unenviable task in adapting themselves to the challenges of the twenty-first century. The jury is out and it is by no means certain that the verdict will be favourable to the monarchy.
> Andrew Morton, *Diana: Her True Story* (1993)

> We no longer give fealty to any institution (or person) simply because of their lineage. Nowadays we rightly want to know whether they perform or not. And on that test, as far as the monarchy is concerned, the jury is out.
> Stephen Haseler, in *Daily Mail* (22 May 1993)

just and lasting settlement. A cliché of politics. Abraham Lincoln talked of a 'just and lasting peace' in his Second Inaugural address (4 March 1865), referring to the end of the American Civil War. President Eisenhower spoke in Geneva (1955) of 'a just and durable peace' and later said, 'we will make constantly brighter the lamp that will one day guide us to our goal – a just and lasting peace'. The 'settlement' version became boringly popular with regard to the Palestinian problem after 1973. When the IRA announced its 'ceasefire' in Northern Ireland (31 August 1994), its statement managed to include the phrase twice: 'the desire for peace based on a just and lasting settlement cannot be crushed ... We believe that an opportunity to secure a just and lasting settlement has been created.'

just deserts. General use, for 'deserved reward or come-uppance'. An inevitable pairing. Date of origin unknown.

> Sentence lengths could be shorter, the only relevant matter being that they should represent a just response to the crime committed. This, broadly, was the doctrine known as 'just deserts', on which much of the Criminal Justice Act 1991 was based.
> *Sunday Times* (1 May 1994)

The father thumps the yob, pulls out his warrant card to reveal he's a policeman, and arrests him. Just deserts for the yob and cheers for the PC? Not in the Britain we have become.
Andrew Neil, *Daily Mail* (9 March 1995)

just good friends. Journalistic use. Or rather the way a person being interviewed expresses to a newspaper (usually) that his or her relationship with another is not sexual or romantic. In James Joyce, *Ulysses* (1922), there occurs the original straightforward form: 'They would be just good friends like a big brother and sister without all that other.' The phrase probably established itself in the US during the 1930s, though in the film of Cole Porter's musical *Silk Stockings* (US 1957), the phrase is used several times as if not clichéd yet. From *Vivien: The Life of Vivien Leigh* by Alexander Walker (1987): 'At Cherbourg, Jack [Mcrivale – Vivien's lover as her marriage to Laurence Olivier was ending in 1960] experienced for the first time the bruising intrusiveness of the British Press who boarded the ship *en masse* to interrogate Vivien's handsome travelling companion. In self-defence, he fell back on the old "just good friends" cliché.' Now only used as a consciously humorous evasion, especially when not true. A BBC sitcom current in 1984 was called *Just Good Friends* and several songs about that time also had the title.

just how serious . . . ? A cliché of broadcast journalism, the invariable start to a thrusting, probing question. In the mid-1970s, Michael Leapman, as diarist on *The Times*, poked fun at the fad and invented a broadcasting character called 'Justow Serious'.

justice. *See* THIS HAS RESTORED MY FAITH . . .

= K =

keep the wolf from the door, to.   General idiomatic use, meaning 'to keep poverty and hunger at bay, to find the elementary necessities needed for survival'. The literal expression occurs in the *Oxford English Dictionary* (2nd edition) as long ago as 1470. In the film *She Done Him Wrong* (US, 1933), Mae West has the line: 'The wolf at my door? Why, I remember when he came right into my room and had pups!' A borderline case. Perhaps no more than a familiar idiom.

> Compassion fatigue has set in . . . If I gave them anything, I would only have to ask for the money back to keep the wolf from my own door.
> *Independent* (1 June 1994)

> Through it all, Dermody could hardly keep the wolf from the door. Appealing to Owenson for assistance he once wrote: 'I have now fasted for a longer time than caused the death of Chatterton.'
> *Irish Times* (11 July 1994)

killer instinct.   General use, to describe the quality of extreme seriousness thought to be required to win in sport and life. Known by 1931 (in a boxing context). A cliché by the mid-twentieth century.

> Already he has given Oxford a lift with his drive, enthusiasm, attack and killer instinct.
> *The Times* (20 February 1973)

> Maybe it's the killer instinct that Seidelman needs to develop. She appears more concerned with keeping her movie politically correct than with making it fun.
> *Washington Post* (10 April 1987)

killer's name, Inspector, is ... AAAAHHHH!   Film script use – where the person identifying the villain succumbs before he has got the name out. Cited in the song 'I Love a Film Cliché' by Dick Vosburgh and

Trevor Lyttelton from the show *A Day in Hollywood, A Night in the Ukraine* (1980).

king's ransom. A huge amount of money, presumably meaning an amount sufficient to release a king from captivity. Used by Christopher Marlowe in *Dr Faustus* (1590). A cliché by 1900.

> Venables made a killing on his 23 per cent shareholding, cashing in the blue chips for around £3 million. Part of that has been invested in his London club Scribes West but he would pay a king's ransom to call off the dogs of war.
> *Daily Mirror* (31 October 1994)

> Lawyers acting for the Princess of Wales in any divorce would ask for a king's ransom, says Frances Gibb.
> *The Times* (15 November 1994)

kiss goodbye. *See* MUST SURELY . . .

kissed by the sun. Journalistic and travel promotion phrase for a spot that gets a lot of sun, as in 'a white-washed village kissed by the sun' – listed in the *Independent* 'DIY travel writers' cliché kit' (31 December 1988).

> 'Welcome to Sebastopol, our beautiful Crimean city, kissed by the sun on the banks of the Black Sea,' trilled the tough lady with the Soviet perm. She hurried us aboard an old bus and we rattled off between blocks of flats.
> *Sunday Telegraph* (9 October 1994)

> I had never before realized how close the two passengers in a car are to each other. Her left arm must have been centimetres away from mine when I changed gear. She kept her legs together and her skirt revealed a splash of skin still kissed by the sun.
> Potboiler novel, quoted in *Guardian* (10 December 1994)

know which side one's bread is buttered on, to. General use, meaning 'to know where one's best interests lie'. Known by 1834. A cliché by the mid-twentieth century – listed in *The Times* (28 May 1984).

> . . . an interviewer who plainly knew which side his bread was buttered. The future isn't hard to see: Dimbleby gets knighted, Diana can get knotted.
> *Evening Standard* (London) (30 June 1994)

> Such voices accuse him of insincerity or, at best, of a heightened sense of pragmatism – in other words, of knowing which side his bread is buttered.
> *Sunday Telegraph* (24 July 1994)

= L =

labour of love.   General idiomatic use, for work undertaken through enjoyment of the work itself rather than for any other reward. Biblical origin: 'Your works of faith and labours of love' – Thessalonians 1:3 (also Hebrews 6:10). A cliché by 1900.

> [Congratulating John Lahr on his book *Prick Up Your Ears*] It all reads so effortlessly! Labour of love must be right. The affection shone through the book.
> Kenneth Williams, letter of 3 September 1978, in *The Kenneth Williams Letters* (1994)

> What of the future for *Viz*? Thanks to the contract publishing business Brown has created a company that could now run without his labour of love.
> *Evening Standard* (London) (16 November 1994)

> They'll write this wonderful tune and a first verse, and then find that the second verse doesn't fit. It drags in all sorts of skills. It's a labour of love and it takes up lots of time. They're so proud of the finished product, though.
> *Times Educational Supplement* (16 December 1994)

> This book has been for me a labour of love.
> Martin Walker, *Words Without Frontiers: The Spread of European English* (1995)

lance the boil, to.   General, especially media, use. Meaning 'to try and solve a problem by making a bold stroke'. Date of origin of this figurative use, unknown. A cliché by the early 1980s.

> Lebanon has now made it possible to involve other Arab states in the process and therefore to come up with a more comprehensive approach than would have been possible otherwise. That is the boil the Reagan plan has helped lance.
> *Economist* (13 November 1982)

> The Treasury rules should be changed to close this loophole and lance the

nasty little boil of councillors awarding themselves poll tax payers' cash without having to account.
Sunday Times (20 August 1989)

Mr Major at least, and at last, has had enough . . . He has been seeking out his closest friends in the trade to discuss how to 'lance the boil'.
Independent (23 June 1995)

'Mr Major has lanced the boil,' he reported confidently at 5.23. This, indeed, quickly became the metaphor of the night. Never was a boil more comprehensively lanced.
Observer (25 June 1995)

land of a thousand contrasts. Travel promotion and general advertising use. Date of origin unknown. 'Land of contrasts' was included in the 'travel scribes' armoury' compiled from a competition in the *Guardian* (10 April 1993).

A Moroccan Summer. This beautiful land of a thousand contrasts is the backdrop to the Austin Reed Spring Summer Collections.
Austin Reed's Spring/Summer catalogue (1995)

land of the living. *See* IN THE . . .

lap of luxury. *See* IN THE . . .

larger than life. *See* HE WAS A BIG MAN . . .

laser-sharp. *See* RAZOR-SHARP . . .

last great wilderness. Journalistic and especially travel writing use. Date of origin unknown. A cliché from the 1970s/80s onwards. Part of the 'travel scribes' armoury' compiled from a competition in the *Guardian* (10 April 1993).

Each year the Highlands of Scotland, Britain's last great wilderness, attract thousands of people seeking a new way of life. But as the new settlers arrive, thousands of young Scots head south in search of qualifications and jobs. Most never return.
Independent (30 June 1994)

The howling of the grey wolf, portrayed for centuries as a bloodthirsty predator to be killed on sight, is being heard in the snow-covered forests of Yellowstone Park this week for the first time in half a century. This is thanks

to an enlightened 'recovery plan' to restore the balance of nature in one of north America's last great wilderness areas.
Irish Times (20 January 1995)

A Highland estate regarded as one of Scotland's last great wilderness areas, that of Knoydart, is likely to be sold following an imminent take-over of its present owner, the Dundee-based Titaghur jute company.
Herald (Glasgow) (11 April 1995)

last-chance saloon.   *See* (DRINKING IN THE) LAST-CHANCE . . .

late great——. A cliché, mostly used by disc jockeys and pop promoters. That death can confer status on a pop star, and do wonders for record sales, is certainly true – however, one feels that the use of 'great' here has often rather more to do with the demands of rhyme than truth. A cliché since the 1950s/60s.

Callaway, 75, earned his spurs as president of textile combine Burlington Industries, subsequently created a vineyard that he sold to Hiram Walker for $14 million, and, as befits a second cousin of the late, great Bobby Jones, turned his talents to golf.
The Times (10 November 1994).

Scottish football will today be given another chance to pay its respects to the late great Davie Cooper – and Hotline callers are anxious for it to be done properly.
Daily Record (1 April 1995)

late lamented ——.   General use, referring mostly to the dead who are still missed. Known by 1859. A cliché by the mid-twentieth century.

One programme, *Subterranea Britannica* (BBC2), was the stuff of the late-lamented *40 Minutes* and at 50 minutes outstayed its welcome.
Herald (Glasgow) (7 May 1994)

Like the time when, as a callow 17-year-old during an Edinburgh Festival-time jam session, Travis suggested to the late, lamented alto saxophonist Joe Harriott that they play something up-tempo.
Herald (Glasgow) (19 January 1995)

laugh.   *See* I FOUND THAT IF I MADE PEOPLE . . . ; LIKE ALL GREAT COMIC CREATIONS . . . ; ONE NEEDS A GOOD . . .

law and order.   Political and journalistic use, but a pairing known in English since 1598. There was a 'Law and Order Party' in the US in the

1840s. The recent cliché status of the phrase dates from 1968 when Richard Nixon was running for the American presidency and decided to pursue the 'law and order vote'. It also became a popular issue in British politics and so widely was the phrase used – and so sloppily spoken – that people took to referring to 'Laura Norder' as if she were a person.

> Laura Norder is adamant . . . more police means less crime, tougher courts lead to fuller jails equals happiness all round. Or so the theory goes.
> George Hume column, *Herald* (Glasgow) (22 September 1994)

leap. *See* ONE SMALL STEP . . .

learned the lesson of. *See* WE HAVE SURELY . . .

leave no stone unturned, to. General use, meaning 'to make every endeavour to find something, to search thoroughly'. From an anonymously published attack on dice-playing, *c.*1550: 'He will refuse no labour nor leave no stone unturned, to pick up a penny.' Also known since 1575 in the form 'no straw unturned'. The expression was used by President Johnson in 1963 when announcing the terms of the Warren Commission's investigations into the cause of President Kennedy's assassination. Diana Rigg neatly twisted the phrase for her collection of theatrical reviews – *No Turn Unstoned* (1982). A cliché by the mid-twentieth century. Cited as a 'silly expression' that had recently been 'killed by the jeers of a few journalists' by George Orwell in 'Politics and the English Language' (*Horizon*, April 1946) – obviously a touch prematurely. Listed in the *Independent* (24 December 1994) as a cliché of newspaper editorials.

> We won't leave a stone unturned until we bring this animal to justice. We'll catch someone for this because they need to be locked up.
> *Daily Mirror* (6 September 1994)

> Police are leaving no stone unturned as they search for a slippery customer who stole a snake.
> *Daily Record* (4 May 1995)

leave severely alone, to. General use, though hardly at all in recent years. Known by 1880. The *Pocket Oxford Dictionary* (1924, but in a 1950s edition) gave it as an example of a cliché.

If the King Street commissars were not so invincibly stupid, they would have insisted that the movement be left severely alone.
Christopher Driver, *The Disarmers* (1964)

leaving. *See* NOTHING IN HIS LIFE . . .

legal loophole. General use, meaning a way of getting round the law. This alliterative phrase was known by 1768. A cliché by 1900.

Legal loophole allows boy rapist to avoid custody.
Headline, *Independent* (12 November 1994)

The closure of a legal loophole which lets Europe dump toxic waste on developing countries as 'recyclable' material has created a profitable new crime: waste smuggling.
Independent on Sunday (1 January 1995)

legend in one's own lifetime/living legend. Both of these phrases are now clichés of tribute. A possibility exists that the first person to whom both were applied (and within a couple of pages of each other), actually deserved them. Lytton Strachey in *Eminent Victorians* (1918) wrote of Florence Nightingale: 'She was a legend in her lifetime, and she knew it . . . Once or twice a year, perhaps, but nobody could be quite certain, in deadly secrecy, she went for a drive in the park. Unrecognised, the living legend flitted for a moment before the common gaze.' Clichés by the 1920s/30s.

Compare: **legend in his own lunchtime**. I recall that in about 1976, Christopher Wordsworth, reviewing a novel by Clifford Makins, a sporting journalist, described the author as having been this. The epithet is now quite frequently applied to other journalists of a certain type. According to Ned Sherrin, *Theatrical Anecdotes* (1991): 'David Climie, the witty revue and comedy writer . . . claims to have invented the phrase "A legend in his own lunchtime" and to have lavished it on the mercurial BBC comedy innovator, Dennis Main Wilson.'

In 1888 [Robert Louis] Stevenson had set out with his family entourage for the South Seas, becoming a legend in his lifetime.
The Oxford Companion to English Literature (1985)

A great many have occupied your chair but it is a measure of your Speakership that you have become a legend in your own lifetime.
Margaret Thatcher, speech (May 1983) marking the retirement of George Thomas, Speaker of the House of Commons

'It's called The Living Legend – The Tony Blackburn Story,' he explains more or less tongue-in-cheek. 'They call me the Living Legend at Radio One . . . I'm known as the Survivor around there.'
Tony Blackburn, disc jockey, quoted in *Guardian* (25 August 1984)

. . . the King of the One-liners, Henny Youngman, who'd befriended me after I'd introduced him on one of the London Palladium shows as 'a rumour in his own lifetime'.
Bob Monkhouse, *Crying With Laughter* (1993), referring to the 1950s

Leading libel lawyer Peter Carter-Ruck once said of him [Lord Goodman]: 'He became a legend in his lifetime.'
Sunday Express (14 May 1995)

lesson. *See* WE HAVE SURELY LEARNED THE . . .

let me/we must nail this lie. Political and public affairs use, meaning 'the lie must be disproved in an open and obvious fashion'. Date of origin unknown. A cliché by the 1980s. Identified as a current cliché in *The Times* (17 March 1995).

The news that yet another independent school is to close down for lack of support should help nail the lie that the better-off in this country are doing better than ever before. In fact, as a Mori survey in one of the Sunday newspapers pointed out, the middle classes in Britain have seldom been in such DIRE STRAITS.
Daily Telegraph (29 June 1994)

I retired in the summer of this year from the headship of Whalley Range High School in Manchester, categorised as the 'worst' school for truancy in the country because of its 14 per cent unauthorised absences. Probably no one is in a better position than I am to nail the lie implicit in this simplistic assertion.
Times Educational Supplement (9 December 1994)

let us go forward together. A political cliché, chiefly made so by Winston Churchill: 'I can only say to you let us go forward together and put these grave matters to the proof' (the conclusion of a speech on Ulster, 14 March 1914); 'Let us go forward together in all parts of the Empire, in all parts of the Island' (speaking on the war, 27 January 1940); and 'I say, "Come then, let us go forward together with our united strength" ' (in his 'Blood, sweat and tears' speech, 13 May 1940). A cliché from then on. It occurs along with other rhetorical clichés during the 'Party Political

Speech' (written by Max Schreiner) on the Peter Sellers comedy album *The Best of Sellers* (1958): 'Let us assume a bold front and go forward together.'

let's do the show (right here in the barn)! Show business and entertainment use, but almost always in affectionate parody. This is taken to be a staple line from the films featuring the young Mickey Rooney and Judy Garland from 1939 onwards. It had several forms: 'Hey! I've got it! Why don't we **put on a show**?'/'Hey kids! We can put on the show in the backyard!' – but a precise example has proved hard to find. In *Babes in Arms* (1939), Rooney and Garland play the teenage children of retired vaudeville players who decide to put on a big show of their own. Alas, they do not actually say any of the above lines, though they do express their determination to 'put on a show'. In *Strike Up the Band* (1940), Rooney has the line: 'Say, that's not a bad idea. We could put on our own show!' – though he does not say it to Garland. A cliché by the late 1940s/50s. 'Hey, why don't we put on a show?' is cited in the song 'I Love a Film Cliché' by Dick Vosburgh and Trevor Lyttelton from the show *A Day in Hollywood, A Night in the Ukraine* (1980).

level playing field. *See* START FROM A . . .

lie. *See* LET ME/WE MUST NAIL THIS . . .

life. *See* IS THERE LIFE AFTER . . . ; REBUILDING ONE'S . . .

light at the end of the tunnel. Political and journalistic use. Meaning 'a sign that some long-awaited relief or an end to some problem is at hand'. The earliest citation in the *Oxford English Dictionary* (2nd edition) is from 1922, and in a non-political context, though George Eliot had expressed the idea of coming out of a tunnel of darkness into daylight in a letter of 1879. In June 1983 the diarist of *The Times* tried to find the first *Tory* politician to have used the phrase. Stanley Baldwin in 1929 was the first, it turned out, followed by Neville Chamberlain at a Lord Mayor's banquet in 1937.

As for Churchill – well, John Colville, his private secretary, seems to quote a *French* source in his diary for 13 June 1940 ('some gleam of light at the far end of the tunnel'), quotes Paul Reynaud, the French PM on 16 June ('the ray of light at the end of the tunnel'), and himself uses it on 31 May 1952: 'I think it is more that he [Churchill] cannot see the light at the end of the tunnel.' But I have been unable to locate the source of Churchill's reported use of the cliché on 3 May 1941.

The old expression was later dusted down and invoked about an end to the Vietnam War. In 1967 New Year's Eve invitations at the American Embassy in Saigon bore the legend: 'Come and see the light at the end of the tunnel.' President Kennedy nearly employed the expression apropos something else at a press conference on 12 December 1962: 'We don't see the end of the tunnel, but I must say I don't think it is darker than it was a year ago, and in some ways lighter.' A cliché by the mid-twentieth century.

Somewhere about this time, a joke was added: 'If we see the light at the end of the tunnel, it's the light of the oncoming train.' Though not original to him, the line appears in Robert Lowell's poem 'Day by Day' (1977). In 1988 I heard of a graffito in Dublin which ran: 'Because of the present economic situation, the light at the end of the tunnel will be switched off at weekends.'

light-hearted look.   *See* —— TAKE A . . .

lights.   *See* WILL THE LAST PERSON TO LEAVE . . .

like.   *See* WE SHALL NOT SEE HIS . . .

like a beached whale.   Mostly journalistic use – for 'stranded', 'high and dry', particularly if any person so described is large and helpless. A cliché by the 1950s.

> [Of R.A. Butler in his later years] He seemed like a benign and decent beached whale washed up on the harder shores of modern Conservatism.
> Peter Hennessy, *Independent* (8 May 1987)

> Beached whale – Michael Billington on a Moby Dick that's all at sea.
> Headline, *Guardian* (19 March 1992)

> Here is stalk-chewing Johnny Depp, who divides his days between tending his oversize Momma – 'Did yer ever see a beached whale on television?' is how he describes her to strangers – and saving his mentally retarded brother Leonardo DiCaprio from suicidal escapades.
> *Financial Times* (5 May 1994)

> Holly Wantuch's trembling Sharla is forced to fellate a chicken drumstick,

Michael Shannon's Chris spatters the kitchen with his blood, Marc A Nelson's lumbering Ansel collapses like a beached whale.
The Times (24 August 1994)

like a bear garden. General use, of a somewhat consciously archaic kind, to describe any disorderly situation. A bear garden was originally a place set aside for bear baiting and thence the term came (by 1743) to be applied to a disorderly place. 'Squabbles and boxings . . . rendering the place more like a bear-garden than a hall of instruction' – John Bristed, *Anthroplanomenus: Being an Account of a Pedestrian Tour through part of the Highlands of Scotland* (1803). Possibly now used out of some confusion with the term 'beer garden', from the German and in English use in the US by 1884. A borderline cliché by the mid-twentieth century.

> Whatever follies this country has fallen into since the war, none seems to me nearly so grievous as the hash we have made of our schools. Teaching is, or should be, one of the most rewarding callings anybody can follow; but it has become a bear garden.
> Godfrey Smith, *Sunday Times* (6 June 1993)

like a coiled spring. General use, especially in attempts at fine writing, to convey tension. Date of origin unknown. 'Each panzer was a coiled spring, oiled/For instant action' – George Macbeth, *A War Quartet* (1969). A cliché by the 1970s.

> His fingers teased until her nipples hardened to desire, and in a great upsurge of longing, she arched her body to the coiled-spring inflexibility of his.
> Anne Hampson, *Stormy Masquerade* (1980)

> Music became metaphor with the terrific surge of self-pride in the playing of the great billowing melody in the first movement; there was a buccaneering, defiant elan in the hectic waltz. There was dignity in the slow movement. And in a crisp and rude version of the witty finale, the tension was as tight as a coiled spring.
> Michael Tumelty, *Herald* (Glasgow) (2 June 1993)

> United will start handsome favourites to become the fourth club this century to complete the coveted league and FA Cup double, with every good reason. Seeing them in training this week, they have appeared as a coiled spring, ready to burst into dramatic life in the May sunshine.
> *Daily Mail* (14 May 1994)

like a dream come true. Journalistic use. What any stroke of luck is to an ordinary member of the public, when reported by journalists, and thus an idiom that has turned into a cliché. Date of origin unknown. A cliché by the 1950s/60s.

The advent of the laser would seem to be a chemist's dream come true.
Scientific American (May 1979)

British radio hams are to be able to talk to an astronaut on board the latest US space shuttle . . . Dr Garriott said: 'This will be a dream come true. I have had this project on my mind since I first became an astronaut.'
The Times (October 1983)

A club cricket enthusiast has inherited a fortune and his own village cricket club from an elderly widow who was a distant relative he never knew . . . Mr Hews, aged 68, a retired company representative, lives in a semi-detached house in Arnold Avenue, Coventry. 'It's like a dream come true,' he said.
The Times (22 October 1983)

At the end of May 1985 Brian MacArthur, in the cramped Covent Garden basement, was experiencing an editor's dream come true.
David Goodhart and Patrick Wintour, *Eddie Shah and the Newspaper Revolution* (1986)

For Susan [George], the purchase of their 17th-century house is a dream come true.
Hello! (13 May 1995)

But the Sheikh's first words after [winning] the race [the Derby] were not for himself. He said: 'This is a dream come true, but my thoughts are now of Alex.'
Independent on Sunday (11 June 1995)

like a fairy tale (princess). Mostly journalistic use. The urge to say that everything in sight was 'like a fairy tale' was, of course, rampant at the nuptials of the Prince of Wales and Lady Diana Spencer in July 1981. Tom Fleming, the BBC TV commentator for the fixture, said the bride was 'like a fairy-tale princess'. Even Robert Runcie, Archbishop of Canterbury, began his address at St Paul's: 'Here is the stuff of which fairy tales are made.' **It was just like a fairy tale** is also a cliché (current by 1860) and now put into the mouths of unsuspecting members of the public by popular journalists when they are trying to describe some rather pleasant thing that has happened to them. As Iona and Peter Opie point out, however, in *The Classic Fairy Tales* (1974), this is a very partial way of looking at such matters: 'When the wonderful happens, when a holiday abroad is a splendid success or an unlikely romance ends happily, we commonly exclaim it was "just like a fairy tale", overlooking that most events in fairy tales are remarkable for their unpleasantness, and that in some of the tales there is no happy ending, not even the hero or heroine escaping with their life.' Clichés by 1950.

> The story from then on is like a fairytale – ending in a link with a fairytale princess. For instead of having to fight for cash and premises, Jackie was handed both on a plate.
> *Today* (17 June 1994)

> Diana Spencer chose her own companions. This fairytale princess has not got dainty feet in glass slippers but lumps of clay.
> *The Times* (6 October 1994)

like a fish out of water.   General idiomatic use, to mean behaving inappropriately for the environment or situation. Known by 1886. A cliché by the mid-twentieth century. Listed as a cliché in *The Times* (28 May 1984).

> 'But,' added the young Wadhamite . . . 'I've heard he's an absolute fish out of water when he's away from the academic world he's accustomed to.'
> Anthony Powell, *Infants of the Spring* (1976)

like a vicarage tea-party.   *See* MAKE —— LOOK . . .

like all great comic creations, he makes you laugh before he opens his mouth.   Used in criticism. 'The test of a real comedian is whether you laugh at him before he opens his mouth' – George Jean Nathan, in *American Mercury* (September 1929). 'Very early on in his stage career Stan [Laurel] had made an interesting discovery: he found that audiences laughed at him before he ever said or did anything' – Fred Lawrence Guiles, *Stan* (1980). A cliché by the 1960s/70s. Robert McLennan MP said it of Barry Humphries as 'Sir Les Patterson' in November 1987.

like coming home.   General use, meaning '(it is) what is appropriate for one; what one feels completely natural or right doing'. Originally, the phrase was used in a near literal fashion: 'I am sure nobody can deny that the house is very small . . . and yet, it feels like coming home again' – Wilkie Collins, *No Name* (1862). Then, more figuratively, Winston Churchill said at a Conservative rally in 1924 (having left the Liberal Party): 'It's all very strange for [his wife]. But to me, of course, it's just like coming home.' In the film *The Garden of Allah* (US, 1936), Marlene Dietrich says 'It's like coming home' about returning to a nunnery. A cliché by the 1970s, perhaps as a result of the film title *Coming Home* (US, 1978).

> For Douglas Hurd, it was just like coming home ... [he] took his place behind the Foreign Secretary's desk.
> *Independent* (31 October 1989)

> [Mclvyn Bragg] 'Actually I found arriving at the BBC was like arriving home ... It was a job I knew I wanted to do.'
> *Independent on Sunday* (17 June 1990)

like opening an oven door. General use, meaning 'it was suddenly, fiercely hot', but especially when referring to the climate. As such, part of the 'travel scribes' armoury' compiled from a competition in the *Guardian* (10 April 1993).

> *Wine* magazine writer Stuart Walton knows a vino that 'offers a blast of roasting pork, like opening the oven door'.
> *Today* (8 May 1995)

like (painting) the Forth Bridge. General use, to describe an endless task. It is popular knowledge that since it was constructed in the 1880s, the steel rail bridge over the Firth of Forth in Scotland has been continuously repainted. That is to say, when they got to the end of it, the painters immediately started all over again (though in 1993 a 'maintenance holiday' was declared and the traditional on average four-yearly application of paint to each part of the structure looked likely to lapse). A borderline cliché by the 1980s.

> Because of the mismatch in the computer criteria used by Western govern ments and industry, a nightmarish task is now involved in explaining the new CoCom rules to companies ... There is talk in CoCom of making its list review a continuous process – 'like painting the Forth Bridge, the minute you finish, you start again,' one official says.
> *Financial Times* (25 July 1984)

> In the far future, small free-roaming insectoids could be set to handle continuous tasks such as cleaning the outside of skyscrapers, or painting the Forth Bridge. Miniature versions could be put to work cleaning pavements and gutters, or the inside of your house.
> *Guardian* (2 August 1984)

> Dealing with social security is a bit like the Forth Bridge, [Peter Lilley] says.

'I suspect I am only halfway across. But if I do get to the other side, I suspect whoever comes after me will have to start at the beginning and repaint all over again.'
Independent (23 May 1995)

like —— was going out of style.   General use, meaning 'was behaving as though this was the last opportunity to do something' (compare AS IF/LIKE THERE WAS/WERE NO TOMORROW). Date of origin unknown, though Eric Partridge, *Dictionary of Catchphrases* (1977), has 'spends money as if it were going out of fashion/style' as a phrase by *c.*1930. A cliché by the 1970s/80s.

The familiar story is smothered in the stalest of prose, in which principles are 'deeply held', people are 'eminently suitable' or spend money 'as though it were going out of style' and a car is driven 'hell for leather'. There was a time when an assiduous editor would have chucked out such a bouquet of clichés, or been moved to less demanding employment. Oh well!
Mail on Sunday (11 September 1994)

And Don Johnson 'hands out money like it's going out of style'.
Daily Mirror (12 December 1994)

limped into port.   General use, but mostly journalistic. Date of origin unknown. A cliché by the mid-twentieth century.

Amid the glare of television lights, the panoply of ecstatic family and friends marking their return, and the flotilla of small boats sounding their klaxons, the fact that the women and their yacht, Heineken, limped in to port behind the 14 other competitors was an irrelevance.
Mail on Sunday (12 June 1994)

The Lupina C limped back to her home port of Kilkeel with her gear in tatters.
Herald (Glasgow) (18 January 1995)

list of the ten most . . .   *See* IN ANYBODY'S . . .

live in a fool's paradise, to.   To experience contentment or happiness based on an incorrect assessment of the circumstances. Known by 1621 (in Robert Burton's *Anatomy of Melancholy*). A cliché by the mid-twentieth century.

They live in a fool's paradise, for rabies has already visited the British Isles. In the latter part of the 19th century a number of deer IN LONDON'S Rich-

mond Park died of the disease. In any case, rabies is carried by many animals other than dogs.
European (31 March 1995)

live in cloud cuckoo land, to.   General use. Meaning 'to have impractical ideas', the expression comes from the name *Nephelococcygia*, suggested for the capital city of the birds (situated in the air), in *The Birds* by Aristophanes (d. *c.*380BC). Listed as a current cliché in *The Times* (28 May 1984).

> The decision to standardize the names of authors may be a big stride for the book world. But it is only a small step towards that cloud-cuckoo-land where everybody speaks and writes English according to the same rules.
> *The Times* (30 May 1994)

> Fund managers have questioned RJB's assessment of the market after 1998 when contracts with power generators, coal's biggest customer, expire. One banker advising an under-bidder said the RJB predictions 'were in cloud-cuckoo-land'.
> *Sunday Times* (27 November 1994)

> Mr Watkinson said that the RMT's claim for 6 per cent [pay rise] mean that the [union's] leadership was 'living in cloud cuckoo land'.
> *Independent* (27 May 1995)

lives.   *See* THIS WIN . . .

living a lie.   General use, but especially journalistic, meaning 'keeping up a pretence'. 'To live a lie' was known by 1770. A cliché by the 1960s/70s.

> Zany Kenny Everett's wife kept her love affair secret from the outside world for four years – to save hurting his feelings. Cuddly Ken knew of the affair. But Lee Everett and her lover, Sweeney actor John Atkin, lived a lie to avoid publicity.
> *News of the World* (2 October 1983)

living legend.   *See* LEGEND IN ONE'S OWN . . .

living life in the fast lane.   Journalistic use, meaning 'living expensively, indulgently and dangerously'. From the association of this lifestyle with 'fast cars' and such. Date of origin unknown, but 'The image usually associated with the superjet, "fast lane" set' appeared in the *Detroit Free Press* (16 April 1978). A cliché by the 1970s.

Controversial racing car genius Colin Chapman lived life in the fast lane.
Daily Star (11 October 1984)

Jackie Stewart lives life in the fast lane. Like any businessman, really.
Advertisement for Toshiba computer (February 1989)

'Life in the fast lane' was how one tabloid newspaper described the short career of Michael VerMeulen, the American editor of *GQ* who died, allegedly of a drug overdose, last week at the age of only 38.
Observer (3 September 1995)

London's. *See* IN LONDON'S —

long hot summer. Mostly journalistic use. *The Long Hot Summer* was the title of a 1958 film based on the stories of William Faulkner and also of a spin-off TV series (1965–6). The film was based on 'The Hamlet', a story published by Faulkner in 1928, which contains the chapter heading 'The Long Summer' (*sic*). Originally, an understandable coinage, this phrase appears, for example, in the opening chapter of Wilkie Collins, *The Woman in White* (1860): 'It was the last day of July. The long, hot summer was drawing to a close.' But the once-bright phrase rapidly turned into a journalist's cliché following the 1967 riots in the Black ghettos of 18 US cities, notably Detroit and Newark. In June of that year, the Rev. Dr Martin Luther King Jr warned: 'Everyone is worrying about the long hot summer with its threat of riots. We had a long cold winter when little was done about the conditions that create riots.' Claud Cockburn's *I, Claud* (1967) has a chapter entitled 'Long Cold Winter'. An almost instant cliché.

It looks as if it will be a long hot summer for the dons of Christ's College, Cambridge, who are once again faced with the tricky business of electing a Master.
Lady Olga Maitland, *Sunday Express* (11 July 1982)

Poles face long hot summer of discontent.
Headline, *Independent* (5 June 1995)

long night. *See* IT WAS GOING TO BE A . . .

long-felt want. *See* FULFIL A . . .

long-suffering wife. *See* PAY TRIBUTE TO MY . . .; TO MY WIFE, WITHOUT . . .

looking bronzed/tanned and fit. Journalistic use. An inevitable pairing when someone (often a politician) RETURNS TO THE FRAY having acquired a suntan, perhaps after earlier being ill, and after ENJOYING A WELL-DESERVED REST. A cliché by the 1920s (see first citation). Alternatively, people in this situation are **looking tanned, rested and fit** or **looking relaxed**. ' "Relaxed" has taken the place of the outmoded "bronzed and fit" ' – *The Times* (16 March 1961).

Epitaph. Here lies a Gossip Writer./Heart Failure Made Him Quit./He met a Famous Person/Who Didn't Look Tanned and Fit.
Anonymous, *Punch* (6 December 1933)

Kennedy arrived . . . looking tanned, rested and fit. My television adviser, Ted Rodgers, recommended that I use television make-up, but unwisely I refused, permitting only a little 'beard stick' on my perpetual five o'clock shadow.
Richard M. Nixon, *Memoirs* (1978)

He's tanned, he's rested, he's ready: Nixon in '88.
T-shirt slogan quoted in *Time* Magazine (22 February 1988)

Eric Burdon: Tan, fit and living in the desert.
Headline, *San Diego Union* (25 March 1989)

Mr Major, looking relaxed and confident, was not going down without a fight. In a warmly appreciated appeal to regional chauvinism, the Prime Minister cast back 1,100 years to the era of King Alfred the Great for reasons to vote Tory in the West Country.
The Times (24 May 1994)

Looking slim, tanned and relaxed [Antonia De Sancha] wore a single white flower in her hair and white high heeled shoes.
Sunday Mirror (4 September 1994)

Bronzed and fit, Anthony and Paul have travelled across 39 American states, mainly by picking up a car in one state and delivering it to another.
Daily Mail (30 September 1994)

Looking tanned and fit after a two-week break at the renowned St James's Club in Antigua, the petite Miss [Elaine] Paige . . .
Hello! (13 May 1995)

Princess Anne, suntanned and relaxed after a working visit to Mauritius, looked a picture of happiness as she danced the night away with her husband Cdr. Tim Laurence.
Hello! (13 May 1995)

lost in the mists of time. General idiomatic use. Date of origin unknown (or, rather, lost in the . . .). A cliché by the 1950s/60s.

> Stockton Castle, which stood at the southern end of the town's High Street on the site that is now the Swallow Hotel, was the focus of the action although the details of what happened have been lost in the mists of time.
> *Northern Echo* (11 May 1994)

> For centuries, in communities like Sartene, Fozzano and Carbini, fanatical pride dictated that family was pitted against family, sworn to seek revenge for deeds that should have been lost in the mists of time.
> *Mail on Sunday* (26 March 1995)

> The origins of Wexford are lost in the mists of time but it is likely that Celtic settlers arrived there in the 2nd century AD.
> Advertisement brochure, Travel for the Arts, London (Autumn 1995)

love. *See* I LOVE IT BUT . . .

love-tug. *See* TUG OF LOVE.

lowest form of animal life. General use in abusive contexts. Originally a straightforward descriptive phrase, as in J.R. Greene *Protozoa* (1859): 'The lowest form of animal life with which we are acquainted.' In the film *Mutiny on the Bounty* (US, 1935), a midshipman is described as the 'lowest form of animal life in the navy'. A cliché by the 1940s/50s.

> These are essentially the tic-tac merchants of the business: the lowest form of financial animal whose computer-quick trading minds feed the screens in the great towers occupied by the new networks.
> *Guardian* (18 October 1994)

lulled into a sense of false security. General use. 'To rock them . . . in the cradle of their false security' – Lord Lytton, *Rienzi* (1835). A cliché by the mid-twentieth century. Eric Partridge, *A Dictionary of Clichés* (5th edition, 1978), has 'lulled to a false sense of security' and adds 'Politicians, please note!'

> But the Australians seemed to be lulled into a false sense of security when scrum-half Edwards was dismissed in the first half.
> *Daily Mail* (18 November 1994)

> The Ombudsman may hold insurers responsible for failure to collect these

premiums if the arrangement has been working well, and the policyholder has been lulled into a false sense of security.
Scotsman (15 February 1995)

lunar landscape. General use. An inevitable alliterative pairing to describe any bleak prospect of a physical, geographical kind. Date of origin unknown – 1960s? A cliché by the 1970s. Part of the 'travel scribes' armoury' compiled from a competition in the *Guardian* (10 April 1993).

That still left our own 340 yards of lunar landscape for the hearse to nego-tiate. There was no way the council would pay two-thirds of that, so out came the old tin bath again – and two narrow strips of concrete were laid.
Herald (Glasgow) (18 July 1994)

The tourists, mostly wealthy Americans, had been drifting through stormy seas for days anticipating their first glimpse of the Antarctic peninsula, and the lunar landscape of dark grey rocky hills patched with snow was not what they had expected.
Observer (26 March 1995)

lunchtime. *See* LEGEND IN ONE'S OWN . . .

lush vegetation. General use, an inevitable pairing. Date of origin unknown. A cliché by the mid-twentieth century. Part of the 'travel scribes' armoury' compiled from a competition in the *Guardian* (10 April 1993).

Upland lakes and ranches, rugged peaks and awesome ravines, and dense forests of Ponderosa pine give way to semi-arid plains, vast peach and apple orchards, lush vegetation and areas so remote that they are still unexplored.
Herald (Glasgow) (5 September 1994)

Even more exhilarating was swimming behind the torrent to stand on a rock ledge and look out through the film of water to the lush vegetation below.
The Times (5 November 1994)

lust and ambition. *See* SAVAGE STORY OF . . .

== M ==

mad.   *See* <small>FRIENDS THOUGHT I WAS . . .</small>

mailed fist.   General use, meaning 'physical force' or, figuratively, 'tough action'. Known by 1897. A cliché by the mid-twentieth century. Compare <small>WITH AN IRON FIST/HAND.</small>

> In Enfield, North London, where Labour ousted the Tories after 26 years, former leader Graham Eustance said: 'Local issues didn't come into it. If John Major doesn't want to lose the next election he must produce the mailed fist and start knocking some heads together, starting with the Cabinet.'
> *Daily Mail* (7 May 1994)

> The Iraqis should not be allowed to renew this threat when the American and British soldiers have gone home. Unless something is done to prevent this then his mailed fist will still be over Kuwait and her neighbours.
> *Financial Times* (15 October 1994)

major setback.   General use, inevitable pairing. Date of origin unknown. A cliché by the mid-twentieth century.

> The result is a major setback for USI's hopes of bringing the non-affiliated universities into the fold.
> *Irish Times* (10 May 1994)

> Sir Hugh's sentiments were shared by stunned Ministers. Armed Forces Minister Jeremy Hanley spoke of the major setback of the crash and praised the 'brave and talented men' who had saved countless lives over the years with their work in Northern Ireland.
> *Daily Mail* (4 June 1994)

make —— look like a vicarage tea-party.   Journalistic use in popular criticism. One which lingers in my memory is from a *Daily Telegraph* review of Alan Sillitoe's novel *Saturday Night and Sunday Morning* (1958): 'A novel of today, with a freshness and raw fury that makes *Room at the Top* look like a vicarage tea-party.' The quote was used on the cover of the paperback of Sillitoe's novel. When Jacqueline Suzann's *Valley of the Dolls* came out in 1966, a publication called *This Week* noted that it made '*Peyton Place* look like a Bobbsey Twins escapade' (the Bobbsey Twins were nice, clean-cut Americans who got into and out of scrapes in juvenile fiction). A cliché perhaps even before this date.

> He surveyed the smoking ruins of . . . a fine old Elizabethan rectory . . . and said: 'It makes the dissolution of the Monasteries look like a vicarage tea-party'.
> *Daily Telegraph* (31 January 1984)

> 'After the Mexican earthquake, they were all jumping up and down saying "Are we prepared?" The next big one here is going to make Mexico look like a Sunday afternoon tea party,' Shah said.
> *Washington Post* (19 April 1986)

> [Charles Saatchi's advertisements] 'made previous campaigns look like Mary Poppins'.
> *Sunday Times* (21 August 1988), quoting an earlier *Sun* profile

> The City would grind to a standstill if I spoke out. What I could reveal would make the film *Scandal* look like a teddy bears' picnic.
> Pamella Bordes, quoted in the *Sun* (16 March 1989) during a political/sexual scandal

make the supreme sacrifice, to. General pompous use. Meaning 'to die for a cause, a friend, etc.', especially in the 1914–18 war. 'These young men . . . have gone down not only to the horror of the battlefield but to the gates of death as they made the supreme sacrifice' – W.M. Clow, *The Evangelist of the Strait Gate* (1916). A (perhaps) forgivable cliché since then.

> Governor Nelson Rockefeller . . . has emerged from the DARK NIGHT OF THE SOUL that afflicts all politicians pondering the supreme sacrifice.
> *Guardian* (22 December 1970)

> Only when we dare to question the necessity for the 'supreme' sacrifice, and examine truthfully the quality of life that all the survivors are destined to lead afterwards . . .
> *Independent* (1 May 1995)

man behind the myth. General use, but chiefly journalistic. What biographies and articles often claim to reveal. Date of origin unknown.

'The Man and the Myth' was the title given to a Kenneth Tynan profile of Humphrey Bogart in *Playboy* (June 1966). A cliché by the 1960s/70s.

> Christopher Dobson and Ronald Payne are looking for the man behind the myth.
> Martin Bell reviewing book *The Carlos Complex* (1977) in the *Listener*

> On Saturday night and Sunday, the festival presents The Middleham Requiem in Middleham Church, a new choral work exploring the real man behind the myth of Richard III, whose northern home was Middleham Castle.
> *Northern Echo* (27 May 1994)

(man) for all seasons. General use, but chiefly promotional and journalistic, to describe an accomplished, adaptable, appealing person. The origin is a description of Sir Thomas More (1478–1535) by a contemporary, Robert Whittington: 'More is a man of angel's wit and singular learning; I know not his fellow. For where is the man of that gentleness, lowliness and affability? And as time requireth, a man of marvellous mirth and pastimes; and sometimes of as sad a gravity: as who say a man for all seasons.' Whittington (*c*.1480–*c*.1530) wrote the passage for schoolboys to put into Latin in his book *Vulgaria* (*c*.1521). It translates a comment on More by Erasmus – who wrote in his preface to *In Praise of Folly* (1509) that More was *omnium horarum hominem*.

The popularity stems from the phrase's use as the title of Robert Bolt's play about Sir Thomas More (1960, filmed 1967). The cliché formula 'a —— for all seasons' was established soon after.

> [Ralph Richardson] was warm and what the public might call ordinary and, therefore, quite exceptional. That was his ability, that was his talent; he really was a man for all seasons.
> Laurence Olivier, *On Acting* (1986)

> She [Margaret Thatcher] has proved herself not the 'best man in Britain' but the 'Woman For All Seasons.'
> Jean Rook, *Daily Express* (in 1982/3)

man in the street. A cliché of journalism, as in: 'Let's find out what the man in the street wants to know/really thinks.' Not a modern phrase. Fulke Greville, the English diarist, used it (entry dated 22 March 1830). A cliché by 1900.

Up to recently, the man in the street might have defined his attitude to

animals in terms of coursing, fox hunting, or dogfighting. If he did not spend time watching live animals being torn apart for entertainment or kick the family dog into the kennel at night, he might class himself as an animal lover while contemplating rack of lamb for dinner.
Irish Times (24 October 1994)

man of the moment. General use, with alliterative appeal. Known by 1871 when Browning wrote of a 'man o' the moment'. A cliché by 1900.

The Man of the Moment . . . The Chemist.
Title of article in *Punch* (28 January 1914)

Here's our man of the moment . . . Hail the conquering hero comes.
Vincent Brome, *Day of Destruction* (1974)

What counts is being man of the moment among the solicitors and powerful corporate clients willing to pay for who they believe is the best.
Mail on Sunday (22 May 1994)

Once the final whistle has blown and the floodlights are dimmed, man of the moment Smith will switch his attention to a more difficult task.
Northern Echo (26 July 1994)

map. *See* SPREAD OUT LIKE A . . .

marital bliss. General use, often ironic. Date of origin 1988. A cliché by the 1920s/30s. Compare NUPTIAL BLISS.

Their marriage ran for more than 30 years, with periods where that impossible state of 'marital bliss' came close to realization.
The Times (7 September 1994)

marker. *See* PUT DOWN A . . .

married. *See* WE'LL GET . . .

matter is receiving my/our close personal attention. General use, especially in official correspondence. Often means the reverse. Date of origin unknown. A cliché by the mid-twentieth century. The phrase 'close personal attention' also has a life of its own:

They said outdoor activities coupled with close personal attention helped the youngsters realise their self worth.
Northern Echo (9 September 1994)

If leaders don't pay close attention to their team members, they will fail: and attention is by definition personal.
Daily Mail (24 May 1995)

matter of life and death. General idiomatic use, meaning that something is very important. Often used in an exaggerated, figurative fashion. Known by 1583. *A Matter of Life and Death* was the title of a Powell and Pressburger film (UK, 1946; known as *Stairway to Heaven* in the US). A cliché by the 1960s/70s.

For Jane Fonda, it has been the quintessential political correctness dilemma of the American Nineties: should she chop, or should she not chop? For Fonda and Co, it may just be a matter of political correctness in the Nineties. For the Indians, it is a matter of life and death.
Observer (27 October 1991)

The Foreign Office said it was doing 'everything possible' to secure the release of Mr Cowley . . . 'It is a very delicate situation, really a matter of life and death. We have to be very careful about how we conduct this matter.'
Observer (27 August 1995)

maze. *See* CAUGHT UP IN A SINISTER . . .

meaningful dialogue. Political use, mainly, but perhaps also in business. American origin, 1960s? Perhaps a coinage that runs parallel to the use of 'meaningful' in the druggy, alternative artistic sense, also from the 1960s (e.g. a pop song's lyrics might have been described as 'very wonderful and very meaningful'). A cliché almost instantly.

We hope that international pressure will be increased and that meaningful dialogue will begin soon in Burma.
Letter to the editor, *Guardian* (22 July 1994)

meet the challenge, to. Mostly political and business use. Date of origin unknown. A cliché by the mid-twentieth century. It occurs along with other rhetorical clichés during the 'Party Political Speech' (written by Max Schreiner) on the Peter Sellers comedy album *The Best of Sellers* (1958): 'If any part of what I say is challenged, I am more than ready to meet that challenge'.

Meet the challenge, make the change.
Slogan, Labour Party Conference 1989

With the Tories reeling from their worst nationwide election defeat in modern times, the Prime Minister marched out to Downing Street to promise: 'I will meet a challenge whenever it comes'.
Evening Standard (London) (6 May 1994)

The World Bank reports: 'Deficiencies in the system of legal education and training and a dearth in appropriate standards of professional ethics, have left legal practitioners complacent and unprepared to meet the challenge of their business clients competing in a global economy.'
Financial Times (15 July 1994)

meet with an untimely end, to. General use, meaning 'to die'. 'Untimely end' known by 1578, 'meet with . . .' by 1890. Identified as a current cliché in *The Times* (17 March 1995).

The only way you can benefit from Barclays' offer is to meet an untimely end. The money will then be just enough to pay for a modest funeral.
Observer (19 February 1995)

melting-pot. *See* THROWN INTO THE . . .

memories. *See* FULL OF . . .

memory lane. *See* DOWN . . .

merciful release. Condolence use, to suggest that a person's death means that they will not have to suffer bodily any further. Also that the relatives of the deceased will have a burden lifted from them. Known by 1901. A forgivable cliché, though less so in other contexts.

I have had a grave week as my mother has just died, aged 84. You say the English always say 'Happy release' at a death. It was really so in her case.
Letter from Evelyn Waugh to Nancy Mitford (18 December 1954)

He was screaming in such agony that I doubt that I or anyone else who heard him will ever be able to forget it. A British medic ran up, pulled out a pistol, and handed it to a captured Argie medic. The man took it with a nod, leaned down, and shot his own comrade in the head. It was a merciful release for a human being in ultimate pain.
Herald (Glasgow) (4 June 1994)

The crowd, traditionally one of the most supine in sport, were comatose long before the merciful release of the Croat's third-set collapse. They were

as desperate to please as a Boy Scout in bob-a-job week, but had no outlet for their enthusiasm.
Daily Telegraph (4 July 1994)

message of —. Cliché of (mostly British) politics, suggesting that the outcome of, say, a by-election should convey a meaning of importance to the leaders of the political parties that have not done well. The *Daily News* (12 April 1919) had: 'The message of Hull [there had been a by-election] is a message for all the world. It is the announcement that this country, whatever its Government may do, will not have a French peace.' A cliché by the 1960s/70s.

'The SDP bubble has burst,' crowed Fallon. 'That is the message of Darlington.'
Time Magazine (4 April 1983)

message of hope. Mostly journalistic use. Date of origin unknown. A cliché by the mid-twentieth century.

Message of hope as 'The Craig' [Ravenscraig steel mill] dies.
Sunday Times (21 June 1992)

Treasury message of hope amid the jitters.
Headline, *Daily Mail* (27 June 1994)

Gary Lineker has sent a message of hope to fellow professional football striker Tim Langford of Wycombe Wanderers, whose three-year-old son is fighting leukaemia. Three years ago the Linekers' baby son George was diagnosed with the disease and is now recovering.
Evening Standard (London) (16 September 1994)

midnight oil. *See* BURN THE . . .

miles of golden sand. Travel promotional and journalistic use. Date of origin unknown. A cliché by the 1960s/70s.

King of them is Mick Parsons, who has a buggy shop at Pembrey in west Wales, with an outlook on three miles of golden sand.
Guardian (21 May 1994)

North of Torbay, Exmouth is the entrance to the River Exe, with an expanse of two miles of golden sand edging the esplanade.
Herald (Glasgow) (4 March 1995)

mission statement. Political and business use, meaning 'a document setting out aims and aspirations'. 1980s origin? A cliché shortly thereafter. Identified as a current cliché in *The Times* (17 March 1995).

> The fact that the public understanding of science was included in the White Paper, and is now part of the mission statement of the research councils, is a great advance and we applaud this enthusiastically.
> *Daily Telegraph* (1 June 1994)

> That was more than just a re-assertion of the company's mission statement. It was almost a threat to the new regime of financial 'bean counters' from the ousted advertising 'suit'.
> *Sunday Times* (8 January 1995)

mistake. *See* THERE MUST BE SOME . . .

M(istc)r ——. Cliché of journalism. Any 'supremo' automatically gets dubbed one of these. *Private Eye* jokingly pointed to the trend by inventing 'Soccer's Mr Football' in the 1960s/70s – which was when the cliché first became noticeable.

> London's new Mr Railway, David Kirby, likes messing about in boats and singing in the choir.
> *The Times* (8 December 1981)

> Last week it was disclosed that Newmarch is to be the new chief executive of the Prudential – or, put another way, Mr Insurance UK.
> *Observer* (9 April 1989)

mists of time. *See* LOST IN THE . . .

modern classic. Mostly publishing but also other promotional use. 'Penguin Modern Classics', for example, were available in the 1960s but the cliché use (often unjustified or too liberally applied) became apparent in the 1970s/80s. Cited in Eric Partridge, *A Dictionary of Clichés* (5th edition, 1978).

> Anna Pasternak, the author of the modern classic *Princess in Love*, has just had the paperback rights to the book returned to her by Bloomsbury. The publisher says the book, about Princess Diana's irresistible romance with James Hewitt, is too downmarket for it.
> *Evening Standard* (London) (5 May 1995)

> This was trans-Atlantic publishing co-operation at its best. We provided

photographs, [Jackie Kennedy Onassis] offered to produce a map of Tsarist Russia, and jointly we edited a script that turned into a modern classic.
Independent (21 May 1994)

moment in time. *See* AT THIS . . .

moment of truth. General use. Meaning 'a decisive turning point, a significant moment', the phrase comes from *el momento de la verdad* in Spanish bullfighting – the final sword-thrust that kills the animal. *Il Momento della Verità* was the title of an Italian/Spanish film (1964) on a bullfighting theme. In *I, Claud* (1967), Claud Cockburn said of European intellectuals who had fought in the Spanish Civil War: 'They proclaimed, however briefly, that a moment comes when your actions have to bear some kind of relation to your words. This is what is called the Moment of Truth.' A cliché by the mid-twentieth century.

'We have 50,000 moments of truth out there every day,' said Carlzon, defining a moment of truth as each time a customer came into contact with the company.
Financial Times (15 September 1986)

moon. *See* IF THEY/WE CAN PUT A MAN ON THE . . . ; OVER THE . . .

moot point. General use. A point that can be argued, is debatable. Known by 1650. A cliché by the mid-twentieth century.

It is a moot point whether they do much good because, like other party machines, the Conservative local unit functions day-in and day-out pretty successfully.
Cleethorpes News (6 May 1977)

Whether these powerful sounds combined well with Sculthorpe's soppily atmospheric string-quartet writing was a moot point. But it still made quite a change from Mozart at the Wigmore Hall.
Daily Telegraph (30 July 1994)

A code of conduct could proclaim what good practice and standards should be, but it was a moot point as to whether a trade union was the best organisation to police ethics, said the official.
Irish Times (31 December 1994)

moral obligation. General use. An inevitable pairing, known by 1729. A cliché by 1900.

Institutions are thrilled that they are allowed to invest in South Africa again. But they feel no moral obligation to do so.
Financial Times (2 June 1994)

Kevin Keegan, the Newcastle United manager, felt 'morally obliged' to go to Old Trafford and attack. Moral obligation and the Four-man Midfield: a philosophical tract that gave us a belter of a match.
The Times (31 October 1994)

more dash than cash. Fashion journalistic use, especially in *Vogue*, for which this slogan appears to have been invented in the 1950s. About clothing which, while stylish, is cheap or – given *Vogue*'s usual standards – cheaper than the norm. It was still being used over *Vogue* features in the 1990s. Also in other contexts:

The march of Waterstone's bookshops through the 1980s high streets owed more to dash than cash. With their bright staff and 'reliable, wide-ranging stock', the stores showed that the marketing flummery of Thatcherism could serve both Mind and Mammon.
Observer (4 September 1994)

If *Vogue* is a reliable financial sounding board we are in for prosperity and great good sense. In the October issue they have said farewell to the More Dash Than Cash section and welcomed back an old-timer called Great Good Buys.
Daily Telegraph (19 September 1994)

more years than I care to remember. *See* AFTER/FOR . . .

mother of parliaments. General use, but mistakenly applied to Westminster. What John Bright, the English radical politician, said in a speech at Birmingham on 18 January 1865, was: '*England* is the mother of parliaments.' Frequently misused, even at the highest levels. Icelanders may well object that they have a prior claim to the title anyway.

There is a huge complacency about the supposed mother of parliaments. Tradition is of the highest value in things that do not matter but a mathematical nonsense in things that do.
Independent (2 May 1994)

movement. *See* THIS GREAT . . .

mum. *See* FOR THE BEST MUM . . .

murky past. General use. An inevitable pairing, known by 1917 and a cliché since thenabouts, too.

> For such a beautiful flower, the tulip has a rather murky past.
> Headline, *Today* (27 August 1994)

> The sight stirred Chatterjee. 'The islands are like that,' he said. 'They appear beautiful, but they have a very murky past.'
> *Financial Times* (29 April 1995)

murmuring fountains. Journalistic use. Date of origin unknown – though it sounds like a translation of a classical author. A cliché by the mid-twentieth century. Listed in the *Independent* 'DIY travel writers' cliché kit' (31 December 1988).

> Sound is important: birdsong in the trees; the splashing and murmuring of the fountains, waterfall and stream.
> *Sunday Telegraph* (26 March 1995)

music or the words. *See* WHICH COMES FIRST . . .

must surely kiss goodbye to . . . Journalistic, often sporting use. Date of origin unknown. A cliché by the 1960s/70s.

> Brazil were undeniably the better team, but if their finishing is as profligate against Italy in Sunday's final they can surely kiss their hopes of a fourth World Cup goodbye.
> *Scotsman* (14 July 1994)

> Wretched Derby can surely kiss the play-offs goodbye after being out-gunned by Burnley, going down 3–1.
> *People* (16 April 1995)

mute witnesses (to the passing of time). General but especially travel journalistic and promotional use, for what buildings and stones (usually) are often described as being. Date of origin unknown, but I recall a French tourist leaflet from Provence in 1959 having the line: *Les pierres parlent à ceux qui savent les entendres* ('the stones speak to those who know how to hear them'). So, a cliché by the mid-twentieth century. 'The old stones of the castle are mute witness to the unrelenting passage of time and the violent forces of history' – listed in the *Independent* 'DIY travel writers' cliché kit' (31 December 1988).

'We have been mute witnesses of evil deeds,' wrote Pastor Dietrich

Bonhoeffer at the end of 1942. 'Are we still of any use? Will our spiritual resistance to what is enforced on us still prove strong enough, and will we still be honest enough with ourselves to rediscover the road to simplicity and integrity?'
Independent (25 August 1994)

To give the situation an extra spin, the couple are standing inside a prehistoric exhibit at the museum where he's a curator. The mute witnesses to this very modern rite are a pair of neanderthal waxworks.
Independent (6 May 1995)

my boy is a good boy.   Drama. What Italian-American mothers invariably say when told that their sons are, in fact, violent criminals or whatever. Observed by Fritz Spiegl in an article on drama cliché lines in the *Listener* (7 February 1985).

my friends . . .   Cliché of politics, and it always presumes rather a lot when politicians make use of this phrase. *Safire's Political Dictionary* (1978) asserts that the first American to do so – noticeably, at any rate – was Franklin D. Roosevelt, who acquired the salutation in 1910 from Richard Connell who was running for Congress at the same time. But Abraham Lincoln had used this form of address on occasions.

In British politics, during a party political broadcast on 4 June 1945, Winston Churchill said: 'My friends, I must tell you that a Socialist policy is abhorrent to the British idea of freedom.' Anthony Eden, in his pained TV broadcast during the Suez crisis (3 November 1956), used the phrase, ingratiatingly, too. But I don't think any British prime minister has done so since. It is hard to imagine Margaret Thatcher ever getting her tongue round it. Nor has anyone tried to find an equivalent of the standard 'My fellow Americans', beloved of US presidents.

It occurs along with other rhetorical clichés during the 'Party Political Speech' (written by Max Schreiner) on the Peter Sellers comedy album *The Best of Sellers* (1958). Identified as a current cliché in *The Times* (17 March 1995).

my regiment leaves at dawn.   Musical comedy and operetta use? It is a line spoken by Groucho Marx in the film *Monkey Business* (1931), preceded by the words, 'Come, Kapellmeister, let the violas throb!' Presumably this is a cliché of operetta, spoken by the soldier to his love as an encouragement to do whatever, but no precise example has been traced. It was certainly the situation in many romantic tangles, even if the line itself was not actually spoken.

my wife and family are standing by me.   Political use, when a sacked or disgraced minister issues a statement. Mostly British politics. Also used when other sorts of people are in difficulties. Date of origin unknown. A cliché by the 1960s. Compare I WOULD LIKE TO SPEND MORE TIME WITH (MY WIFE) AND FAMILY.

> The informal family photographs are very fetching and they will look as good framed on an Islington mantelpiece as they did in print, but they have begun to be as ubiquitous as those of a disgraced Tory minister whose wife has declared that she is standing by him.
> *Daily Mail* (3 October 1994)

> Sex attacks PC jailed for three months ... He added that Turner's wife was standing by him, but the family now faced losing their police home in Forbes Road, Falkirk.
> *Scotsman* (28 October 1994)

my wife doesn't understand me.   Cliché of seduction, uttered by a married man in order to gain sympathy. Date of origin unknown. A cliché by the mid-twentieth century.

> Nor would the Mrs Mellors and Norrises face public humiliation without some daft, unsisterly bat somewhere believing that a breathy 'My wife doesn't understand me' justifies indulging a genital itch.
> *Guardian* (2 May 1994)

> These women are reviled for leading married men astray, when they are often the ones who have been lured into hotel rooms with sweet promises and sympathetic stories about, 'how my wife doesn't understand me'.
> *Daily Mirror* (10 May 1995)

myth.   *See* MAN BEHIND THE ...

= N =

nail into the coffin. *See* DRIVE ANOTHER . . .

nail this lie. *See* LET ME/WE MUST . . .

naked as nature intended. General use. Compare 'Stripping as they ran, till, when they touched the sands, they were naked as God had made them, and as happy as He intended them to be' – Rudyard Kipling, 'Propagation of Knowledge' (1926) from *Stalky & Co.*   Used as the title of the most famous British nudist film, in the 1950s – as confirmed by this extract from the sketch 'Naked Films' by Steven Vinaver in the book *That Was the Week That Was* (ed. Frost & Sherrin, 1963): 'Two-fifty-eight, entered Gala Royal to see "Naked as Nature Intended". Three-thirty, down to the Cameo Moulin for "My Bare Lady".' A cliché from around this time.

> But most men will be cringeing in sympathy with Charles. He must have felt like he was caught in one of those terrible nightmares – you know, the ones where you find yourself in the High Street as naked as unforgiving Mother Nature intended.
> *Daily Mirror* (8 September 1994)

name of the game. *See* —— IS THE . . .

nasty, brutish and short. General use, to describe life. A quotation from Thomas Hobbes, *Leviathan, or the Matter, Form, and Power of a Commonwealth, Ecclesiastical and Civil*, Chap. 13 (1651). In this treatise of political philosophy, Hobbes sees man not as a social being but as a selfish creature. The state of nature in which he resides is one in which there are: 'No arts; no letters; no society; and which is worst of all, continual fear and danger of violent death; and the life of man, solitary, poor, nasty, brutish, and short.' The last portion of this bleak view has fallen victim to over-quoting, as Philip Howard, Literary Editor of *The Times*, noted on 15 August 1984. He warned of the danger that: 'We become so fond of hackneyed quotation that we trot it out, without thinking, at every opportunity.' He gave, as his example, 'the one about the life of man being "solitary, poor, nasty, brutish, and short," just to let everybody know that I am an intellectual sort of chap who reads Hobbes in the bath'. Curiously, later that year, on 1 November, when *The Times* had a first leader on the assassination of Mrs Indira Gandhi, it began by observing that world figures know all too sickeningly well 'the continual fear and danger of violent death' that Thomas Hobbes identified as a condition of man. And added: 'With that awful daily awareness, now goes for some a reminder of his definition of life as nasty, brutish and short.'

nationwide hunt/search.   Journalistic use. Date of origin unknown. A cliché by the 1960s/70s. Listed by Keith Waterhouse in *Daily Mirror Style* (1981) as a phrase to be avoided.

> A citizen's arrest . . . ended the nationwide hunt.
> *Daily Telegraph* (9 November 1978)

> A nationwide hunt has been launched for the vanished strawberries of Britain, the dozens of flavourful old varieties that may be lurking in gardens and country estates.
> *The Times* (12 May 1994)

> 'We can sometimes do a nationwide search,' confesses Ms Ormiston . . . 'but it's a nightmare, takes ages, and I only do it if someone is very insistent.'
> *Independent* (9 June 1994)

> To the chagrin of critics of the award, pollution levels and the number of environment-friendly initiatives were not taken into consideration in the nationwide search for the cleanest city.
> *Independent* (4 May 1995)

Nazi jackboot(s).   General use, to encapsulate the horrors of Nazism in the Second World War. A cliché by the 1950s.

> Looking back on that visit of the late forties, I had not appreciated just how recently those Nazi jackboots had strutted down the Champs Elysees.
> *Herald* (Glasgow) (23 August 1994)

> We may learn from Janus and Janus that 11 per cent of American men and women have had personal experience of dominance/bondage, but instead

of that news satisfying our curiosity, it merely prompts more detailed questions . . . Are Nazi jackboots still in favour?
Independent on Sunday (25 April 1993)

need one's own space, to.   General use, most often in the context of breaking away from a partnership or marriage in order that the persons involved may be able to grow and flourish independently. From American psycho-babble, perhaps dating from the 1960s/70s. A cliché by the 1980s.

[Elizabeth Taylor said] that she and Larry Fortensky have agreed to a trial separation, 'Larry and I both need our own space now.'
Independent (1 September 1995)

needs no introduction.   Chairpersons' and presenters' use. From my *Best Behaviour* (1992): 'A good chairman is hard to find, though even a bad one is preferable to professional toastmasters with their noisy gavel-banging, and pompous if not incompetent introductions. The chairman should introduce the speaker with the minimum of words. There is no point in saying that the "speaker needs no introduction" if you then plough through his biography.' A cliché by the mid-twentieth century.

Elaine Myers needs no introduction to nitelifers.
Leader (Durban) (7 May 1971)

negotiating table.   *See* TO THE . . .

neither fair to you nor true to myself.   Speechmakers' pompous use. It occurs along with other rhetorical clichés during the 'Party Political Speech' (written by Max Schreiner) on the Peter Sellers comedy album *The Best of Sellers* (1958): 'For if I were to convey to you a spirit of false optimism then I should be neither fair to you nor true to myself.'

nerve centre.   General use, mostly journalistic, for the centre of control of any organization. 'Wall Street is the great nerve centre of all American business' – James Bryce, *The American Commonwealth* (1888). A cliché by the mid-twentieth century. Mocked by Tom Stoppard in the play *Night and Day* (1978): 'Commandeered it as the nerve centre of Mageeba's victorious drive against the FORCES OF DARKNESS, otherwise known as the Adoma Liberation Front.'

A 'nerve centre' opens today opposite Victoria Station for cross-Channel steamer car traffic.
Daily Telegraph (30 November 1959)

Palatable platitudes at the nerve centre of chic – Wet, liberal, self-righteous rap for those who can't stomach the hard stuff. Adam Sweeting on the Disposable Heroes of Hiphoprisy.
By-line, *Guardian* (10 June 1992)

nestling in the valley. Travel journalistic use. Date of origin unknown. Part of the 'travel scribes' armoury' compiled from a competition in the *Guardian* (10 April 1993).

For our first night we chose the Hotellerie du Prieuré St Lazare from the Crystal Holidays brochure. It seemed about the right distance from the ferry and it looked appealing: 'Nestling in the Loire Valley, at the crossroads of Anjou, Touraine and Poitou, stands the Royal Abbey of Fontevraud . . .'
Daily Telegraph (11 June 1994)

Joanna Trollope's domestic bliss in Gloucestershire is much chronicled. The house of honey-coloured stone, nestling in a valley with roses, wisteria, trout stream, and farmhouse kitchen where she sometimes bops to Elvis and where sits the famous Aga, gibes about which are wearing thin.
Valerie Grove, *The Times* (31 March 1995)

nice girl like you. *See* WHAT'S A . . .

nice place you got here. Film script use, mainly. Dick Vosburgh and Trevor Lyttleton included this film phrase in their catalogue song 'I Love a Film Cliché', which was included in the Broadway hit, *A Day in Hollywood, A Night in the Ukraine* (1980). In it, they gave the longer version – the one uttered by a gangster with a lump in his jacket, viz: 'Nice place you got here, blue eyes. Be too bad if something was to . . . happen to it!' At this point, the heavy usually knocks over an ornament, as a warning.

Often, one hears the version 'nice *little* place you've got here' – used with equal amounts of irony about a dump or somewhere impressively grand. However, in the film *Breakfast at Tiffany's* (1961), it is said almost straight. In *Laura* (1944), Dana Andrews says to Clifton Webb, 'Nice little place you have here, Mr Lydecker' with feint quotation marks round it.

Eric Partridge's *Catch Phrases* seems to think it all started in Britain in the 1940s, but I feel sure the film use must have started in the US in the 1930s. It is also said to have been popularized around 1942 by the BBC radio show *ITMA*, following a visit to Windsor Castle by the star Tommy Handley. A cliché by the 1950s.

> To this day [Stevie] Wonder habitually talks about 'seeing' and catches out sighted friends by walking into unfamiliar rooms, taking a 'look' around and saying: 'Hey, nice place you've got here.'
> *Independent* (13 May 1989)

night. *See* (AS SURELY) AS NIGHT FOLLOWS DAY . . .

nightmare. *See* DREAM TURNED TO A . . .

nipped in the bud. General use, meaning 'arrested or checked at the very start'. Known by 1606. Listed in the *Independent* (24 December 1994) as a cliché of newspaper editorials.

> A promising career was virtually nipped in the bud when the leg-spinner was savaged – chiefly by Aamir Sohail and Javed Miandad – and finished with match figures of 33–0–184–0.
> *Daily Mail* (27 June 1994)

> When covering by Pritchard twice nipped danger in the bud, even these worker Bees began to drone in the heat.
> *Observer* (7 May 1995)

no/an axe to grind. *See* HAVE NO/AN AXE . . .

no pun intended. *See* IF YOU'LL EXCUSE THE PUN!

Northern fastness. General quasi-literary use, for a stronghold. Always in the North for some reason. Date of origin unknown. A cliché by 1900.

> In four countries – Greenland, Finland, Norway and Sweden – you can visit Santa centres where you can meet the 'real' Santa Claus in his 'real' Northern fastness, tour his workshop and, of course, spend lots of money on souvenirs, in restaurants and on such suitable activities as taking a sleigh ride.
> *Financial Times* (24 December 1994)

not a pretty sight. General use, for something that looks particularly unpleasant. Observed by Fritz Spiegl in an article on drama cliché lines in the *Listener* (7 February 1985). Usually said about the appearance of a body that has been involved in an accident or death.

Take a long, hard look at this picture. No, it's not a pretty sight but, sad to say, it's the brutal face of Britain, 1994.
People (11 September 1994)

In-yer-face investment banking, as practised by Swiss Bank Corporation, is not a pretty sight. Swiss Bank has specialised in upsetting the City's establishment, rather as S.G. Warburg did 30 years ago.
Daily Telegraph (14 January 1995)

not for everyone, maybe.   Travel journalistic use – when summing up the attractions of a particular holiday. Part of the 'travel scribes' armoury' compiled from a competition in the *Guardian* (10 April 1993).

not lost but gone before.   Condolence and bereavement use. According to W. Gurney Benham, *Cassell's Book of Quotations* (1907), 'Not lost but gone before' was the title of a song published in Smith's *Edinburgh Harmony* (1829), and it is one of the standard epitaphs now imprinted on countless graves. It may have been popularized by its use as the title of a poem by Caroline Norton (1808–77), which goes:

> For death and life in ceaseless strife,
>   Beat wild on this world's shore,
> And all our calm is in that balm –
>   Not lost but gone before.

The variant form occurs in *Human Life* (1819) by Samuel Rogers:

> Those whom he loved so long and sees no more,
> Loved, and still loves – not dead – but gone before.

However, according to *H.L. Mencken's Dictionary of Quotations* (1942), the phrase occurs in one of Alexander Pope's epitaphs for 'Elijah Fenton, Easthampstead England' (*c.*1731) – though this one is not included in *Pope's Poetical Works*:

> Weep not, ye mourners, for the dead,
>   But in this hope your spirits soar,
> That ye can say of those ye mourn,
>   They are not lost but gone before.

And to Philip Henry (1631–96) is ascribed the couplet:

> They are not *amissi*, but *praemissi*;
> Not lost but gone before.

Seneca wrote: *Non amittuntur sed praemittuntur* ('They are not lost but sent before'). So the concept is, indeed, a very old one. The simple phrase 'gone before' meaning 'dead' was well established in English by the early sixteenth century.

In *Heaven's Command* (1973), James Morris quotes the epitaph on Lt Christopher Hyland of the 62nd Regt., who died in Bermuda in 1837:

> Alas, he is not lost,
> But is gone before.

In 1982 I was told of a woman's gravestone in Canada 'some years ago' that had:

> Dry up your tears, and weep no more,
> I am not dead, but gone before,
> Remember me, and bear in mind
> You have not long to stay behind.

nothing in his life became him like the leaving it. Obituary and tribute use. An allusion to Shakespeare, *Macbeth*, I.iv.7 (1606) where Malcolm says it of the murdered Thane of Cawdor: '. . . he died/As one that had been studied in his death,/To throw away the dearest thing he ow'd,/As 'twere a careless trifle.' Sometimes adapted and used figuratively to describe the way a person has relinquished a position with dignity. A cliché by 1900.

> So farewell then, Kelvin. Nothing became Sydney Carton's life so well as the leaving of it, and that must surely be true of Kelvin's disappearance from the Sky.
> *Guardian* (5 August 1994)

> Yesterday, Reynolds's detractors – Spring, Bruton and Harney included – sang fulsome praises of the man they had just buried [or, rather, the Irish Prime Minister they had just forced out of office]. 'You have done your best, Taoiseach . . . You have stood up for the family in Irish life . . . Nothing became him so well as his leaving . . . It was his finest hour', and so on.
> *The Times* (18 November 1994)

nowhere. *See* ON THE ROAD FROM . . .

no-win situation. A struggle that cannot be won. 'No-win' has been known since 1962 and a cliché shortly thereafter.

Both attack Washington for a 'no-win' war policy.
Economist (5 November 1966)

Under Michael Grade, Channel 4 is in a no-win situation – too commercially successful for its own goods and still managing to shock.
Observer (11 Sunday 1995)

nudity. *See* IT'S ABSOLUTELY VITAL . . .

nuptial bliss. General use, slightly facetious or ironical for the supposed contentment of the wedded state. Date of origin unknown. A cliché by the mid-twentieth century. Compare MARITAL BLISS.

Just when Michael Jackson thought he could enjoy a few quiet weeks as a married man, another expensive lawsuit from a young boy is about to disrupt his nuptial bliss. A summons has been mailed to his hideaway in the Trump Tower.
Sunday Times (27 November 1994)

nutshell. *See* IN A . . .

= O =

—— **of a lifetime.** *See* HOLIDAY ...

—— **of all time.** General use, whenever a superlative needs needlessly heightening. Probably of American origin, date unknown. A cliché by the mid-twentieth century.

> By now we have all learned ... to substitute 'Russia' for the 'Soviet Union' in our reporting, our discourse and – increasingly – in our national consciousness. The change symbolizes one of the great, transforming, peaceful revolutions of all time.
> *Washington Post* (26 June 1992)

of paramount importance. General use. Known by 1877. A cliché by the mid-twentieth century.

> Bull, of paramount importance to Taylor's promotion plans, limped off after aggravating scar tissue around his hamstring but not before creating the 11th-minute winner.
> *Daily Telegraph* (15 August 1994)

> The executive said: 'We will be asking British Gas for evidence that they will be in a position to discharge their duty. Safety is of paramount importance and must not be jeopardised.'
> *Daily Telegraph* (30 December 1994)

> They were of 'paramount importance', Mr Ruggiero said, not simply because they covered a big chunk of international commerce but because they were the first TEST OF THE CREDIBILITY of the WTO which superseded the General Agreement on Tariffs and Trade in January.
> *Financial Times* (4 May 1995)

—— **of the century.** Promotional and advertising use. The *San Francisco Examiner* (13 April 1895) described the murder of two pretty girls by a Sunday school superintendent as 'the crime of a century'. This last points to a likely American origin for the format. A review of Amanda M. Ros's novel *Irene Iddesleigh* in the magazine *Black and White* (19 February 1898) was headed 'The Book of the Century'. The Empire Hotel, Bath (opened 1901), had lavatory bowls with the slogan 'The Closet of the Century' written around the rim. The Australian film *Robbery Under Arms* (1907) was promoted on a Melbourne poster as 'The Picture of the Century'. There were two films, both called *Crime of the Century*, in 1933 and 1946. More recently there was a British TV quiz called *Sale of the Century* (1970s/80s). A cliché from about this period. The 1981 Royal nuptials were dubbed by *Time* Magazine in a 1983 advertisement as 'the wedding of the century'.

of which more anon.   General use, as a light-hearted way of closing down a train of thought. Date of origin unknown. Only a borderline cliché as it is inoffensive and still quite fun.

> True, would-be floaters such as TeleWest and General Cable have thought better of it, but that still leaves the likes of 3i and Eurotunnel (of which more anon).
> *Independent on Sunday* (29 May 1994)

—— of yesteryear.   General use, consciously quaint and quasi-poetic. 'But where are the snows of yester-year?' was coined by D.G. Rossetti to translate *d'antan* in his translation (1870) of the famous line from François Villon's *Grand Testament: Mais où sont les neiges d'antan?* The format was a cliché by the 1970s/80s.

> Where were the klongs of yesteryear, all those colorful canals, criss-crossing the city?
> *National Geographic Magazine* (July 1967)

> Were progressives of yesteryear any less rigorous in rooting out real or imagined anti-semitic references than the new politically correct bully boys and girls are in rooting out, say, homophobic references?
> *Sunday Telegraph* (2 February 1992)

official.   *See* —— AND THAT'S . . .

on a collision course.   General and journalistic use. The original naval use of the term was known by 1944. The figurative use was current by the 1960s and a cliché shortly thereafter. Listed in the *Independent* (24 December 1994) as a cliché of newspaper editorials.

The great powers are now headed on a collision course over Berlin.
New Statesman (21 July 1961)

[The city council's] policies on development and road building . . . set it on a collision course.
The Times (8 January 1973)

The Arts: Collision course on the voyage round Columbus – Two films are planned to celebrate the anniversary of the explorer's famous arrival in America. David Gritten charts progress in the year's hottest clash in filmmaking.
By-line, *Daily Telegraph* (8 February 1992)

on bended knee.   General use, to mean 'in a suppliant position, deferring to another' as though to a ruler or other person in high authority. 'With one accord/On castleyard and all around the people sink on bended knee' – Marie A. Brown, *Nadeschda* (1878). A cliché by 1900.

The offer was met with a hostile reception from Mrs Lennox [Gulf War widow]. 'I'm not going on bended knee and expose all my financial details in order to benefit. It's not what my husband gave his life for,' she said.
Daily Telegraph (6 May 1994)

For the first time in his life, or almost the first time (you can never tell with this man), Ballesteros went on bended knee to the USGA to get an invitation.
Independent (7 May 1994)

on Day One/Two/Three . . .   Travel journalistic use. Part of the 'travel scribes' armoury' compiled from a competition in the *Guardian* (10 April 1993).

So on the afternoon of Day 5 we took a little drive up to a pretty mountain village and ate feta in a tiny taverna PERCHED ON A HILLside while swallows dived and goats ambled around us.
Kathryn Flett, *Observer* 'Life' Magazine (30 April 1995)

on the road from —— to nowhere.   General use, signifying that a place (or a person) is in an obscure position (or is not getting anywhere). Date of origin unknown. A cliché by the 1970s. Now mostly journalistic. Mocked by Tom Stoppard in the play *Night and Day* (1978): 'This time last week Jeddu was a one-horse town on the road from Kamba City to nowhere.'

My uncle's farm is on the road to nowhere . . . They often don't see a new face for months on end.
E. Coxhead, *One Green Bottle* (1951)

People on foot on a hot road . . . walking from nowhere to nowhere.
Guardian Weekly (21 March 1970)

once in a lifetime (experience). General use, but often in travel promotion and advertising. Known by 1908. 'The thrill that comes once in a lifetime' – heading, H.T. Webster, *Our Boyhood Thrills* (1915). A cliché by the mid-twentieth century, perhaps helped by the Moss Hart/George S. Kaufman play title *Once In a Lifetime* (1930, filmed US, 1933) and the song title sung by Anthony Newley with lyrics by Leslie Bricusse (1961).

The *Mail on Sunday* is giving two families of four (two adults, two children) a once-in-a-lifetime chance to experience this spectacular celebration of horsemanship from the comfort of one of Wembley Arena's new fully-catered VIP boxes.
Mail on Sunday (4 September 1994)

'It's a once-in-a-lifetime experience,' agrees Kate Edwards, who has come with her husband, Nick. 'Except we do it every year!'
Independent (19 December 1994)

'People are going for once-in-a-lifetime experiences which tend to be expensive,' says James Daunt of Daunt Books, the . . . travel bookshop that is the scene of much pre-honeymoon browsing.
Independent (15 September 1995)

one day all this will be yours, my son. General use, perhaps nowadays only in parody use. Spoken by a proud father gesturing proprietorially over his property. Compare from Rudyard Kipling's story 'The Brush-wood Boy' (1895): ' "Perfect! By Jove, it's perfect!" Georgie was looking at the round-bosomed woods beyond the home paddock, where the white pheasant-boxes were ranged . . . Georgie felt his father's arm tighten in his.

' "It's not half bad – but *hodie mihi, eras tibi* [what's mine today will be yours], isn't it? I suppose you'll be turning up some day with a girl under your arm . . ." '

A borderline cliché by the mid-twentieth century.

One day my son all this might *not* be yours.
Headline to Albany Life assurance advertisement (December 1981)

One day, my boy, all this *won't* be yours.
Headline to National Provident life assurance ad (the same month as above)

One day, my son, all this will be yours – but not just yet.
Glenmorangie whisky advertisement (December 1982)

one needs a good laugh in these difficult times.   Conversational use.
I noticed this occurring with some regularity in the 1970s/80s in letters
from radio listeners, though I expect they had been saying this since the
beginning of the Second World War, if not of the First. However, a cliché
since 1980, say. This citation is not quite typical of the use:

. . . awarded for providing a perfect 'night out' for Mayfest audiences, a
hilarious and well-crafted comic vehicle for a great Scottish cast, and a
damned good laugh at a time when Scottish theatre really needs it.
Scotland on Sunday (8 May 1994)

one small step for ——, one giant leap for ——.   Mostly journalistic use,
echoing what Neil Armstrong claimed he said when stepping on to the
moon's surface for the first time on 20 July 1969 was 'That's one small step
for a man, one giant leap for mankind'. The indefinite article before 'man'
was, however, completely inaudible, thus ruining the sense. A cliché from
very shortly afterwards.

Small step for non-white mankind.
Headline, *The Times* (29 October 1983)

Up to 10.75% – one small step for your money, one giant leap for your
interest rate. You'll be OVER THE MOON to discover you only need £1,000
to open a Capital Choice account at the Alliance & Leicester.
Advertisement (July 1989)

A small step for man; a giant leap for plastic frogs.
Headline, *Independent* (9 May 1992)

Robert Bryhn, of the Swedish advertising agency which dreamt up the idea
[of an advertising billboard in space] said in London yesterday: 'This is a
small step for the people behind the project but a giant leap for modern
marketing'.
Independent (12 August 1995)

One small step is better than a giant leap in cost.
Headline, *Observer* (27 August 1995)

one thing is certain.   Journalistic use, mainly. Date of origin unknown.
A cliché by the 1970s.

One thing is certain, no matter what asset value Lasmo believes is appropriate, it will play no part in the thinking of Enterprise.
Lloyd's List (13 June 1994)

Whatever happens when [Sibson and Kaylor, boxers] explode into belligerent action . . . at Wembley on Tuesday, one thing is certain: for the loser there will be nothing left except a rubble of wrecked hopes.
Sunday Express (25 November 1984)

Most of these stones are huge and look extremely heavy, being three feet high, two feet wide and over two feet thick. They come in all shapes and sizes but one thing is certain: the majority could not have been lifted by even two men.
Guardian (11 May 1995)

ongoing situation or —— **situation.**   General use. For several years in the 1970s and 80s, starting in April 1976, *Private Eye* waged a campaign against the unnecessary addition of the word 'situation' in situations where the speaker thought it added something to the sentence. The column was entitled 'Ongoing situations'. This succeeded in making the matter a well-known joke but did not entirely put an end to the practice. Oddly, as long ago as 22 August 1934, *The Times* was drawing attention to the trend: 'A popular dodge at present is to add the word "situation" or "position" to a noun; by this means, apparently, it has been discovered that the most pregnant meanings can be expressed with the least effort. The "coal situation" remains unchanged; the "herring position" is grave.' A cliché, however, from the 1970s onwards. 'Ongoing situation' was identified as a still current cliché in *The Times* (17 March 1995).

Whereas a hedge situation at Altwood Road, Maidenhead in Berkshire, belonging to you overhangs the highway known as Altwood Road, Maidenhead aforesaid, so as to endanger or obstruct the passage of pedestrians . . .
An employee of the Royal Borough of Windsor and Maidenhead wrote to a householder and asked him to trim a hedge in these words (reported 1981)

'[John Lennon] asked if I had ever tried [heroin]. I told him that while he was in India with the Maharishi, I had a sniff of it in a party situation . . .'
Yoko Ono, quoted in Peter Brown and Steven Gaines, *The Love You Make* (1983)

Much has been learned since the first Whitbread [round-the-world yacht race] in 1973/74 when, tragically, three men died in man overboard situations . . .
High Life Magazine (September 1993)

Whether a conifer will recover from wind burn depends on the severity. If a severe draught is an ongoing situation, then recovery is unlikely.
Herald (Glasgow) (16 July 1994)

According to the British Airport Authority: 'The thing about security is that we review it constantly and we certainly wouldn't be making any reductions. The process of review never stops, it's an ongoing situation.'
Financial Times (5 September 1994)

only time will tell. A cliché especially of broadcast news journalism and used by reporters to round off a story when they can't think of anything else to say. The proverbial expression has existed since 1539. A cliché since the 1960s/70s. *Time* Magazine (March 1984) quoted Edwin Newman, a former NBC-TV correspondent, on a continuing weakness of TV news: 'There are too many correspondents standing outside buildings and saying, "Time will tell." ' (Indeed, the 'only' is often omitted.)

'One only has to go to any other country and to see what happens when the Civil Service is not a bulwark, when it does not have the traditions of our Civil Service.' Only time will tell whether that bulwark is now about to be undermined.
Scotsman (14 July 1994)

Time alone will tell whether the French continue to shop for boys' names on our side of the Channel.
Mail on Sunday (11 June 1995)

oo-la-la or **oh-la-la.** Mostly journalistic use, to express the naughtiness commonly associated with the French. Known by 1940. A cliché by the 1950s. Listed by Keith Waterhouse in *Daily Mirror Style* (1981): 'This foreign-desk phrase, believed to be extinct, was sighted recently in the *Sun*.'

The ooh-la-la French maid.
Spectator (24 July 1959)

Those two great standbys of French fashion, quality and a little bit of ooh-la-la.
The Times (10 April 1973)

orgasm like a cork bursting from a bottle of champagne. Popular simile especially in cheap fiction. Date of origin unknown. A cliché by the mid-twentieth century.

Maxine was now heedless of anything except her urgent need for Charles, and their sexual tension swiftly built up to a climax as violently explosive as the cork bursting from a bottle of champagne.
Shirley Conran, *Lace* (1982)

out-Herod Herod, to.　General use. A literary allusion, often adapted in the form 'to out something something' and meaning to go beyond the extremes of tyranny (or whatever activity is under consideration) as usually perceived. The allusion is to Herod's slaughter of all the children of Bethlehem (Matthew 2:16). The precise formulation of the phrase occurs in Shakespeare's *Hamlet*, III.ii.8 (1600) when the Prince is instructing the actors not to go over the top: 'O! it offends me to the soul to hear a robustious periwig-pated fellow tear a passion to tatters . . . I would have such a fellow whipped for o'erdoing Termagant; it out-herods Herod: pray you, avoid it.' (Termagant and Herod both featured in medieval mystery plays as noisy violent types.) Popular in the nineteenth century, a cliché by the end of it.

Italian composers essaying the more classical forms are impelled to out-Herod Herod in the seriousness and Teutonicism of their productions.
Westminster Gazette (2 October 1901)

In an act of gross unfairness that even out-Thatchered Thatcher, one-in-four of all workers were sentenced to a three-year standstill. And in an act of gross meanness, that even out-Scrooged Scrooge, the Government's punitive pay policy, unlike any other since the last war, offers no protection whatsoever for the poorest-paid.
Herald (Glasgow) (31 December 1993)

oven door.　*See* LIKE OPENING . . .

over the moon.　General use, but especially journalistic and sporting. In about 1978, two cliché expressions became notorious in Britain if one wished to express either pleasure or dismay at the outcome of anything, but especially of a football match. The speaker was either 'over the moon' or AS SICK AS A PARROT. 'Over the moon' is probably the older of the two phrases. Indeed, in the diaries of May, Lady Cavendish (published 1927) there is an entry for 7 February 1857 saying how she broke the news of her youngest brother's birth to the rest of her siblings: 'I had told the little ones who were first utterly incredulous and then over the moon.' The family of Catherine Gladstone (*née* Gwynne), wife of the Prime Minister, is said to have had its own idiomatic language and originated the phrase. However, the nursery rhyme 'Hey diddle diddle/The cat and the fiddle,/The cow jumped over the moon' dates back to 1765 at least and surely conveys the same meaning. Besides, the Rev. Sydney Smith was reported in 1833 as having said 'I could have jumped over the moon'.

The specific application to football was already in evidence in 1962, when Alf Ramsey (a team manager) was quoted as saying, on one occasion, 'I feel like jumping over the moon'.

The clichéd use probably began because of the remorseless post-game analysis by TV football commentators and the consequent need for players and managers to provide pithy comments. Liverpool footballer Phil Thompson said he felt 'sick as a parrot' after his team's defeat in the 1978 Football League Cup Final. Ironically, *Private Eye* fuelled the cliché by constant mockery, to such an extent that by 1980 an 'instant' BBC Radio play about the European Cup Final (written on the spot by Neville Smith according to the outcome) was given the alternative titles *Over the Moon/Sick as a Parrot.*

> 'I am over the moon,' M. Roux said yesterday ... he quickly denied, however, that his brother [another celebrated restaurateur] would be 'sick as a parrot.'
>
> Albert Roux, restaurateur, on gaining three stars in the *Michelin Guide* and quoted in *The Times* (21 January 1982)

> A hospital spokeswoman yesterday said Martin was in a 'stable but serious condition'. Mrs Hunisett said: 'I am over the moon. I never thought I would see my son alive again.'
>
> *Independent* (21 June 1995)

own space. *See* NEED ONE'S . . .

oxygen of publicity. *See* STARVE(D) OF . . .

= P =

packed courtroom. Mostly journalistic use. Date of origin unknown. Noted as a cliché in the *Sunday Telegraph* (19 September 1982).

> The chief prosecutor told a packed courtroom that the seven had been 'actively engaged in preparations to overthrow the lawful government by armed rebellion.'
> *Financial Times* (8 February 1983)

> A teenager who spent more than a week in jail for refusing to testify against a US congressman finally took the stand yesterday and said he paid her to have sex with him when she was 16. Beverly Heard, 19, a former campaign worker for Representative Mel Reynolds, told a packed courtroom she had sexual intercourse many times with the Democrat, who is 43.
> *Herald* (Glasgow) (8 August 1995)

painting the Forth Bridge. *See* LIKE . . .

pall of fear. Journalistic use. Date of origin unknown. A cliché by the 1960s/70s. 'The pall of fear hangs heavy over the STRIKE-TORN city today' – cited by Malcolm Bradbury in an article on clichés in *Tatler* (March 1980).

> Nor is it only Hikkaduwa that is living under a pall of fear. The 60-mile road from the capital, Colombo, was deserted last week. It was the same for 100 miles in every direction.
> *Sunday Times* (13 November 1988)

> Despite the massive security force presence at the stadium and a peace pact between police and ANC marshals until midnight tonight, a pall of fear hangs over the country. Mr Hani's murder has plunged the country further into economic decay and poverty, and signalled to the country's political leaders that time is rapidly running out.
> *Evening Standard* (London) (19 April 1993)

par for the course. General use, meaning 'what you would expect', derived from golfing. Known by 1947. A cliché by the 1960s/70s. Identified as a current cliché by Howard Dimmock of Westcliff-on-Sea in a letter to the *Sunday Times* (31 December 1989).

> Some midnight assignations, a bit of bonking and a good deal of philosophizing are obviously par for the course.
> *Venue* Magazine (26 April 1985)

parameter(s). General use, meaning 'limits, boundaries' – from scientific terminology. Date of origin unknown, but given the quotation marks in the first citation, the popular, figurative use may have begun in the 1960s. A cliché by the 1970s.

> The fact that Nixon was willing to make his chastisement public suggests ... that the President at least understands 'the parameters of the problem'.
> *Time* Magazine (3 August 1970)

> Mr Murdoch has made his feelings on this subject very clear to me and I am determined that, as he says, the *News of the World* will strive to maintain the best practices of popular investigative journalism within the agreed parameters of the code of conduct.
> *The Times* (12 May 1995)

> Using the simulator, cars can be developed and tested without actually building them: instead, the parameters of suspension design and aerodynamics can be loaded into the computer and proven with a hard drive around the virtual landscape.
> *Daily Telegraph* (13 May 1995)

paramount importance. *See* OF PARAMOUNT ...

pardon the pun. *See* IF YOU'LL EXCUSE ...

parliaments. *See* MOTHER OF ...

parlous state/times. General use. An inevitable pairing. 'Thou art in a parlous state, shepherd' – Shakespeare, *As You Like It*, III.ii.42 (1598). A cliché by 1900.

> It does not seem like it, but there are 14 other artists at the Serpentine, representing Germany, France and New York, as well as ex-Goldsmiths'. They demonstrate that things are in as parlous a state abroad as here.
> *Evening Standard* (London) (15 May 1994)

Basingstoke council has spent £12 million on it. That is courageous in these parlous times. And the Anvil is not short of surprises.
The Times (21 May 1994)

past one's sell-by date, to be.   General use, popular and journalistic. The phrase 'sell-by date', referring to the date when perishable foodstuffs should be sold, was known by 1973. In a figurative sense, especially when a person is thought to be 'over the hill', the phrase became popular in the late 1980s. A cliché soon after.

I suspect the *Neighbours* phenomenon has reached its peak anyway, though not yet its 'sell-by' date.
Observer (4 February 1990)

Once described by an over-enthusiastic newspaper as 'one of London's most eligible bachelors', Stacpoole is now grey, portly and, at 55, looking rather past his sell-by date.
Today (1 September 1994)

Wood and his ilk are well past their sell-by date and it amazes me that they have been able to exert such a huge influence on the sport.
Observer (8 January 1995)

'I'm what they call past my sell-by date, but I've worked at fitness and motivation and that's kept me going longer than most.'
Graham Gooch, cricketer, quoted in *Sunday Express* Magazine (14 May 1995)

patriot.   *See* TRUE . . .

patter of little/tiny feet.   General use, in phrases indicating that small children are present or babies are expected in a household. Longfellow has 'patter of little feet' in 1863. A borderline cliché by the 1960s/70s.

Expectant motherhood these days is marked less by the patter of tiny feet than the tinkling of cash registers.
The Times (29 October 1977)

Newlyweds Nicolas Cage and Patricia Arquette are expecting the patter of tiny feet.
Hello! (13 May 1995)

pay bonanza.   *See* BONANZA.

pay tribute to my long-suffering wife.   Authors' cliché from the acknowledgements section of their books (compare TO MY WIFE,

WITHOUT WHOM . . .) but the phrase 'long-suffering wife' on its own is a cliché also. Known by 1969 – in *Time* Magazine, for example.

> The movie stars John Goodman from TV's Roseanne as larger-than-life Fred and Elizabeth Perkins as his long-suffering wife Wilma.
> *Northern Echo* (31 May 1994)

> Its main characters are a hard-drinking, foul-mouthed father, his long-suffering wife (whom he beats regularly) and a family variously embroiled in gangs, tragedy and corrective institutions.
> *Independent on Sunday* (16 April 1995)

> I must now pay tribute to the long-suffering good nature of my wife Sally and my two daughters . . . they have lived through this project with me for a number of years.
> Martin Walker, *Words Without Frontiers: The Spread of European English* (1995)

pendulum. *See* POLITICAL . . .

people of goodwill. General pompous use, especially journalistic. Date of origin unknown. A cliché by 1900. Listed in the *Independent* (24 December 1994) as a cliché of newspaper editorials. Compare Malcolm Muggeridge on writing leading articles for the *Guardian* in the 1920s: 'Many an uplifting sentence did I tap out . . . expressing the hope that moderate men of all shades of opinion would draw together, and that wiser counsels would yet prevail.'

> Dr Carey, in his address of welcome, called on people of goodwill to pray that 'there may be built a worldwide community where all acknowledge one another as true brothers and sisters, where war shall be no more'.
> *Daily Telegraph* (6 June 1994)

> Failing a guarantee from the RUC that Sunday's parade will be rerouted, LOCC again calls upon all people of goodwill, irrespective of political affiliation, to support our peaceful protests.
> *Irish Times* (22 April 1995)

perched on a/the hill, to be. Travel journalistic use. Date of origin unknown. A cliché by the 1970s/80s. Part of the 'travel scribes' armoury' compiled from a competition in the *Guardian* (10 April 1993).

> So on the afternoon of Day 5 we took a little drive up to a pretty mountain village and ate feta in a tiny taverna perched on a hillside while swallows dived and goats ambled around us.
> Kathryn Flett, *Observer* 'Life' Magazine (30 April 1995)

perfectly clear.   *See* I WANT OT MAKE IT . . .

pick up the pieces, to.   General use, meaning 'to try and win some compensation from an apparently hopeless situation'. Known by 1904. A cliché by the mid-twentieth century.

'If anything does go wrong it'll be nice having you around to pick up the pieces.'
Rich Perry, *Dead End* (1977)

'There's nothing to be said. It has happened and nothing's going to bring him back,' said Ann Ingram [mother of man sentenced to death and electrocuted in the US]. 'Now we must pick up the pieces of our lives.'
Independent on Sunday (9 April 1995)

pieces.   *See* PICK UP THE . . .

pipeline.   *See* IN THE . . .

plague.   *See* AVOID — LIKE THE . . .

play into the hands of . . . , to.   General use, meaning 'to act so as to give an advantage to an opponent'. Known by 1705. A cliché by 1900. Cited as a 'dying metaphor' by George Orwell in 'Politics and the English Language' (*Horizon*, April 1946).

In some ways the people who do these things play into our hands. The public are horrified by these actions and become more sympathetic to what we are trying to do.
Sunday Times (29 May 1994)

The Secretary of State's pre-budget sternness may just be a ploy to deflate expectations and make a small increase in arts funding look like a big one, but the current crisis does play into the hands of those who say that all the National Lottery will achieve is lots of lovely buildings with nothing going on inside them.
Sunday Times (6 November 1994)

pleasure.   *See* STATELY . . .

point in time.   *See* AT THIS MOMENT . . .

point of no return.   *See* REACH/PASS THE POINT . . .

pole position. *See* IN POLE . . .

police. *See* HELPING THE . . .

policemen. *See* YOUR . . .

political capital. *See* RESTORE . . .

political dynamite. Journalistic use. Date of origin not known. A cliché by the mid-twentieth century.

> Spokesmen of the People's Party, aware of the political dynamite involved in any large-scale attack on the nationalized empire, have stressed that their aim is to 'de-politicize' rather than de-nationalize.
> *Economist* (9 February 1963)

> He had reason to be cautious for the proposal . . . had been naked, political dynamite.
> W. Haggard, *The Hardlines* (1970)

> However innocent his intentions, Atherton must have been aware that every grain of dirt represented a stick of political dynamite. Certainly, England can no longer go on pontificating to Pakistan or any other country in the world now that their captain has been caught with dirt on his hands.
> *Daily Mail* (25 July 1994)

> David Hart, general secretary of the National Association of Head Teachers, said the figures confirmed teachers' worst fears: 'There is no doubt we are facing the biggest funding crisis in many a long year, maybe SINCE TIME IMMEMORIAL and I think Professor Smithers' figures are political dynamite.'
> *Times Educational Supplement* (7 April 1995)

political pendulum (can only swing so far). Journalistic use. The idea of a political pendulum swinging one way or the other is often evoked to portray the changing fortunes of the parties. This particular use of it was listed in the *Independent* (24 December 1994) as a cliché of newspaper editorials.

> It is noteworthy that, historically, the swing in the political pendulum away from the direction of full employment and the welfare state, where it pointed in the post-war political climate, has been accompanied by a parallel revival of monetarism.
> *Guardian* (29 August 1994)

Yet if the political pendulum swing of the 1960s made Cilla famous, she followed its backward sweep. At the last election she came out for Major, whom she swears she still fancies.
Observer (18 December 1994)

The consequent further economic slowdown in the economy would undermine Mr Major's soothing claim that the economy is coming right and Tory MPs need only hang on for a further year to see the political pendulum swing back their way.
Guardian (2 May 1995)

pretty sight. *See* NOT A . . .

principled stand. *See* TAKE A . . .

psychological moment. *See* AT THE . . .

public pressure. *See* YIELD TO . . .

pun. *See* IF YOU'LL EXCUSE THE . . .

punters. *See* WHAT THE . . .

pure genius. General use. An inevitable pairing. Dryden wrote in 1695: 'Art being strengthened by the knowledge of things may be . . . sublim'd into a pure Genius.' Borderline cliché, possibly caused by the phrase's widespread use as an advertising slogan for Guinness from the 1980s onwards.

Pergolesi's Stabat Mater . . . is a work of pure genius, one for which . . . I would gladly give both of Bach's Passions and feel that I had greatly profited by the exchange.
Financial Times (1 December 1983)

Who else other than an enormously capable person, would have thought of it? Here we are with some 3 million people for whom every day is much like a May Day and what do we do? We move a Bank Holiday 'to August or October'. Pure genius.
Observer (11 October 1992)

832 pages of pure genius.
Advertisement for John Irving, *A Son of the Circus* in the *Observer* (3 September 1995)

put an issue on the front/back burner, to.   General, but chiefly business and journalistic use, from the US. Meaning either to bring something to the forefront of attention or to relegate it. Derived from cooking. Both versions known since the 1940s. In 1945, 'cooking on the front burner' was American 'jive talk' for 'the tops'. Both versions clichés from the 1970s.

> With Mr Khruschev showing no interest in the Anglo-American proposals, the test ban . . . will have to be put on the back burner, as the Americans have it.
> *The Times* (26 April 1963)

> The whole issue is now on the front burner with the flame turned up high.
> *The Times* (26 September 1970)

> After a slow start in July 1991, the G7 nations are finally putting this issue on the front burner. A senior British official said that the problems of refugees would dominate the G7 meetings in July.
> *Independent on Sunday* (5 June 1994)

> If it is found that reporters or photographers did practise deception to enter Farm Place in order to expose Lady Spencer no serious person would seek to defend them. The issue of privacy generally will be right back on the political front burner.
> *Evening Standard* (London) (5 April 1995)

> The way I see it, anybody thinking of proposing a cooling-off period should pause, hold back, stall, keep it on ice, put it on the back burner, REST ON HIS OAR, and desist – at least for a period.
> *Sunday Telegraph* (30 April 1995)

put bums on seats, to.   Media use, referring to the abilities which any form of entertainment has to attract an audience. Origin possibly American but date unknown. A cliché by the 1970s.

> Bottoms on seats – Sir Peter Hall's policy for the National Theatre.
> *Spectator* (10 May 1980)

> The massed Partick Thistle fans in the audience were ecstatic, everyone else looked a mite baffled. But that's your fragmented post-modern culture, isn't it? It makes no claim to universality; just puts neatly-labelled bums on seats.
> *Guardian* (11 May 1993)

One guy fronted me up the other week and demanded to know: 'What are you going to do about it?' Moi? He suggested that if I gave them a bigger push through the arts page it would put bums on seats.
Herald (Glasgow) (24 February 1994)

put clear blue water between, to.   General but especially journalistic and political use, for separating one thing clearly from another – in regulations, policing, conflicts of interest, etc. Specifically in connection with the British Conservative party – an attempt to differentiate its policies from those of its opponents, specifically what right-wing Tories believe they need to put between themselves and Labour. *Clear Blue Water* was the title of a collection of speech extracts published by the Conservative minister Michael Portillo in September 1994. Identified as a current cliché in *The Times* (17 March 1995).

The anti-European rhetoric of Mr Portillo highlighted the Right's belief that the party has to move in its direction in order to put 'clear blue water' between the Conservative Party and the new-look Labour Party of Tony Blair ... But Mr Major is resisting this, wanting to remain in the centre ground and arguing that 'clear blue water' already exists over the minimum wage and Scottish devolution.
Scotsman (13 October 1994)

'Margaret Thatcher put clear blue water between herself and Labour,' he wrote from his Hampstead home. 'She won all three general elections into which she led the Conservative Party. John Major should learn the lessons of history.'
Times Educational Supplement (7 April 1995)

Commercial radio ... took more than half of radio listening hours for the first time. Justin Sampson, head of strategic planning at the Radio Advertising Bureau, said: 'There is now clear blue water between commercial and BBC radio.'
Independent (5 August 1995)

Leaving [the European Court] ... would be a piece of anti-European theatre that the party would love ... it would also put clear blue water between government and opposition.
Andrew Marr, *Independent* (28 September 1995)

put down a marker, to.   General use, especially in public affairs. Meaning 'to stake a claim, make it obvious what your intentions are or your position is' (often in order to cover yourself in the future). Derived from the use of markers in sports and games. Date of origin unknown. A cliché by the 1980s.

The package sets down a marker for the competition.
Observer (20 October 1983)

Next day he could find not so much as a sentence about his gripe anywhere in the paper . . . Still, he consoled himself with one of his favourite phrases: he had 'put down a personal marker'.
Nigel Rees, *The Newsmakers* (1987)

If the Brazilians put down a marker for the Latin American countries on Monday evening, then Germany and Spain kept the European flag flying bravely yesterday when they served up what many felt was the best match of the tournament so far in their 1–1 draw in the Soldier Field in Chicago.
Irish Times (22 June 1994)

The IAAF reacted indignantly yesterday to the legal marker put down by Modahl's solicitor, who accused the governing body of prejudicing her forthcoming hearing by failing to release information about her initial test and failing to supply the remains of the sample used for the B test to her medical advisers.
Independent (12 September 1994)

Anne Simpson, director of PIRC, said: 'I believe that if we win, it will bring about a SEA-CHANGE in pay policies. If we can put down a marker, I think other companies will take note.'
The Times (8 April 1995)

put on a show. *See* LET'S DO THE SHOW . . .

= Q =

quality time (together).   Mostly journalistic, in family and relationship studies. Meaning 'time spent in beneficial interaction with a partner or, especially, with a young child'. Of American origin by the 1980s and a particularly irritating cliché soon after coinage.

> Her mother is an engineer who has read too many articles on quality time and relating to kids.
> *San Francisco Sunday Examiner & Chronicle* (12 June 1988)

> As Nathan tells Emery: 'People with girlfriends tend to get non-productive. They spend a lot of "quality time" together; they dawdle. They learn how to make cappuccino; they join AA; they rent *Dances with Wolves* and cry together when Two Socks dies.'
> *The Times* (19 May 1994)

> Now I am the last person to look down on Spanish package holidays . . . They allow families to spend quality time together, away from distractions.
> *Herald* (Glasgow) (8 October 1994)

quantum jump/leap.   General use, meaning 'a sudden large advance or increase', originally used with a specific scientific meaning. 'Quantum jump' was known by 1927, 'leap' by the 1970s. In both cases, the use of the word 'quantum' is unnecessary, especially when it is not understood. Clichés by the 1970s.

> The imperial Presidency did not begin with Richard Nixon although under him abuses of the office took a quantum leap.
> *New Yorker* Magazine (13 June 1977)

question of ——.   Mostly broadcasting use, when framing programme titles. As in *A Question of Sport/Confidence/Stars/Politics* etc. I was responsible for *A Question of Degree* (about graduate unemployment, BBC Radio,

1970) and that particular phrase has been around for a long time (*Punch*, 7 December 1910, for example).

Many titles are also put in the form, *The Body/The Week/Sport In Question*. Both forms were clichés by about 1980.

question-mark still hangs over . . .   Mostly media use, meaning 'there is still uncertainty or doubt'. Date of origin not known. A cliché by the 1980s.

> There is uncertainty about what should be done with their sprawling barracks. Many British officers' houses have been put on the market and snapped up, but a question mark hangs over the main complex.
> *The Times* (14 May 1994)

> Inkatha envisages a team of 'facilitators' rather than arbitrators, but a question mark hangs over the party's course of action if the mediators decide against it. 'We will cross that bridge when we come to it,' said Chief Buthelezi.
> *Daily Telegraph* (6 March 1995)

Compare JURY IS (STILL) OUT ON —

= R =

radio.   *See* BECAUSE THE SCENERY IS BETTER.

raging torrent.   General use. An inevitable pairing – the words have been together since at least 1603. A cliché by 1900.

> It is a raging torrent at present, fed by thousands of mountain streams swollen by the wet season.
> *Today* (17 May 1994)

> But nobody warned you about the flooding. Come the winds and rains of winter, the water rises and the gurgling stream becomes a raging torrent.
> *Daily Mail* (1 April 1995)

rank and file.   Political use, referring to the ordinary membership of – particularly – the British Labour Party. Originally, a military term akin to 'foot soldiers' as opposed to the officer class. Date of origin not known, but known in this context by the 1940s, as in the first citation. A cliché by the 1960s.

> Oratory ... stratospherically above the plain, blunt, and fairly honest opinions held by the rank and file of Newark Labour.
> J.W. Day, *Harvest Adventure* (1946)

> Senior Newham Labour councillor Graham Lane admitted today there had been some annoyance amongst rank and file party members that Mr Kellaway, a Liberal Democrat councillor, had been allowed to return so easily to the Labour fold.
> *Evening Standard* (London) (10 June 1994)

rapturous applause.   General use. An inevitable pairing. Known by 1853. A cliché by 1900.

> No wonder ... that the first plink of those conciliatory ping-pong balls produced rapturous applause.
> *Daily Telegraph* (3 December 1971)

The rapturous applause which greeted the voluntary 90-piece orchestra, the 140-strong choir in blue, green, yellow and red, and conductor Noel Tredinnick was enough to make any visitor question whether they had become dislocated in time and found themselves at a concert with the demi-God of rock, Eric Clapton, who had occupied the stage a few weeks earlier.
The Times (15 April 1995)

rash act.   General use. An inevitable pairing. Known by 1886. A cliché by 1900.

This helps to explain Pasqua's rash act in lecturing Algerian leaders and initiating contacts with fundamentalists in exile living in Germany. Theoretically that should be the task of the foreign minister, Alain Juppé.
European (19 August 1994)

No matter how much sympathy one feels for the sacked drivers, this seems to have been an extraordinarily rash act. What possessed them?
Guardian (29 April 1995)

ravages of time.   General use, slightly literary and self-consciously archaic. 'If Mrs Evergreen does take some pains to repair the ravages of time' occurs in R.B. Sheridan, *The School for Scandal*, II.ii (1777). A cliché by 1900.

Despite the ravages of time, fine comics for sale still turn up. 'I bet there's a whole box of Batman No 1 in someone's attic,' Mr McAlpine says.
The Times (30 July 1994)

Reading his great reviews I'm filled with a mixture of admiration and rancorous envy. The writing is so sharp, the detail so illuminating that great performances seem to have been miraculously preserved from the ravages of time.
Independent on Sunday (30 October 1994)

razor-sharp accuracy/analysis/wit . . .   General use, but chiefly journalistic and promotional. As an adjectival phrase, 'razor-sharp' was known by 1921. A cliché by the 1960s. A recent variant has been **laser-sharp**.

A witty, razor-sharp satire on monogamy.
Advertisement, *New York Review of Books* (25 October 1979)

[Reginald Maudling's] mind was razor-sharp, one of the best I have encoun-

tered, and it remained so through all the mistakes and misfortunes of his business life.
John Cole, *As It Seemed To Me* (1995)

Bill Ashton's charges return with a hustling big-band set, recorded live at Ronnie Scott's. It goes without saying that the section work is laser-sharp; even more welcome is the sensitivity and restraint shown by the soloists.
The Times (19 March 1995)

reach/pass the point of no return, to. General use, from flying (where, at such a point, there is not enough fuel available to cover the same distance home again.) Known by 1941. A cliché by the 1950s/60s. Now almost exclusively figurative use only.

Scholars may well 'have passed the point of no return' in this matter.
Oxford Diocesan Magazine (20 October 1977)

Schumacher's View: Monaco could have been my point of no return.
Headline, *European* (27 May 1994)

reaches —— that —— never do. General use but popular in Britain through advertising. Compare the American proverb first recorded by Gelett Burgess in *Are You a Bromide?* (1907): 'The Salvation Army reaches a class of people that churches never do.' Popularized as a result of the long-running slogan for beer in Britain: 'Heineken refreshes the parts other beers cannot reach.' This has been used on and off since 1975.

Much parodied – in graffiti: 'Courage reaches the parts other beers don't bother with'; 'Joe Jordan [Scottish footballer] kicks the parts other beers don't reach'; 'Hook Norton ale reaches the parts Heineken daren't mention'; 'Mavis Brown reaches parts most beers can't reach'; 'Vindaloo purges the parts other curries can't reach'. A cliché by the late 1970s.

When I think of our much-travelled Foreign Secretary [Lord Carrington] I am reminded of . . . the peer that reaches those foreign parts other peers cannot reach.
Margaret Thatcher, speech at Conservative Party Conference (1980)

real Haiti/Borneo/Spain . . . Travel journalistic use, mostly – with 'the real Spain' being by far the most common construction. Meaning 'the part of a traveller's destination away from the artificial life of the tourist resorts'. Part of the 'travel scribes' armoury' compiled from a competition in the *Guardian* (10 April 1993).

The tourist authorities are certainly conscious of the potential of inland Spain – 'real' Spain.
Guardian (21 April 1986)

Consisting of two tiers of arches running for more than half a mile and more than 90 ft high in places, it is just one of the extraordinary sights to be found in the city and a shining example of the real Spain.
Guardian (6 March 1987)

Another tick on the mental Filofax inscribed 'The Real Spain.' But then, the whole journey from Malaga had been the real Spain, as if constructed ahead of me in Potemkin Village style by Ministry of Tourism workmen eager to dispel the old image of paella-and-chips.
Guardian (2 June 1990)

The Costa Brava was named 76 years ago by poet and journalist Ferran Agullo in recognition of its ruggedness. It is also known as 'The Gateway to Spain', but those who treat it as such, hurtling down the A17 autopista in search of 'the real Spain' further south, miss out on the best bit of all.
Sunday Telegraph (10 July 1994)

The few tourists who make it as far as Santa Cruz identify themselves by noisily slurping Fanta, and carrying the air of having stumbled upon the real Spain. But economically, the real Tenerife is back there on the beach.
Independent (15 April 1995)

real sense. *See* IN A VERY . . .

rebuilding one's life. Journalistic use, describing the process of coming to terms with a divorce or separation or with a death. Very much part of the *Hello!* magazine vocabulary, where it almost acquires euphemistic force in putting a positive angle on something that may, in reality, be wretched. Date of origin not known. A cliché by the early 1990s.

Bitterness is not an emotion Joan understands and she began rebuilding her life with the help of the decent Irish people who showered her with letters of sympathy and gifts.
Daily Mail (1 September 1994)

As the Princess has matured, so she has worn her hair ever shorter. Last year, busy rebuilding her life, she tried out a more severe look in her second Vogue cover.
Daily Mail (1 February 1995)

It seemed everyone except me was part of a happy couple. I dealt with it by

burying myself in my work. Although I went on a few blind dates, I wasn't
ready for romance so I concentrated on rebuilding my life.
Daily Mail (20 April 1995)

recipe for disaster.   General use. Date of origin not known. A cliché by
the 1970s.

'The track will have to be open for extensive schooling beforehand and
I'm not happy about the incorporation of three regulation fences including
an open ditch,' said Nicholson. 'I think they should stick to cross-country
fences, otherwise it could be a recipe for disaster.'
Guardian (24 November 1994)

He said the suggestion that the Government might grant recognition to the
breakaway Garda Federation, which he referred to as an 'illegal organization', was a 'recipe for disaster'.
Irish Times (10 May 1995)

redeeming feature(s).   General use. An inevitable pairing. Known by
1901. A cliché by the mid-twentieth century.

The state was ruled not by Britain but by the Diwan of Travancore,
Sir Ramaswamy Iyer, of whom it could truly be said that he was an
UNMITIGATED SCOUNDREL with no redeeming features.
The Times (26 November 1993)

He was barely gracious in his parting remarks afterwards. Wimbledon, for
him, did not have one redeeming feature, he said.
The Times (28 June 1994)

The redeeming feature of this tiresome programme was Evening Songs,
to Dvorak, by Smok's fellow-Czech choreographer Jiri Kylian gentle, soft,
lyrical, folksy and short.
Sunday Times (9 April 1995)

redefined.   *See* WHO REDEFINED —

re-draw.   *See* SINGLEHANDEDLY . . .

refurbished.   *See* COMPLETELY . . .

regal splendour.   General use. An inevitable pairing. Date of origin not
known. A cliché by the mid-twentieth century.

Sitting in the regal splendour of the Foreign Office, Hurd explains . . .
Daily Telegraph (1 June 1994)

To crown the occasion, there was the royal yacht Britannia – her days now numbered – moored in regal splendour in front of the Tower of London.
Guardian (1 July 1994)

regiment. *See* MY REGIMENT LEAVES . . .

reinvent the wheel, to. General use, meaning 'to go back to basics, with a view to doing things better or more freshly'. Often used pejoratively of someone who is doing so unnecessarily or out of ignorance. Or, in the form, 'let's not reinvent the wheel', as an injunction not to waste time by going over the obvious. Probably of American origin, since the 1970s. A cliché since the following decade.

'It used to be you almost had to reinvent the wheel to get funding,' said Daniel Cobb, dean of the faculty at the small liberal arts college in West Virginia.
Washington Post (16 July 1984)

'I don't think a leader of the western world can run a foreign policy that isn't consistent without great danger,' says Eagleburger, 'You can't reinvent the wheel every time because people have got to have some sense of continuity.'
Washington Post (12 August 1984)

The notion of 'reinventing' can also be applied to almost anything apart from the wheel:

The blurb says of the *Vox* characters [in a novel by Nicholson Baker] that in their 166 pages of conversation they are 're-inventing sex'.
Independent (7 March 1992)

A spring reborn in the world's oldest democracy, that brings forth the vision and courage to reinvent America.
President Clinton, inaugural speech (20 January 1993)

relaxed. *See* LOOKING BRONZED . . .

Renaissance man. General use, especially media. Meaning 'anyone who is accomplished in more than one field, but who is (these days) rather less than a polymath'. Originally used to describe anyone who displayed the educated, civilized, practical virtues of the idealized Renaissance man. Known by 1906. A cliché since the 1970s.

> Young people in their teens and twenties for whom [Orson] Welles was Renaissance man reborn.
> Kenneth Tynan in *Show* (October 1961)

> At 50, Hood is the Renaissance man of sailing; he designed, cut the sails and outfitted *Independence*, the first man in history to control every aspect of a 12-tonner from drawing-board to helm.
> *Time* Magazine (8 August 1977)

> I once told him [actor David Buck] that he was 'the Renaissance man of radio'. He thought that uproarious.
> Letter to the editor, *Radio Times* (11 February 1989)

> Michael Swann, a big man in every way, was a Renaissance figure, scholar, scientist, soldier . . .
> Marmaduke Hussey, appreciation of Sir Michael Swann in *The Independent* (24 September 1990)

> Of the people I have known well, [Conor Cruise O'Brien] is as near to a Renaissance man as any.
> John Cole, *As It Seemed To Me* (1995)

See also HE WAS A BIG MAN . . .

rendezvous with destiny.   Political, speech-making use, mostly. Derived from Franklin D. Roosevelt: 'There is a mysterious cycle in human events. To some generations much is given. Of other generations much is expected. This generation of Americans has a rendezvous with destiny' – speech, Democratic convention (1936). A cliché whenever used after this.

> All Mr Heath's justified complacency as he watches the Labour Party destroying itself will avail him little if, come the next General Election, his own rendezvous with destiny turns out to be an appointment in Samarra.
> *The Times* (28 June 1973)

Indeed, any phrase incorporating the word 'destiny', especially in alliterative couplings, sounds like a cliché as soon as it is coined. In late 1980s Britain, a number of funeral directors flirted with the slogan **dignity in destiny.**   Then there is **day of destiny.**

[Tony] Blair was in no doubt about the historical significance of yesterday's

event. In an impromptu speech after the vote was declared, Blair hoped it would be 'a day of destiny for our party and our country'.
Sunday Times (30 April 1995)

rest. *See* ENJOYING A WELL-DESERVED . . .

rest is history. General use, cutting off a biographical anecdote. Date of origin not known. A cliché by the early 1980s.

There across all the papers was the photograph of me presenting the Queen Mother with her chart, under the caption 'Astrologer Royal'. Well, the rest, as they say, is history.
Russell Grant, *TV Times* (15 October 1983)

The rest, one might say pompously, is history. Except that in my case the opposite was true. What it had been was history. What it was to be was not history at all.
Alan Bennett, having described his transition from Oxford history don to Broadway revue artist, speaking at a seminar, Nuffield College, Oxford, in 1986

rest on one's oars, to. General use. Meaning 'to suspend efforts, to take things easy, to glide along without doing anything' – as in rowing when oars are lifted out of the water and the arms rested upon them. As 'to lie on one's oars', known by 1726. A cliché by 1900. Listed in the *Independent* (24 December 1994) as a cliché of newspaper editorials.

They also know that they cannot afford to rest on their oars because Hungary, whose population is only one-quarter of Poland's, has pulled in twice as much foreign investment.
Herald (Glasgow) (4 July 1994)

rested and fit. *See* LOOKING BRONZED . . .

restore political capital, to. Journalistic use mainly. The phrase 'political capital' was known by 1818. A cliché by 1900. Listed in the *Independent* (24 December 1994) as a cliché of newspaper editorials.

While hardliners have made political capital out of the Central Bank's rouble debacle, the Russian President has remained cocooned in his Kremlin offices, offering no reassurance to the people and making no concerted attempt to restore confidence in the leadership.
Daily Telegraph (31 July 1993)

return. *See* REACH/PASS THE POINT OF NO . . .

return to the fray, to. General use, meaning 'to resume work or activity'. Derived from the Middle English word 'fray' meaning 'conflict, fighting', but now used only in a figurative way. A cliché by the mid-twentieth century.

> Happily, the mechanism in the form of Rule 19 is in place to do that if the club deem fit, but to protect both the good reputation of players like Gary who are keen to return to the fray and the competitive prospects of his club-mates, it would seem that a change is in order.
> *Herald* (Glasgow) (19 July 1994)

> Scotland consider a return to the fray.
> Headline, *Sunday Times* (25 September 1994)

rich and famous. General use, but mostly journalistic. An inevitable pairing. The first example I have noted is in the film *Breakfast at Tiffany's* (US, 1961). The usage has become completely set in concrete since a film with the title *Rich and Famous* (US, 1981). An American TV series *Lifestyles of the Rich and Famous* was established by 1986. So, a cliché by the 1980s.

> The [Press] Council's assistant director, said yesterday that lawyers acting for the rich and famous were becoming aware of the fast track system for getting speedy corrections of untruths.
> *Independent* (4 April 1989)

> Miss Navratilova is extraordinarily rich and famous and can, therefore, do pretty much as she likes. However, it is alarming when such prominent people do such silly things, because they only encourage deviant behaviour in other, more impressionable people.
> *Daily Mail* (23 June 1994)

rich beyond the dreams of avarice. General use, consciously archaic. 'Dream of avarice' on its own was known by 1678. Dr Samuel Johnson used 'rich beyond . . .' in 1781. A cliché by 1900.

> Brazil's social conditions still have a long way to go, as do even its advanced industries. The vast gap between rich and poor, which has widened in recent years, seems to many (not just the left) offensive in itself. Yet it does not matter greatly, if at all, that a few are rich beyond the dreams of avarice.
> *Economist* (29 April 1995)

ride roughshod over, to. General idiomatic use, meaning 'to tyrannize, domineer, treat roughly'. Derived from the type of horse shoe which has nails projecting from it to enable the horse to gain a firm foothold on difficult ground. Known in the literal sense by 1688 and figuratively by 1813.

> Sociologists are notorious for their use of generalizing terms that ride roughshod over the particularities of history.
> *Times Literary Supplement* (11 February 1977)

> *The Client* isn't as well made as Peter Weir's *Witness*, but it's a lot dirtier. Schumacher shows how the authorities ride roughshod over the poor, ignoring their civil rights, caring nothing for their safety.
> *Observer* (23 October 1994)

ride the whirlwind, to.   General idiomatic use, meaning 'to be in a commanding position especially in time of trouble'. Possibly coined by Joseph Addison when writing about the 1st Duke of Marlborough in *The Campaign* (1705), a celebration of the Battle of Blenheim: 'And pleas'd th' Almighty's orders to perform,/Rides in the whirlwind, and directs the storm.' Henry Buckle in his *History of Civilisation in England* (1857) had: 'To see whether they who had raised the storm could ride the whirlwind.' A cliché by 1900.

> With his overall Commons majority already down to 18 and his Government fighting on several other damaging policy fronts, Mr Major is riding a whirlwind.
> *Daily Mail* (21 May 1993)

Even more of a cliché is **whirlwind romance**, to describe an engagement or marriage following a brief courtship. Mostly journalistic use. Known by 1969 and a cliché already by then.

> He ended his letter asking his parents to look after his fiancée, Debbie Turley, whom he planned to marry after a whirlwind 10-day romance.
> *Today* (10 March 1989)

right.   *See* SOMEWHERE TO THE . . .

ring of steel.   Mostly journalistic use, to describe something which is surrounded by armaments, preventing escape. Adolf Hitler said in a speech on the Italian armistice in 1943: 'Tactical necessity may compel us once and again to give up something on some front in this gigantic fateful struggle, but it will never break the ring of steel that protects the Reich.' (Translation from *Hitler's Words*, ed. Gordon W. Prange, 1944.) A cliché by the 1960s.

The place [Warsaw] is just a ring of steel.
Reporter on BBC TV *Nine O'clock News* (17 December 1981)

Ring of steel around islands.
Headline over report on the Falklands War, *The Times* (30 April 1982)

Syrian steel rings Arafat.
Sunday Express (8 October 1983)

The [White House] mansion's £20 million 'ring of steel' security, including ground-to-air missiles, failed to stop a Cessna smashing into the south lawn.
Daily Record (13 September 1994)

ring the changes (on), to. To go through all the variations. Derived from bell-ringing. Known by 1614. A cliché by 1900.

I prefer to keep all walls as free as possible of electric wiring by having everything at roof level. This isn't as limiting as it sounds. You can still ring the changes between spots, chandeliers, rise-and-fall pendants to suit decor or mood and with the minimum of work.
Herald (Glasgow) (18 June 1994)

ringing declaration (of principle). Mostly political and journalistic use. Date of origin not known. Listed in the *Independent* (24 December 1994) as a cliché of newspaper editorials.

It seems to have become clear to Mr Heffer that it would be folly to present a predominantly right wing Cabinet with some kind of ringing declaration of radical socialist principle. In his view, a severely practical document was needed, in which the radicalism was presented as realism.
Guardian (28 March 1988)

road. *See* ON THE . . .

rock 'n' roll. *See* —— IS THE NEW . . .

rocks. *See* HEADING FOR THE . . .

roll. *See* HEADS MUST/WILL . . .

—— roller-coaster. Mostly journalistic use, to describe anything that is chaotic in its progress. After the kind of switchback railway in amusement parks, which were known by this name by 1888. Phrase used figuratively by 1957. A cliché by the 1960s.

It might follow from this that Budget 2 is just a STORM IN A Commons tea-room TEA-CUP, a one-day wonder to be easily forgotten as the political rollercoaster buckets onwards.
Guardian (9 December 1994)

After Michael Foot defeated Denis Healey for the leadership of the Labour Party in November 1980, Her Majesty's opposition was on a dizzying rollercoaster, and so was I.
John Cole, *As It Seemed To Me* (1995)

Most defectors appear to come unstuck. Only a few – like Churchill – have ridden the rollercoaster with aplomb.
Independent (9 October 1995)

romance. *See* RIDE THE WHIRLWIND.

rooted objection. General use. An inevitable pairing. Known by 1810. A cliché by 1900.

Surprisingly, the most rooted objection to donated eggs and to ovarian transplants comes from Lady Warnock, former mistress of Girton College and the guiding light behind the Warnock Report on Human Fertilization.
Daily Telegraph (26 July 1994)

Polling confirms what anecdote and personal experience suggest, which is that so far, most English voters have no rooted objection to Scottish Home Rule and are, if anything, mildly in favour.
Independent (17 January 1995)

rough old trade. Journalistic use – a phrase principally applied to politics, and not to be confused with 'rough trade' in the homosexual sense (sadistic, violent). Date of origin unknown. A cliché by the early 1990s.

Terry departs to Provence with more friends and fewer enemies than anyone I know in our rough old trade [literary journalism].
Sunday Telegraph (4 January 1987)

Berg, now 79 but still sprightly enough to climb unassisted into the ring and still a handsome and lucid advertisement for a rough old trade [boxing].
Independent (1 December 1988)

I have often remarked – it may perhaps have become something of a cliché – that politics is a rough old trade. But not since we ceased executing Ministers some time in the late seventeenth century has it been quite as rough as it is under Mrs Margaret Thatcher.
Alan Watkins, *Observer* (21 January 1990)

roughshod. *See* RIDE . . .

round up the usual suspects. *See* USUAL SUSPECTS.

rude awakening. General use, meaning an 'arousal from complacency'. An inevitable pairing. Known by 1895. A cliché by 1900.

> Anyone visiting this year's Grosvenor House Antique Fair . . . with the object of buying antiques on the cheap is in for a rude awakening.
> *Daily Telegraph* (12 June 1971)

> After that rude awakening Ruddock wrote to every player in his squad explaining that they were simply not fit enough.
> *Independent* (8 May 1995)

—— rules OK. Street language use, but also in advertising. This curious affirmative is said to have begun in gang-speak of the late 1960s in Scotland and Northern Ireland, though some would say it dates back to the 1930s. Either a gang or a football team or the Provisional IRA would be said to 'rule OK'. Later, around 1976, this was turned into a joke with numerous variations – 'Queen Elizabeth rules UK', 'Rodgers and Hammerstein rule OK, lahoma' and so on. It soon became an all but unstoppable cliché. In 1981, Virginian rubbed tobacco was advertised beneath the slogan, 'Virginian Rolls OK' and a French cigarette beneath *Gauloises à rouler, OK.* In 1982, I was asked by BBC Radio to present a series on local government. 'Yes,' I said, 'I will – as long as you don't call it "Town Hall Rules OK".' Two weeks later, they rang back to say, 'We've chosen that title you suggested.' And they had. I only spoke it through gritted teeth. A cliché by the late 1970s.

> Golf rules OK?
> Headline, *Observer* (13 November 1983)

rumour hath it. General, consciously archaic, use to introduce information that one has heard. Used in a literal way by 1705. A cliché by the mid-twentieth century.

> Shakespearian scenarios: rumour hath it that Deborah Warner is writing a screenplay of *Measure for Measure* while Ian McKellen has been working on a potential screen adaptation of *Richard III.* . .
> *Independent* (26 April 1994)

run. *See* THIS ONE WILL . . .

runaway success. General use, journalistic and promotional. 'Runaway sale' was recorded by 1953. Also **runaway best-seller.** Clichés all by about 1970.

His plan was a runaway success.
Botham & Donnelly, *Valentino* (1976)

Q has taken on the weeklies and won, and in doing so has changed the face of rock journalism in Britain ... Arguably, its runaway success owes much to its purging of rock-press habits that have alienated generations of weekly readers.
Guardian (28 November 1994)

= S =

said and done. *See* WHEN ALL IS . . .

salient point. General use, meaning 'a prominent point or one of conspicuous relevance in argument'. Known by 1838. A cliché by 1900.

> He also misses one salient point in his argument.
> Bryan Forbes, letter to the editor, *Independent* (13 June 1995)

salt of the earth. General use, meaning 'the best of mankind'. From Jesus Christ's description of his disciples in Matthew 5:13: 'Ye are the salt of the earth: but if the salt have lost his savour, wherewith shall it be salted?' Which suggests, rather, that they should give the world an interesting flavour, be a ginger group, and not that they were simply jolly good chaps. The New English Bible conveys this meaning better as 'you are salt to the world'. A borderline cliché now, especially when detached from its biblical source.

> My message is not the one I would have liked to send on my retirement from the health service. Those who work in it are the salt of the earth but have been let down by politicians in the grip of dogma.
> *Independent* (20 January 1995)

sand. *See* SUN, SEA . . .

sardonic grins. *See* EXCHANGE . . .

satisfactory conclusion. *See* BROUGHT TO A . . .

savage story of lust and ambition. Cliché of the type used to promote films and books. This was actually used on posters for the film *Room at the Top* (1958). The combination of 'lust and ambition' was known by 1681.

say.   *See* BEFORE DEALING WITH THAT . . .

saying.   *See* IT GOES WITHOUT . . .

says.   *See* —— THAT SAYS IT ALL.

schoolboy.   *See* AS EVERY SCHOOLBOY KNOWS.

scrapheap/scrapyard.   *See* CONSIGN SOMEONE . . .

sea change.   *See* SUFFER A . . .

sea of upturned faces.   Cheap literary and journalistic use. From Mrs Radcliffe, *The Italian* (1797): 'The thousand upturned faces of the gazing crowd'; from Sir Walter Scott, *Rob Roy*, Chap. 20 (1817): 'I next strained my eyes, with equally bad success, to see if, among the sea of upturned faces which bent their eyes on the pulpit as a common centre, I could discover the sober and businesslike physiognomy of Owen'; from Harriet Martineau, *French Wines and Politics* (1833): 'A heaving ocean of upturned faces.' A cliché by 1900. 'Among literary and journalistic clichés, "a sea of upturned faces" must rival "the PACKED COURTROOM" for frequency of appearance in print' – *Sunday Telegraph* (19 September 1982).

> In reality, celebrities doubtless clambered wild over upturned faces for a chance of a guest spot on Morecambe and Wise, but to know this for a fact would spoil an important illusion.
> *The Times* (16 May 1994)

> From the roof of the guild hall, fireworks scatter burning embers on upturned faces. Those of us in the portico rush out into the crowds to get a glimpse of all those angels in the sky.
> *Financial Times* (24 December 1994)

> Welles enthusiastically accepted the new title [*Citizen Kane* in 1939/40]; apart from anything else, no one had been able to think of a suitable one (his secretary's proposal of *A Sea of Upturned Faces* being only the least satisfactory).
> Simon Callow, *Orson Welles: The Road to Xanadu* (1995)

seasons.   *See* MAN FOR ALL . . .

secret.   *See* BEST-KEPT . . .

security. *See* LULLED INTO A SENSE . . .

seething/sizzling cauldron. Mostly journalistic use. A cliché by the 1980s.

> Plucky British athletes . . . who ran their lion hearts into THE ground in the sizzling cauldron THAT IS Perth.
> BBC TV *That Was the Week That Was*, (1962–3 series)

> The Turks are not averse to reminding their allies on occasion of their strategic value, especially now that political developments in neighbouring countries have emphasised Turkey's relative stability. Compared with the seething cauldron in the Middle East, Turkey is a 'still centre' of solidity.
> *Financial Times* (17 January 1986)

> Yet Brett has again begun to prise the lid off this gently seething cauldron when he writes that 'danger as well as beauty stalks through this score, and it is never quite exorcised by those fairies'.
> *Observer* (28 October 1990)

> In the abyss there seethes a giant cauldron, with the Conservative Party in meltdown.
> *Mail on Sunday* (26 June 1995)

select few. General use. An inevitable pairing. Known by 1817. A cliché by 1900.

> For a select few in the field, the season started anew yesterday. Of the 150 players competing in the Canon European Masters, fewer than a fifth can have realistic hopes of making the 1995 Ryder Cup team, but for them yesterday may have been the start of something big.
> *Guardian* (2 September 1994)

> Since Jim's shop Fish Alive became one of a select few British tropical fish importers to get his hands on the rare but beautiful fish, they have been making a name for themselves in North-East fish fancying circles.
> *Northern Echo* (4 May 1995)

sell-by date. *See* PAST ONE'S . . .

seminal classic/work. General use. Date of origin not known. Clichés by the 1980s.

> Now that the CUTTING EDGE of British folk humour no longer lies with the seaside postcard, the onus has long since passed to the T-shirt. The lavatory

is no longer the prime mirth-maker it was. Much use, however, is made of language taboos 'Same s***, different day', or the seminal classic, 'Brits On The Piss Tour 90' (or whichever year).
Sunday Times (21 August 1994)

Though this dish has a long history in Burgundy, it was not really introduced to Britain until 1960, by Elizabeth David in her seminal work, *French Provincial Cooking.*
Independent on Sunday Magazine (14 May 1995)

David Finegold and David Soskice reported in a seminal article in 1988 . . .
Will Hutton, *The State We're In* (1995)

Kenneth Arrow conceded in a seminal article in the *Guardian* . . .
Will Hutton, *The State We're In* (1995)

send a coded message, to.   Journalistic and political use – as explained in the citation, i.e. not in the literal sense. A cliché by the 1990s.

Political speeches described as coded are . . . not speeches in code but euphemisms designed to express disagreeable sentiments about something or somebody in terms less distasteful and more face-saving to the somebody in question than the blunt statement of fact would be.
The Times (31 December 1981)

serious consideration.   *See* DESERVING OF . . .

set alarm bells ringing, to.   Journalistic use, meaning 'to alert'. Date of origin not known. A cliché by the 1970s.

The trio moved off in a yellow Mini and as they drove west the resemblance between Mr Waldorf and Martin began to ring alarm bells among the police.
The Times (20 October 1983)

The committee chairman, Mr Sam Nunn . . . interrupted a committee hearing on nuclear weapons to make the announcement, immediately setting off alarm bells in Washington.
Guardian (3 February 1989)

The decision early this summer to cut the price from £1.5m to £750,000, however, sent alarm bells ringing through the business. Is English wine facing a crisis?
Independent on Sunday (14 August 1994)

A very middle class murder ... She thinks something else Roger said to her that morning set alarm bells ringing. He had said that his parents had decided to visit friends in the South of England and had left him in charge of the house.
Daily Mail (16 February 1995)

severely. *See* LEAVE ...

shame of our ——. Journalistic use. Date of origin not known. A cliché by the 1960s.

The shame of our prisons.
Headline, *Observer* (3 May 1981)

Not the shame of football hooligans, not the shame of our Government, not the shame of permanent sleaze, but the shame of almost a thousand years, years defiled in an instant.
The Times (5 May 1995)

shockwaves were felt. Mostly journalistic use. Known in its original scientific use – concerning explosions – by 1907. In the figurative sense, a cliché by the mid-twentieth century.

When the Biba empire finally toppled, the shock waves were felt so far abroad that it seemed unbelievable that they were caused by what was really only a smallish shop in a smallish city.
Sally Brompton, *Observer* (4 September 1983)

Here, eleven Japanese photographers respond to the shockwaves felt in a country at present seemingly locked in an identity crisis.
Guardian (14 June 1994)

When it happens, the cost in lives and property will be many times that of this week's disaster – and the economic shockwaves will be felt all over the world, including Britain.
Daily Mail (19 January 1995)

shoulder to shoulder. *See* STAND/FIGHT ...

show. *See* LET'S DO THE SHOW ...

show must go on. Show business use and figuratively in other situations. This seems to have been originally a circus phrase, though no one seems able to turn up a written reference much before 1930. *The Show Must*

Go On was the title of a film in 1937 and of an Ira Gershwin/Jerome Kern song in *Cover Girl* (1944). In 1950 the phrase was spoken in the film *All About Eve* and, in the same decade, Noël Coward wrote a song which posed the question '*Why* Must the Show Go On?' So, a cliché from about this period.

> The day that my heart bled for the Queen: Pride, dignity and a passionate belief that the show must go on.
> Headline, *Daily Mail* (19 October 1994)

> Manager Lucy Watson, 27, decided the show must go on and offered reduced-price tickets to punters as they left.
> *Daily Record* (5 April 1995)

sick and tired. General use. An inevitable pairing, known by 1783. A cliché by 1900.

> Ordinary people are sick and tired of people who can well afford to pay the full going rate for attendance at the theatre and ballet getting away with being subsidized by the rest of us.
> Terry Dicks MP, House of Commons speech (May 1988)

> President Bush complained he was 'sick and tired' of attacks on Defense Secretary-designate John Tower.
> *Independent* (7 March 1989)

> The 94-year-old Dame Pattie responded by describing Keating as a 'disgrace' and a 'monster.' 'He has spoiled my faith in everything we had and I'm sick and tired of it,' she said.
> *Independent* (7 September 1995)

sick as a parrot. *See* AS SICK . . .

sigh of relief. *See* HEAVE A . . .

sight for sore eyes. General use, referring to something that is a pleasant or welcome sight. In *Are You a Bromide?* (1907), the American writer Gelett Burgess castigated people who spoke in clichés. Among the 'Bromidioms' he listed was: 'You're a sight for sore eyes!' Jonathan Swift had earlier included it among the clichés in his *Polite Conversation* (1738).

> He has legs that don't quite match, a lolloping stride, an ungainly style, and a name that gives him no chance, but Kevin Twaddle was a sight for sore

eyes as he did his own thing for St Johnstone in their 2–2 draw with St Mirren in Paisley.
Herald (Glasgow) (14 November 1994)

Here's a sight for sore eyes: the winners of the Spectacle Wearer of the Year Awards.
Daily Record (15 February 1995)

silent majority. Political use. An inevitable pairing. On 3 November 1969 President Richard Nixon gave a TV address on Vietnam and called for the support of a particular section of US opinion – 'the great silent majority of my fellow Americans', by which he meant Middle America or at least, that part of the US not involved in the vociferous anti-war protest movement. The previous year, in his speech accepting the Republican nomination, Nixon had already addressed this theme: 'The quiet voice in the tumult and the shouting . . . the voice of the great majority of Americans, the forgotten Americans – the non-shouters.' Earlier, the phrase had been used in the nineteenth century to describe the dead, as also the 'great majority'. A cliché when invoked in the 1970s/80s.

silent witness. General use. Known by the time of William Cowper's poem *The Task* (1784): 'Act as a silent witness to countless invasions . . .' A cliché by 1900. Compare MUTE WITNESSES.

There weren't many other people around, and no one said a thing, though one or two mothers looked disapproving. Finally, I couldn't bear being a silent witness any longer, so I went over and asked her to stop. 'I'm her nanny,' she said angrily. 'It's none of your business what I do.'
Independent on Sunday (2 October 1994)

More than anything, now, Taggart wanted to meet the man who had found the body. For everything in this case came down to the footprints. Snow was the silent witness.
Daily Record (24 December 1994)

since/from time immemorial. General use. Known by 1775 in the US. A cliché since 1900.

It's been the custom here from time immemorial or thereabouts.
Cartoon caption in *Punch* (29 April 1925)

David Hart, general secretary of the National Association of Head Teachers, said the figures confirmed teachers' worst fears: 'There is no

doubt we are facing the biggest funding crisis in many a long year, maybe since time immemorial and I think Professor Smithers' figures are POLITICAL DYNAMITE.'
Times Educational Supplement (7 April 1995)

singlehandedly re-draw the political map of ——. Mostly media use. A possible cliché in the UK, but probably only borderline. I base this assumption on a satirical reference in *Private Eye* (4 December 1981) to Margaret Thatcher or Shirley Williams: 'Singlehandedly she has redrawn the political map of Britain.'

sinister maze. *See* CAUGHT UP IN A . . .

situation. *See* ONGOING . . .

sizzling. *See* SEETHING/SIZZLING CAULDRON.

snow-capped mountains/peaks. General use, especially travel journalistic. Both versions known by the 1870s. A cliché by 1900. Part of the 'travel scribes' armoury' compiled from a competition in the *Guardian* (10 April 1993).

> On a four-day official visit to Morocco, the indomitable Ms Boothroyd had travelled from Marrakesh with a friend on Easter Saturday high into the snow-capped Atlas Mountains for lunch.
> *Guardian* (19 April 1995)

> The plants look quite at home in North Wales. Behind looms the northern edge of the Welsh mountains, presided over by the snow-capped mass of Snowdon.
> *Daily Telegraph* (29 April 1995)

so you think you can ——? Media use. Irritating title of an occasional series of BBC TV quizzes from 1965 to the early 1980s that tested the viewers' and experts' knowledge and/or ignorance of various subjects. The first was *So You Think You Can Drive?* Other topics covered included everyday law, health and money matters. An instant cliché.

[Something] of *[Somebody]*. Publishing and authorship use. In *Are You a Bromide?* (1907), the American writer Gelett Burgess castigated people who spoke in clichés. Among the 'Bromidic titles' of novels and short stories he listed was the construction 'The Something of Somebody'.

He noted specifically: *The Courting of Dinah Shedd* and *The Damnation of Theron Ware*.

somewhere to the right of Genghis Khan.   General use, to describe someone's politics, if they are thought to be right-wing or fascist. Popular in the UK by the early 1980s. Genghis Khan (*c*.1162–1227) was a Mongol ruler who conquered large parts of Asia and, rightly or not, his name is always equated with terror, devastation and butchery. Occasionally, the similarly unpleasant Attila the Hun has had his name substituted in the expression. A cliché from the early 1980s.

> Of course, in those days, the union leaders were well to the right of Genghis Khan.
> Arthur Scargill, president of the National Union of Mineworkers, quoted by John Mortimer in the *Sunday Times* (10 January 1982)

> Close friends say he [Kenneth Clarke] has been an emollient force behind the doors of the Department of Health, but Genghis Khan would have looked like a calming influence alongside his ebullient ministers David Mellor and Edwina Currie.
> *Independent* (28 January 1989)

son.   *See* ONE DAY ALL THIS WILL . . .

sorely missed.   Obituary use, but forgivable as are most clichés of bereavement. Date of origin unknown. A cliché by 1900. Less forgivable in other contexts.

> Those members, including The Rev. Francis Moss, who died during the year under review will all be sorely missed.
> Annual Report and Accounts, The Prayer Book Society (December 1994)

> Shahbaz missed the England game and Wednesday's final qualifying match against Belarus and his team has sorely missed his leadership, and skill.
> *Irish Times* (2 December 1994)

> But it is steaming up the Hudson that the QE2 makes her connection with New York. The sight of a liner docking on the piers, a sight available from countless Manhattan windows, stirs a collective memory, and the QE2 would be sorely missed.
> *Daily Telegraph* (2 January 1995)

> With 7,484 runs in 116 Tests Haynes's experience may be sorely missed in the six-match series.
> *Daily Telegraph* (26 April 1995)

space. *See* NEED ONE'S OWN . . .

speculation was rife. General use. An inevitable pairing. Date of origin unknown. A cliché by the mid-twentieth century.

Mr Clinton is so weak that Washington is already rife with speculation about which Democrat might take him on, but as he moves sharply to the Right, he is working hard to protect his left flank.
The Times (26 January 1995)

Speculation had been rife that Dr Kohl would have been forced into a grand coalition with the opposition SPD later this year if the liberals had lost in the Hesse election and a second poll scheduled in the state of North Rhine-Westphalia in May.
Guardian (20 February 1995)

spelled. *See* —— THAT SPELLED ——

spending spree. General use, but mainly journalistic. Alliteratively inevitable. Known by 1956. A cliché by then, too.

Ladbroke . . . aside from the £50m spending spree planned on hotels, is quite happy to welcome no-limit betting.
The Times (12 April 1973)

But Roma, anxious to recoup some of the cash spent on a 15 player close season spending spree, have slapped a transfer fee of at least $5 million on his head.
Irish Times (4 July 1994)

According to the IFS, the Chancellor should not be cutting taxes, nor could he risk raising them to make sure the public do not raid their piggy banks for a spending spree.
The Times (13 October 1994)

spread out like a map (below). Travel journalistic use, mostly. Date of origin not known. A cliché by the 1960s/70s. Part of the 'travel scribes' armoury' compiled from a competition in the *Guardian* (10 April 1993).

After a night at the welcoming Il Nationale hotel, we headed out of town on a marked footpath beside the castle. Steps led upwards until Levanto looked like a map far below.
Sunday Telegraph (15 May 1994)

His vertiginous perspectives were new, and look how the tracery of the balcony itself becomes the near-abstract subject of the picture. Look down

at the island refuge in the middle of the carrefour. Look down upon the tree below, and the circular grating at its base, and the bench beside it, set out like a map.
Financial Times (11 October 1994)

stand head and shoulders above . . . , to.   General use, meaning 'to be distinctly superior in achievement'. Date of origin not known. A cliché by the mid-twentieth century. Listed as a cliché in *The Times* (28 May 1984).

Life was more than head and shoulders above the other news magazines. It was a legend.
Punch (16 October 1974)

This is particularly disconcerting news for those of us who, at 5ft 6in, have always secretly relished the idea that, if magically transported back to the days of Good Queen Bess, we would have stood head and shoulders above the riffraff.
Sunday Times (22 May 1994)

Burgess, who might be described as a Shankill Road socialist, brings a personal passion to his subject that lifts it head and shoulders above the usual sludge of academic sociology.
Sunday Times (14 August 1994)

stand/fight shoulder to shoulder with, to.   General idiomatic use. Date of origin not known. A cliché by 1900. 'Stand shoulder to shoulder' cited as a 'dying metaphor' by George Orwell in 'Politics and the English Language' (*Horizon*, April 1946).

I like seeing my political opponents standing shoulder to shoulder on a burning deck.
Iain Macleod, quoted in *Observer* (18 December 1967)

In any other era, Pete Sampras would be celebrated simply as the most brilliant tennis player of his generation. A man able to stand shoulder to shoulder across the ages with Laver, Hoad, McEnroe or Borg.
Today (30 June 1994)

Like entertainment-starved squaddies attending some up-country ENSA concert party, we sweated shoulder-to-shoulder, desperate to have Massive Attack's hipness conferred upon us.
Herald (Glasgow) (10 December 1994)

standard by which all —— will be measured.   General use. A cliché of approval. Known by 1878. A cliché by the mid-twentieth century.

A new standard by which all thoroughbred driving machines will be measured.
Time Magazine (14 December 1981)

standing by me.   *See* MY WIFE AND FAMILY ARE . . .

star.   *See* YOU'RE GOING OUT A YOUNGSTER . . .

start from a level playing field, to.   General but especially political and public affairs use. Meaning 'to begin an enterprise with no participant having an advantage over another or with no unfairness involved'. Known in the US by 1988. A cliché in the UK by 1993. Identified as a current cliché in *The Times* (17 March 1995).

> We would in effect be saying 'Here are the arms: fight it out'. That is the policy of the level killing field.
> Douglas Hurd, British Foreign Secretary, in a letter to the *Daily Telegraph* (5 April 1993) on lifting the arms embargo in Bosnia in favour of Muslims only

> Tears flowed when the axe fell. 'The programme [TV soap *Eldorado*] had a lot of baggage attached to it,' said Ms Hollingworth. 'We did not start from a level playing field because there was so much antipathy.'
> *Independent on Sunday* (2 May 1993)

starve(d) of the oxygen of (publicity).   Political and journalistic use. Date of origin unknown, though modern use of the phrase stems chiefly from Margaret Thatcher's pronouncement to an American Bar Association meeting in London (15 July 1985): 'We must try to find ways to starve the terrorists of the oxygen of publicity on which they depend.' Identified as a current cliché in *The Times* (17 March 1995).

> In this ludicrously competitive atmosphere, in which companies deprived of the oxygen of publicity gasp for survival, they resort to ever bolder ways of attracting audiences.
> *Independent* (20 July 1994)

> After 15 years, even parrots get bored, particularly those without the remotest possibility of a larger cage, nor even the prospect of a bell or a mirror to play with. Gasping for the special oxygen, that of publicity, they snatch at any mouthpiece.
> *Independent* (27 November 1994)

stately pleasure dome.   Journalistic and pop music use, alluding to the poet Samuel Taylor Coleridge's lines from *Kubla Khan* (1816): 'In Xanadu did Kubla Khan/A stately pleasure-dome decree.' A cliché by the 1970s/80s. Part of the 'travel scribes' armoury' compiled from a competition in the *Guardian* (10 April 1993).

The Pleasure Dome
Title of a collection of Graham Greene's film criticism (1972)

Welcome to the Pleasure Dome
Title of album and song by Frankie Goes to Hollywood (1985)

We would be turning ourselves into not just a non-reproductive society but an unproductive, hedonistic society. Here comes the stately pleasure dome. What kind of beings emerge from a society that does away with all consequences of sexual behaviour?
Sunday Times (1 May 1994)

Politics govern artistic activity in France and Italy. President Mitterrand a stately pleasure dome decreed, and thence stem all the Bastille's problems.
The Times (12 September 1994)

Ihilani means 'heavenly splendour', and my idea of a decent five-star heaven would definitely include this stately pleasure dome overlooking a tranquil, translucent lagoon.
Guardian (14 January 1995)

status quo. *See* SUPPORTERS OF THE ...

steed. *See* TRUSTY SWORD.

step. *See* ONE SMALL ...

stone. *See* LEAVE NO ...

stop. *See* WHEN THE —— HAD TO ...

storm in a tea-cup. General idiomatic use. Meaning 'a short-lived dispute about nothing of importance'. Date of origin not known. A cliché by 1900. Listed as still a cliché in *The Times* (28 May 1984).

Shadow Foreign Secretary Geoffrey Rippon said he was astonished by the angry reaction to his call for a force of citizen volunteers ... he insisted that the row was a 'storm in a teacup'.
Daily Mirror (9 September 1974)

Village hit by storm in tea cup.
Headline, *The Times* (26 July 1994)

Storm in Bradford tea cup.
Headline, *The Times* (26 September 1994)

It might follow from this that Budget 2 is just a storm in a Commons
tea-room tea-cup, a one-day wonder to be easily forgotten as the political
ROLLER-COASTER buckets onwards.
Guardian (9 December 1994)

strife-torn ——. General use, but especially journalistic. Known by
1884. A cliché by the mid-twentieth century. 'The PALL OF FEAR hangs
heavy over the strife-torn city today' – cited by Malcolm Bradbury in an
article on clichés in *Tatler* (March 1980).

The 36-year-old pacifist leader from strife-torn Northern Ireland
declared . . .
Arab Times (14 December 1977)

For strife-torn Cambodia, that is understandable – for Scotland it is to our
shame that we do not set a better example in how we legally protect our
natural inheritance in perpetuity for the benefits and enjoyment of present
and future generations.
Letter to the editor, *Scotsman* (23 May 1994)

stuff that dreams are made of. General use, by way of inaccurate
quotation of Prospero's words from Shakespeare, *The Tempest*, IV.i.156
(1612): 'We are such stuff/As dreams are made *on*' – it is definitely 'on' not
'of' (though Shakespeare did use the 'of' form elsewhere). A cliché by the
mid-twentieth century.

The stuff that dreams are made of.
Last line (spoken by Humphrey Bogart) of film *The Maltese Falcon* (1941)

Stuff What Dreams Are Made Of
Title of Cambridge Footlights revue (1964)

Stuff that dreams are made on.
Headline, *Guardian* (9 May 1988)

style. *See* LIKE —— WAS GOING OUT OF . . .

suffer a sea change, to. General use, especially journalistic. A grandilo-
quent and irrelevant way of saying 'change', alluding to the line from

231

Shakespeare, *The Tempest*, I.ii.401 (1612). However, when Ariel sings 'Suffer a sea-change into something rich and strange' he does actually mean a change caused by the sea. A cliché by the 1980s.

> I sensed, as apparently Jim Callaghan also sensed in the course of the campaign, that a sea change had occurred in the political sensibility of the British people. They had given up on socialism – the thirty-year experiment had plainly failed – and were ready to try something else. The sea change was our mandate.
> Margaret Thatcher, *The Downing Street Years* (1993)

> The shares bounced briefly, but are already almost back to where they were before the figures were released. Yet there are signs of a sea-change in investor behaviour, with funds flowing strongly into unit trusts even when shares generally are not doing well.
> *Independent on Sunday* (5 June 1994)

> Anne Simpson, director of PIRC, said: 'I believe that if we win, it will bring about a sea-change in pay policies. If we can PUT DOWN A MARKER, I think other companies will take note.'
> *The Times* (8 April 1995)

> Today the [Oxford Union's] finances stand on a solid footing . . . This sea-change is due in large part to the wise guidance of Lord Goodman.
> Harvey McGregor, in the *Independent* (27 May 1995)

> Interest rates have reached their peak . . . according to Roger Bootle, a leading City economist. His forecast marks a sea-change in the sentiment sweeping through the markets.
> *Independent on Sunday* (4 June 1995)

suitable for children of all ages (from nine to ninety).   Promotional use, folksy local radio talk in the UK. The core phrase is 'children of all ages'. Since the 1950s/60s and an instant cliché.

> Obscenities are so frequently used on television that they are regarded as acceptable parlance; children of all ages and classes use obscene language in public.
> Letter to the editor, *Daily Telegraph* (16 May 1994)

> Top of the toys . . . It will occupy children of all ages for hours on end and might well produce the next era of construction engineers.
> *Daily Record* (2 December 1994)

summer.   *See* LONG HOT . . .

sun, sea, sand (and sex). Travel journalistic and promotional use. The origin of this slogan is not known, though in the 1939 film version of *The Four Feathers* the Sudan is referred to, with similar alliteration, as 'sun, sweat and sunstroke'. In 1972, I interviewed a group of children born in London of West Indian parents, who were about to pay their first visit to Barbados. When I asked one of them what he expected to find there, he quite spontaneously said: 'All I know is, it's sun, sand and sea.' We used this line as the title of a BBC Radio programme which reported their reactions before and after the visit. Clearly, the child had absorbed the phrase at an early age. It is never very far away. Several songs have the title. A cliché since the 1970s, then. Part of the 'travel scribes' armoury' compiled from a competition in the *Guardian* (10 April 1993).

> Sun, sand and sea are no longer enough for the Yuppie generation of fun-seekers.
> Photo caption in the *Observer* (26 June 1988)

> We bought the beachfront land [in Barbados] a couple of years ago. Sunshine, sand and sea, it's the STUFF THAT DREAMS and travel brochures ARE MADE OF.
> Bob Monkhouse, *Crying With Laughter* (1993)

> Sea, sand and celebration: a guide to the Brighton Festival.
> *Big Issue Weekly* (1–7 May, 1995)

supporters of the status quo. General use, but mainly journalistic. Date of origin not known. A cliché by the mid-twentieth century. Listed in the *Independent* (24 December 1994) as a cliché of newspaper editorials.

> Sebastian Coe, as clean-cut and as mother-in-law-friendly as Andrew, has GONE THE WHOLE HOG and become a Conservative MP. How far does this reflect a trend? Have the moral leaders become young fogeys; or pillars of the Establishment; or supporters of the status quo?
> *The Times* (28 September 1994)

supreme sacrifice. *See* MAKE THE . . .

swan song. General use, meaning 'a farewell action, the last work or performance of a writer or actor or musician'. From the erroneous belief that swans sing just before they die. Not known in this figurative sense until the 1890s. A cliché by the mid-twentieth century. Cited as a 'dying metaphor' by George Orwell in 'Politics and the English Language' (*Horizon*, April 1946).

A swansong for Martina, the finest there ever was.
Headline, *Sunday Times* (19 June 1994)

Red, unlike *Blue* or *White*, failed to carry off a major film festival prize, but is easily the most entertaining and accessible of the trilogy. The director has announced his retirement, so it is also quite possibly his swansong.
Sunday Telegraph (13 November 1994)

sweeping changes.   General use. Date of origin not known. A cliché by the mid-twentieth century.

This is a case where the sweeping changes taking place in building societies should be made fully transparent.
Observer (10 July 1994)

Lady Howe's report on the future of our cathedrals recommends sweeping changes, including the introduction of walkie-talkies for vergers and a new system of counting admissions electronically.
Sunday Times (16 October 1994)

sweeping powers.   General use, meaning 'the taking of measures that are wide in effect'. Date of origin not known. A cliché by the mid-twentieth century. Compare DRASTIC POWERS and DRACONIAN POWERS.

There is nothing like a clean sweep, and Berge's successor, Hugues Gall, decided to remove the music director Myung-Whun Chung, who, as the only successful employee of the Bastille, had acquired sweeping artistic powers.
The Times (12 September 1994)

swingeing cuts.   General use, especially journalistic. Cuts (i.e. economies, reductions in manpower etc.) that are wide ranging and also severe. Date of origin not known. A cliché by the 1980s.

The threat to the Eurofighter comes with the RAF expecting to feel the full force of swingeing cuts.
Daily Mail (11 July 1994)

Film-makers have been ordered to make swingeing cuts to the thriller *The Color Of Night* if they want it to get a lucrative 15 certificate.
Today (2 August 1994)

swordsman.   *See* BEST SWORDSMAN IN ALL FRANCE.

= T =

table. *See* IT DOES HELP IN A CROWDED RESTAURANT . . .

tacit approval. General use. An inevitable pairing, meaning 'unspoken or understated approval'. Date of origin unknown. A cliché by the mid-twentieth century.

> Protected by stringent privacy laws (of which Pythoud approves), married French politicians, businessmen and ordinary citizens enjoy affairs with the tacit approval of society in general, and often that of women, too.
> *European* (19 August 1994)

tacit support. Mostly journalistic use, meaning 'unspoken or under-stated support'. An inevitable pairing. Date of origin unknown. A cliché by the mid-twentieth century. Mocked by Tom Stoppard in the play *Night and Day* (1978): 'Sources close to President Mageeba are conceding that the peasant army of the ALF has the tacit support of the indigenous population of the interior.'

> They accuse [the Communist Party] of . . . soft-lining tacit support of Premier Giulio Andreotti's minority government.
> *Time* Magazine (28 March 1977)

> His target is the Party of Democratic Socialism (PDS), reformed rump of the former East German communist party, which he denounces as 'red-painted fascists'. And the message is that the SPD can only hope to unseat him in Bonn with the tacit support of those communists.
> *Financial Times* (26 September 1994)

tail wagging the dog. *See* CASE OF THE . . .

take a light-hearted look (back) at . . . , to. Media use, as in the promo-tion of satirical radio programmes so as to suggest that they will not give offence. Almost certainly applied to the BBC Radio 4 programme *Week Ending* in 1970/1. A cliché from then on.

> He can afford now to take a light-hearted look back at his numerous disasters. 'There were times my car was bogged up to the axles and I knew I wouldn't be found for ages. It pissed down for days, my booze and food ran out.'
> *Sunday Telegraph* (15 May 1994)

> Skits, I suppose, though I don't like the word; humour, though I don't like that very much either – too close to the BBC's 'light-hearted look at'.
> Alan Bennett, *Writing Home* (1994)

take a principled stand, to.   Listed in the *Independent* (24 December 1994) as a cliché of newspaper editorials.

> Mr Howard said this hardly squared with claims of a principled stand against his party's anti-Europe policy at the time. Roy Hattersley had chosen not to mention Labour's commitment to withdrawal in his 1983 election address and Mr Howard asked why Mr Blair did not do the same.
> *Evening Standard* (London) (7 July 1994)

> 'We weren't being puritanical about it, nor did we have a principled stand against advertising as such, but the *News of the World*, for God's sake. In the event the campaign went ahead, without our involvement, and we had an expensive meeting with a lawyer who explained in the nicest possible way that there was little we could do about it.'
> *Guardian* (28 April 1995)

take one's breath away, to.   General use, meaning 'to be astonished – in a way that impresses one or the reverse'. Known by 1900. One of the clichés cited by Ted Morgan in *Somerset Maugham* (1980) as having been used by the writer in his efforts to achieve a 'casual style'.

> Two years ago my husband and I went to southern Corsica and fell in love with it. Bonifacio – with its tall, thin renaissance houses on top of a rock – took our breath away, just as it did Corsica's most famous son, Napoleon.
> *Daily Mail* (15 October 1994)

take the bull by the horns, to.   General idiomatic use, meaning 'to seize the initiative and not to shrink from dealing with a difficult problem'. Known by 1711. Identified as a current cliché by Howard Dimmock of Westcliff-on-Sea in a letter to the *Sunday Times* (31 December 1989).

'What we need is someone on the park to take the bull by the horns and shout and motivate.' Celtic go into the Hampden clash reflecting on the difference two months have made.

Daily Record (9 November 1994)

take up the cudgels (for/on behalf of), to. General use, meaning 'to fight on behalf of'. Known by 1869. A cliché by 1900. Cited as a 'dying metaphor' by George Orwell in 'Politics and the English Language' (*Horizon*, April 1946).

Already, Christopher Columbus has emerged as the villain of the piece: the man who set the tone for the vandalism that followed. But both the man, and what followed, have been misrepresented. A Columbus scholar at Oxford takes up the cudgels.

By-line, *Economist* (21 December 1991)

tale. *See* TELLS ITS OWN . . .

tanned. *See* LOOKING BRONZED . . .

television. *See* FILMING FOR . . .

tells its own tale about the society we live in. Journalistic use. Date of origin not known. A cliché in the 1980s.

From today, Guardian Food and Drink will appear every Friday as a separately edited page, cut loose from women. This message tells its own tale about the society we live in.

Guardian (5 October 1984)

ten most. *See* IN ANYBODY'S LIST OF . . .

tender mercies. General use, ironically of attention and care thought unlikely to be in the patient's best interest. But also as a slightly facetious or old-fashioned way of referring to someone's care. A biblical phrase from Proverbs 12:10. A cliché by the mid-twentieth century.

Smaller . . . traders and manufacturers . . . left to the tender mercies of the open property market.

Listener (17 June 1965)

From Miss Aitken's tender mercies in his father's primary school he went to the junior high, a short bus ride away in Lochgilphead, and then on to the

greater glory of the old grammar school at Dunoon on the far tip of the Cowal peninsula.
Sunday Times (15 May 1994)

terms. *See* IN NO UNCERTAIN . . .

test of credibility. Journalistic use, mainly. Date of origin not known. A cliché by the 1960s/70s. Listed in the *Independent* (24 December 1994) as a cliché of newspaper editorials.

World Bank sees Nepal project as test of credibility.
Guardian (7 November 1994)

Clifford has published a guide which lists all the vanity publishers in Britain, and gives an indication of their relative share of hoodwinking. To test the credibility of each firm, he compiled a collection of poems and submitted these for comment.
Scotland on Sunday (5 February 1995)

On a weekend that was meant to test the credibility of the Doncaster Panthers as Budweiser League title challengers they lost twice.
Guardian (13 March 1995)

OJ prosecutors test credibility of a psychedelic Nobel laureate.
Headline, *Guardian* (11 April 1995)

They were 'OF PARAMOUNT IMPORTANCE', Mr Ruggiero said, not simply because they covered a big chunk of international commerce but because they were the first test of the credibility of the WTO which superseded the General Agreement on Tariffs and Trade in January.
Financial Times (4 May 1995)

testimony. *See* BEARS ELOQUENT . . .

—— that almost got away. Journalistic use, referring to any neatly missed opportunity. Based presumably on the angler's 'this was a fish that almost got away'. 'Yes, that's the one that got away' is the caption, referring to an empty fish tank, of a *Punch* cartoon (12 October 1938) – and one of many *Punch* cartoons using the phrase in that decade. A British film with the title *The One That Got Away* (about an escaped prisoner) was released in 1957. A cliché by the mid-twentieth century.

It was the anniversary that almost got away. The *Daily Mail* was the only

newspaper to celebrate the opening of the first launderette in Britain 45 years ago last week.
Sunday Times (8 May 1994)

— that is —. Mostly portentous promotional and journalistic use. Identified as such in a BBC TV *That Was the Week That Was* sketch about sports journalist 'Desmond Packet' (in the 1962–3 series): 'Plucky British athletes ... who ran their lion hearts into the ground in the SIZZLING CAULDRON that is Perth.' Could this use derive from the format used so notably by Edgar Allan Poe in *To Helen* (1831): 'The glory that was Greece/And the grandeur that was Rome'?

This is a unique opportunity to see these classic films and either re-live or experience for the first time the genius that is Hitchcock.
Advertisement for an old Alfred Hitchcock film shown in London (November 1983)

These are of course the dog days, when news is scarce, when sane human beings do anything to escape the sub-tropical steambath that is Washington DC in late August.
Independent (23 August 1995)

— that says it all. Journalistic use, most usually in a photo caption describing a look or smile. A cliché by the 1960s/70s.

— that spelled —. Journalistic use. A cliché by the 1960s/70s.

The Ding-Ding special that spelled love for Sid and Jan Parker will take a trip DOWN MEMORY LANE ... to celebrate their 25th wedding anniversary. The happy couple will kiss and cuddle on the top deck of the No. 44 bus, just like they did when they were courting.
Sun (15 October 1983)

— that time forgot. Mostly journalistic use. After *The Land That Time Forgot*, the novel by Edgar Rice Burroughs (1924; filmed UK, 1974). A cliché by the 1960s/70s.

Campaign for the children that time forgot.
Headline, *Observer* (30 April 1995)

Tedious? That's the way we like it ... Angela Pertusini goes to Frinton, the town that time forgot.
Independent (12 May 1995)

Male, white millionaire supremacists only need apply to play on this stretch of land time forgot.
Daily Telegraph (7 April 1995)

that was once ——. Journalistic use: 'The blazing ruin that was once . . .' etc. A cliché by the 1960s/70s.

that's another page turned in the book of life. Conversational reflection on a death. One of the numerous clichés of bereavement, designed to keep the awfulness of death at bay by means of comfortingly trite remarks. A cliché from about 1960 when I heard it spoken after the first funeral I attended. However, the notion of life as a book whose pages turn can be invoked on other occasions as well. On 1 September 1872, the Rev. Francis Kilvert wrote in his diary: 'Left Clyro for ever. A chapter of life closed and a leaf in the Book of Life turned over.' In its original biblical sense, the said book is a record of those who will inherit eternal life (as in Philippians 4:3 and Revelation 20:12).

that's what —— **is all about.** Mostly journalistic use and most frequently in sporting contexts. The basic notion is 'winning is what it's all about' (and never mind all that nonsense of the Olympic motto). Often ascribed to Vince Lombardi, coach and general manger of the Green Bay Packers pro-football team from 1959, in the form 'Winning isn't everything, it's the only thing', it had nevertheless been said earlier by John Wayne as a football coach in the 1953 movie *Trouble Along the Way*. President Nixon's notorious Committee to Re-Elect the President in 1972 had as its motto: 'Winning in politics isn't everything; it's the only thing.' Compare 'That's what love is all about', a line in the song 'The Love Bug Will Bite You' by Pinky Tomlin (1937).

> Football is a physical game. It's about stamina and strength and players battling for each other. A lot of people knock those qualities – but that's what English football is all about.
> Ron Saunders, Aston Villa manager on the League title in 1981, quoted in Ball & Shaw, *The Book of Football Quotations* (1984)

> Whoever plays best is going to win . . . this is what the game is all about.
> Peter Purves, commentating on BBC TV *Championship Darts* (22 September 1983)

> Air France's Concorde. Rediscover what flying is all about.
> Advertisement (*c.*1983)

the —— that is ——. *See* —— THAT IS ——

there are two kinds of ——. General use. In *Are You a Bromide?* (1907), the American writer Gelett Burgess castigated people who spoke in clichés. He drew attention to the tiresome attempt to classify acquaintances – a 'common sport of the thinker' – in such sayings as: 'There are two kinds of persons – those who like olives and those who don't'; 'there are two kinds of women – Daisy, and the Other Kind.'

> There are two kinds of people in the world – those who divide the world into two kinds of people and those who don't.
> Graffito from the University of Texas, in Haan & Hammerstrom *Graffiti in the Southwest Conference* (1981)

> The world, he said, was divided into two groups of people: those who went about 'throwing bricks through windows' and producing memorable phrases, and the glaziers and window cleaners. His wife fell into the latter camp, who received less attention but tended to do more good.
> *The Times* (7 April 1995)

there must be some mistake, officer. Drama use. What middle-class people say on being challenged or arrested by a police officer. Observed by Fritz Spiegl in an article on drama cliché lines in the *Listener* (7 February 1985).

there'll be dancing in the streets tonight. Journalistic use – to signify celebration of or elation at some victory. A cliché by the mid-twentieth century. Tom Stoppard in an extended parody of sports journalism in the play *Professional Foul* (1978) has: 'There'll be Czechs bouncing in the streets of Prague tonight as bankruptcy stares English football in the face.'

> Hoots hombre! They'll be dancing in the streets of Tenerife when a swinging, singing band of Highlanders jets in next month.
> *Sunday Mail* (19 February 1995)

> The city registered that, against the expectations of many, the ceasefire had lasted a full 12 months; but still nobody danced in the streets.
> *Independent* (1 September 1995)

> I shall be dancing in the streets when hunting is banned by a Labour government because it will be the first attack on this rotten lifestyle.
> Alan Amos, *Independent* (6 September 1995)

these are dynamite! or **it's dynamite!**   Journalistic use. Expressions members of the public tend to use when talking to newspapers (but seldom in real life). Clichés by the 1960s/70s.

> I call it goddam urgent. It's dynamite.
> Peter Cheyney, *I'll Say She Does* (1945)

> 'These are dynamite in terms of brand names,' said Mr Alan Woltz, LRC's American born chief executive of the past five years. 'To us they make a good fit.'
> *Financial Times* (29 September 1984)

> Mr Little rushed to the *Sun* offices to study the photographs and said: 'These are dynamite.'
> *Sun* (10 December 1984)

> 'Wait till you see the set and the titles we've designed [for a TV current-affairs show] . . . It's dynamite.'
> Andrew Neil, quoted in the *Independent on Sunday* (25 September 1994)

—— **they call it** —— or —— **they are calling** ——.   Journalistic use. A strange stylistic device. A cliché by the 1970s/80s.

> Strange goings-on behind the closed doors of that exotic building just off Great Queen Street, Covent Garden . . . Freemasons' Hall they call it, a secret world, a world of secrets.
> *Independent* (19 May 1995)

> In Hong Kong, they are calling the political retirement of Lydia Dunn the end of an era.
> *Independent* (16 June 1995)

they came ——.   Funereal journalistic use. The chief thing is to start with the word 'they' but it is almost as important to follow this with 'came'. A cliché by the 1960s/70s. Also found in this context: **they buried their own**.

> They scattered the ashes of a proud Scots lassie yesterday on a cold Welsh hillside.
> Report on the funeral of Jennie Lee, *Observer* (27 November 1988)

> They came, 541 of them, across half a world [to the Falklands] to dedicate the war memorial on a treeless hillside above Blue Beach, where British forces first stepped ashore.
> *The Times* (11 April 1983)

thinking man's/person's/woman's ——. Mostly journalistic use, although as long ago as 1931, Pebeco toothpaste in the US was being promoted as 'The Toothpaste for Thinking People'. However, I think it was Frank Muir who set the more recent trend (now almost a cliché) when he talked of British broadcaster Joan Bakewell as 'the thinking man's crumpet'. That was in the 1960s. Much later, Chantal Cuer, a French-born broadcaster in Britain, said she had been described as 'the thinking man's croissant' and Janet Suzman, the actress, as 'the thinking man's Barbara Windsor'. A cliché formula by the 1980s.

Frank Delaney – the thinking man's Russell Harty.
Sunday Times (16 October 1983)

Frank Delaney – the thinking man's Terry Wogan.
Guardian (17 October 1983)

The thinking woman's Terry Wogan, TV's Frank Delaney.
Sunday Express (30 October 1983)

His performance as a trendy and hung-up LA painter in *Heartbreakers* made him the thinking woman's West Coast crumpet.
Observer (13 September 1987)

One member of the Government said: '[Kenneth Clarke's] the thinking man's lager lout.'
Independent (28 January 1989)

It was chaired by Nick Ross, the thinking woman's newspaper boy.
Observer (29 January 1989)

Hobbies magazine in 1977 described Descartes as 'The thinking man's philosopher'; *Boating Magazine* (1984) described the Mansfield TDC portable toilet as 'the thinking man's head'; *Horizon* (1965) called Lake Geneva, 'the thinking man's lake'; and, *Esquire* (1986) called actor William Hurt, 'the thinking man's asshole'.
Summary from *Spy* Magazine (February 1989)

this great movement of ours. British Labour Party use. Sometimes abbreviated to 'THIGMOU' or 'THIGMOO'. Compare from a speech by Harold Wilson in Huddersfield (May 1951): 'This Party of ours, this Movement of ours . . . is based on principles and ideals . . . This movement of ours is bigger than any individual or group of individuals.' A cliché noted by the early 1980s.

This is not the first time that 'Ginger Jack' had placed himself at the services of Thigmoo – This Great Movement of Ours. Four years previously, he signalled his determination to run against the Communist Jack Adams as deputy general secretary of the TGWU.
Independent on Sunday (7 May 1995)

In those days (not so long ago) the [Building Societies Association]'s monthly lunches would be followed by a proclamation of the mortgage rate. It was at such post-prandial moments that the societies liked to refer to themselves as this great movement of ours.
Daily Telegraph (19 May 1995)

this green and pleasant land. General and especially journalistic use. An over-loved quotation from William Blake's short preface to his poem *Milton* (1804–10) which has come to be called 'Jersualem' as a result of the immensely popular musical setting (1916) by Sir Hubert Parry. The song has become an alternative British national anthem:

> I will not cease from mental fight,
> Nor shall my sword sleep in my hand,
> Till we have built Jerusalem,
> In England's green and pleasant land.

A cliché by the mid-twentieth century. 'Up and down our green and pleasant land' is included in the parody of sportswriters' clichés included in the book *That Was The Week That Was* (1963).

How is it that, if the New Zealand flatworm's habit of slurping up the good old British earthworm will devastate this green and pleasant land, New Zealand seems a very green and pleasant land, far from an arid wasteland?
Letter to the editor, *Independent* (17 January 1995)

Thomas, who regards himself as an immigrant in the so-called green and pleasant land, asserts that the Co-op movement 'has always had an ethical position. It has been one of the congress resolutions for years. The bank has always had a desire to live up to these standards but we never publicised the fact.'
Observer (9 April 1995)

As the environment is increasingly threatened by developers, the concerned classes are rising up to save our green and pleasant land. Sheila Hale reports from the front line.
By-line, *Harpers & Queen* (May 1995)

Young call for green and pleasant land.
Headline, *Independent* (15 May 1995)

this has restored my faith in British justice. Journalistic use. What members of the British public invariably say, when prompted by journalists, after winning a court case.

Mrs Dallaglio, of Barnes, south-west London, who lost her 19-year-old daughter Francesca, said after the ruling: 'This has restored my faith in British justice. I am overwhelmed.'
Independent (11 June 1994)

A jubilant Mr Chichester said his faith in British justice had been restored. 'I was very glad that the cloud hanging over my head for five months has been conclusively removed by the court.'
Independent (12 November 1994)

this one will run and run. General but especially promotional use. From the satirical magazine *Private Eye*'s collection of catchphrases, this can be said of anything, especially of a political dispute or a strike, but was originally the sort of extract taken from critics' notices that theatrical managements liked to display outside theatres to promote their shows. Said originally to have derived from a review by Fergus Cashin of the *Sun*. Identified as a cliché in the 1970s and thus rendered unusable again in its original context.

So this one will run and run. And why not? It has already been running for 18 months since the Downing Street Declaration and for nine since the IRA ceasefire.
Guardian (27 May 1995)

And, like the best soap operas, this one will run and run. The 35-year-old Tan has been acquitted of that charge – although found guilty of uttering a death threat. Boland is now launching a civil suit against her. 'I have to keep this case alive,' he said. 'I hope something will come out of it – but I have to do this, as a mission.'
Observer (28 May 1995)

this thing is bigger than both of us. Film script use, where 'this thing' = 'our love', of course. Now only usable in parody. No citations of original use available. All I have examples of is the ironic use of the phrase. I am told that Milton Berle popularized it, satirically, in his American radio and

TV shows in the US of the 1940s and 50s. In Britain, Frank Muir and Denis Norden did a similar job in their scripts for BBC radio's *Take It From Here* (1947–58). For example, this extract from their *Hamlet* with Hollywood subtitles: 'Oh, dear Ophelia, I have not art to reckon my groans but that I love thee best. ("Don't fight this thing, kid, it's bigger than both of us").' In the 1976 remake of *King Kong*, with the giant ape brushing against the side of the house they are sheltering in, Jeff Bridges as Jack Prescott says to Jessica Lange as Dwan, 'He's bigger than both of us, know what I mean?'

> And would Ackroyd have died for Brian? He shakes his head. 'Because I'm quite a hard person and there was something else that was bigger than both of us and that was my work. I lived for that and Brian lived for me.'
> *The Times* (12 September 1994)

> The advocacy of these young players is almost defiantly assertive. There are no rules of engagement here: just an impassioned, up-front manner with dynamic, larger-than-life contrasts between action and repose, and an over-riding sense that 'this music is bigger than both of us'.
> *Independent* (16 December 1994)

> Hugo Young's heart is in the right place, and mine is there too. But this thing is bigger than both of us.
> Letter to the editor, *Guardian* (11 February 1995)

this town ain't big enough for both of us/the two of us.   Western film script use, where it might be said by the villain to the sheriff or to anyone else who is trying to bring him to book. He is, of course, suggesting that the other person will have to get out of town in order to make the room. By the 1940s? No original citations available. Commonly evoked in parodies from the 1950s onwards.

> 'This Town Ain't Big Enough For Both Of Us'
> Title of song by Sparks (1974)

> When the cop discovers that Landry has designs on his wife, the scene is set for a violent showdown. This town ain't big enough for the two of 'em.
> *Herald* (Glasgow) (8 April 1995)

this win/good fortune/stroke of luck will not change our lives.   What members of the public invariably tell journalists. A cliché by the early twentieth century.

Man [a boozer propping up the bar] who has drawn a runner in the Irish Sweep (to reporter): 'Put dahn as 'ow, if I win, it won't make no difference to my way o' life.'
Caption to cartoon by Chas. Grave, *Punch* (16 March 1932)

The two men [National Lottery winners], wearing newly-bought clothes, adopted the TIME-HONOURED approach of saying the enormous win would not change their lives.
Daily Mail (13 June 1995)

throbbing metropolis. Journalistic use, mostly. Date of origin not known. A cliché by the mid-twentieth century.

In his view Auchtermuchty . . . is an outpost of human decency in a world festering with immorality: in a word, Brigadoon. But fleeting through its sleepy streets en route to the throbbing metropolis of Cupar, visitors may detect that beneath its douce exterior lurks another, darker, Auchtermuchty.
Scotland on Sunday (4 September 1994)

Miles from the throbbing metropolis where bands blithely go about their hearty pop business, a slumbering beast is rousing itself from its morose torpor.
Scotsman (30 November 1994)

thrown into the melting-pot, to be. General idiomatic use, meaning that something is going to be scrapped and a new beginning made or that ideas are going to be put into an imaginary 'pool' and mixed together. From the image of the process of making things from metals that have been melted down. A cliché by the mid-twentieth century. 'The jackboot is thrown into the melting-pot' is cited by George Orwell in 'Politics and the English Language' (*Horizon*, April 1946) as a metaphor where the images clash.

He said the whole question would be thrown into the melting pot in an 'audit' of EU legislation which he secured as part of the Maastricht Treaty package.
Daily Mail (9 June 1994)

Many of today's artists . . . have used the millennium as a metaphor for the post-nuclear, post-Aids culture in which politics, economics, sexual identity, and religion have been thrown up into a melting pot of uncertainties.
Guardian (8 April 1995)

thumbnail sketch. General use. Known by 1852. A cliché by 1900, but only borderline.

> There is also a thumbnail sketch of each club's activities.
> *Lloyd's List* (14 July 1994)

> Sir, Tim Dickson's piece on W. Edwards Deming . . . gave a sensitive and accurate thumbnail sketch of a man whose ideas and achievements are often misunderstood and hence often misrepresented.
> Letter to the editor, *Financial Times* (7 January 1995)

thunderous applause. General use. Known by 1892. A cliché shortly thereafter. Compare **tumultuous applause** (known by 1942) and RAPTUROUS APPLAUSE.

> Mr Mandela arrived at parliament led by a police motorcycle escort. He walked into the chamber to thunderous applause.
> *Independent* (10 May 1994)

> The most vituperative contribution, widely televised, came from a gentleman who turned out to have travelled from Glasgow to stir the pot at what was supposedly a meeting for locals to question the candidates under Christian auspices. There was no doubt whose interests his efforts were intended to serve, and the FoC coalition rewarded him with tumultuous applause.
> *Herald* (Glasgow) (29 June 1994)

> Salle earned himself tumultuous applause on a victory lap but there was no doubt that it was Sally who was the crowd's favourite as the meeting started.
> *Daily Mail* (10 September 1994)

tightly knit community. *See* CLOSELY KNIT . . .

time. *See* I WOULD LIKE TO SPEND MORE . . . ; —— OF ALL TIME; ONLY TIME WILL TELL.

time bomb waiting to go off. General, but especially journalistic, use. A cliché by the mid-twentieth century.

> Hugh Pennington, professor of bacteriology at Aberdeen University, described the spread of E. coli 0157 as 'A time bomb waiting to go off'.
> *Independent* (20 June 1995)

time forgot. *See* —— THAT . . .

time has passed by ——. Cliché of travel writing and advertising, and especially of film travelogues. Memorably completed in the commentary to Muir and Norden's sketch 'Balham, Gateway to the South' (1948): 'Time has passed by this remote corner. So shall we.' Compare: **time has stood still**: 'In this fishing village, where a jumble of neat white-washed houses tumble down the tangle of cobbled streets towards the busy harbour, time seems to have stood still for centuries' – listed in the *Independent* 'DIY travel writers' cliché kit' (31 December 1988). Replaced latterly with the suggestion that the place is **in a time warp** (part of the 'travel scribes' armoury' compiled from a competition in the *Guardian* (10 April 1993).

time-honoured ritual. General use. Date of origin not known. A cliché by the mid-twentieth century.

> For the BBC, Tom Fleming could find clichés of his own. He gave us 'the time-honoured ritual of a British royal occasion'.
> *The Times* (30 July 1981)

> Time-honoured ritual comes under threat: The confusing arguments for and against British Summertime.
> Headline, *Herald* (Glasgow) (22 October 1994)

time immemorial. *See* SINCE/FROM . . .

tip of the iceberg. General use. An indication that a greater and more significant amount of something remains hidden. Based on the well-known fact that only one-ninth of an iceberg projects above the water level. A relatively modern expression, recorded by 1969. A cliché shortly after this.

> . . . the Sixties – 'The Violent Decade', I'm calling it. Of course, the outstanding instances were the ghetto riots and the assassinations of public figures . . . But I have a theory that they were only the tip of the iceberg.
> *Cosmopolitan* (November 1974)

> It will deepen the hole that the Government is in, because it makes it look as though Ridley's outburst was the tip of the iceberg. People are now aware it was not just a rash outburst by one Cabinet eccentric, but reflected deep prejudice within the Cabinet.
> *Independent* (16 July 1990)

The assistant chief constable said the fraud may also have involved organised crime. 'We're just at the tip of the iceberg,' Mr Albon added.
Independent (7 September 1995)

tip the scales, to.   General use, to decide the outcome of something that is in doubt by adding a little weight to some element of it. From the use of scales in weighing objects. A cliché by the mid-twentieth century. Listed as a cliché in *The Times* (28 May 1984).

Women tip the scales against diet dictators.
The Times (13 April 1992)

Instead, as has happened before, the factor that may tip the scales in favour of an increase will be the fear that the Government will lose credibility with the markets by doing nothing.
Guardian (1 May 1995)

A 1lb swing in the weights this time is unlikely to be enough to tip the scales in favour of Shambo, three lengths further adrift in third at Newbury.
Irish Times (11 May 1995)

tissue of lies.   General use. Date of origin not known but probably nineteenth century as 'falsehoods' or 'misrepresentations'. A cliché by the 1970s/80s.

In 1911 he died, having months before in an apoplectic outburst from the Bench accused those in the House of Commons who had sought to criticise him five years earlier of 'a tissue of lies'.
Herald (Glasgow) (1 June 1994)

to my wife, without whom ...   Book dedication and acknowledgements use. Date of origin unknown. P.G. Wodehouse was already poking fun at the style in his dedication to *The Heart of a Goof* (1926): 'To my daughter Leonora without whose never-failing sympathy and encouragement this book would have been finished in half the time.' A cliché by the mid-twentieth century. These days, knowing that it is a cliché, the writer often substitutes some jokey variant. But that is almost a cliché, too.

To Jill, Without whom, Whose, Who has been my constant, Who has always, Who ...
Peter Spence, *Some of Our Best Friends Are Animals* (1976) (However, every word from after the second is crossed out.)

To Kerry, without whom I would probably never have begun this book, and to Walter, without whom I would certainly never have finished it.
Maria Zimmer Bradley, *The Catch Tray* (1979)

For Jeffrey, to whom, without this book . . .
Brian Innes, *The Red Baron* (1983)

This book is dedicated to Alexander (356–23BC) without whom, nothing.
(Alison) Spedding, *The Road and the Hills* (1986)

For the three mothers in my life, ladies without whom . . .
Stephen Sheppard, *For All the Tea in China* (1988).

And finally, my thanks to Jean Aitchison, without whom . . .
John Ayto, *The Longman Register of New Words* (1989)

Plenty of male writers have been, and are, surrounded by facilitating women (the cleaner, the cook, the typist, the fender-off-of-callers, the muse) although usually just one woman plays all the roles, rewarded by the usual sentence in the acknowledgements that begins, 'Finally, thanks to my wife, without whom . . .'
Independent (29 June 1994)

See also PAY TRIBUTE TO MY LONG-SUFFERING WIFE.

to the negotiating table.　　Political and journalistic use, for where negotiations take place. Date of origin unknown. A cliché by the 1960s.

The poverty-ridden grape pickers, most of them semi-literate Mexican-Americans, have brought the wealthy grape growers to the negotiating table.
The Times (14 July 1970)

The EU leaders had been called back to the negotiating table after an 8–3–1 split, with Mr Major alone in promoting Sir Leon. Mr Delors made it clear he did not want the EU summit to descend into chaos.
Independent (25 June 1994)

toe the line, to.　　General use. Meaning 'to conform to the defined standard of any group' (as though lining up at the starting line of a race or in military drill). Known by 1813. A cliché by 1900. Cited as a 'dying metaphor' by George Orwell in 'Politics and theEnglish Language' (*Horizon*, April 1946).

Germany agrees to toe line on Bosnia: Chancellor puts unity before his 'moral' position against blanket arms embargo.
Headline, *Financial Times* (1 December 1994)

token gesture.   General, and especially journalistic, use. Meaning 'an action or contribution that is mostly symbolic and does not significantly materially help'. Date of origin not known. A cliché by the 1980s.

> Britain made a token gesture, with doctors boarding planes arriving from India to spray cabin and cargo areas with disinfectant and question crews about passengers' health.
> *Daily Mail* (30 September 1994)

tomorrow.   *See* AS IT/LIKE THERE WAS/WERE NO . . .

tower of strength.   General idiomatic use. A possible origin: Tennyson, *Ode on the Death of the Duke of Wellington* (1852): 'O fall'n at length that tower of strength.' In the Bible, God is often called a 'strong tower'. A cliché by 1900.

> Special mention must be made of Miss Dorothy Swerdlove who . . . has proved a tower of strength on the details of the American theatre.
> Phyllis Hartnoll, *Oxford Companion to the Theatre* (1983 ed.)

> Though doubtless willing to swap his personal triumphs for the right result, Simon Langford, the veteran full-back, was a tower of strength, scoring all Orrell's points and defusing just about everything that Catt kicked at him.
> *Daily Telegraph* (30 January 1995)

town.   *See* THIS TOWN AIN'T BIG . . .

tradition.   *See* IN THE TRADITION OF ——

tragedy struck when . . .   Journalistic use. Date of origin not known. A cliché by the mid-twentieth century. Listed as to be avoided, by Keith Waterhouse in *Daily Mirror Style* (1981).

> Para's fatal mistake . . . tragedy struck when, as a safety measure, Captain Kelly switched on his torch to show his position.
> *Today* (12 May 1994)

> Since then the Mondeo has covered around 1,700 miles without complaint, although tragedy struck when a strong wind tore off some garage roofing, which clouted the car, denting a wing and cracking the windscreen.
> *Daily Telegraph* (6 August 1994)

transports of delight.   General use. Date of origin not known for the original sense of what you get carried away in when ecstatic. Flanders and Swann then gave the title 'A Transport of Delight' to a song about a London bus (1960) in *At the Drop of a Hat*. Subsequently it became a cliché of travel writers and other journalists when dealing with transport arrangements. Part of the 'travel scribes' armoury' compiled from a competition in the *Guardian* (10 April 1993).

One great thing about running an event on your own estate is being invited to drive or ride all manner of rare machines. Last year's transports of delight were a Maserati A6GCM grand prix car and a Manx Norton.
Independent (18 June 1994)

Few transports of delight at tramline plan for Grafton Street: Too much to lose in a thoroughfare that inspires strong affection? – A CIE project team has proposed running a modern tram line down Grafton Street.
Headline, *Irish Times* (29 October 1994)

In the pink on transport of delight . . . This is the Beauty Express, a new alternative transport mode . . . [where] Michelle caresses your feet as part of her special herbal-wrap pedicure.
Headline and text, *Independent* (21 June 1995)

trials and tribulations. General use. An inevitable pairing. Date of origin not known. A cliché by the 1960s/70s. The Australian *Macquarie Dictionary*'s example of a cliché (1981).

The phantom pilots go up with an instructor for a twice-yearly check-out in the trials and tribulations of spinning.
RAF News (27 April 1977)

Only 10 of the party were in New Zealand – its own indication of the vast difference between the position that obtained then and now. But for all the trials and tribulations of that tour two years ago and Ireland should have won the first Test some benefits of real consequence emerged as a result of it.
Irish Times (14 May 1994)

trouble flared when . . . Journalistic use. Known by 1913 in the US. A cliché by the mid-twentieth century. Condemned by Keith Waterhouse in *Daily Mirror Style* (1981).

Trouble flared when police took loudspeakers off a truck which had been prepared for use at a rally by the militant Hamas Islamic Resistance Movement and Islamic Jihad.
Daily Mail (19 November 1994)

Trouble flared when the two sets of fans descended on the pub for drinks before the tie at Villa Park, Birmingham. Insults were traded before fighting broke out.
Daily Mail (10 April 1995)

troubled waters. *See* FISHING IN . . .

true patriot. General use. Known by 1809. A cliché by 1900. 'Marshal Pétain was a true patriot' is cited as a 'meaningless' or 'consciously dishonest' phrase by George Orwell in 'Politics and the English Language' (*Horizon*, April 1946): 'The person who uses [this kind of phrase] has his own private definition, but allows his hearer to think he means something quite different.'

> The country's reputation has also been denigrated in an insulting and demeaning manner. No true patriot would talk of their country in some of the terms that have been used, Mr Reynolds said.
> *Irish Times* (3 June 1994)

> 'He was a true patriot. He was strong for Korea and I was terribly upset by his death,' said Nahomi Kim, a North Korean who lives in Tokyo.
> *Daily Telegraph* (20 July 1994)

trusty sword. General, consciously archaic use. Known by 1558. Also in Edmund Spenser: 'His trusty sword, the servant of his might' (1596) and William Shakespeare, *A Midsummer Night's Dream*, V.i.330 (1594): 'Come, trusty sword,/Come, blade, my breast imbrue!' A cliché by 1900. The most recent citation might appear to be an attempt to break away from the cliché by rearranging it:

> If it falls to me to start a fight to cut out the cancer of bent and twisted jour-nalism in our country with the simple sword of truth and the trusty shield of British fair play, so be it.
> Jonathan Aitken MP, statement (10 April 1995)

Compare the inevitableness of **trusty steed** (date of origin unknown).

> He [an American] actually wrote 'Send me a photo of you, and your car, so I can see you standing beside your trusty steed.'
> Letter of 9 November 1971 in *The Kenneth Williams Letters* (1994)

tug of love. Journalistic use, meaning 'a conflict of affections', especially in relation to disputes between parents over the custody of their children.

The Tug of Love was the title of a comedy by Israel Zangwill (1907). A cliché by the mid-twentieth century. Also **love-tug**, listed by Keith Waterhouse in *Daily Mirror Style* (1981).

> Back home in the arms of her mother, a tiny tug-of-love girl sleeps peacefully. The girl . . . had been taken to California after being snatched by her father.
> *Daily Mirror* (21 March 1977)

> A Scots tug-of-love mum is on the run with her baby daughter after walking out on her American husband.
> *Daily Record* (22 September 1994)

> Tug-of-love mother Sarah Dodds is today looking forward to moving into a new home and starting a new life with her two-year-old daughter.
> *Daily Mail* (24 April 1995)

two kinds of ——. *See* THERE ARE . . .

== U ==

unaccustomed as I am to public speaking. Speechmaking use. A long established cliché and still with us. From William Thackeray, *Pendennis*, Chap. 71 (1848–50): 'I'd like to read a speech of yours in the *Times* before I go – "Mr Pendennis said: Unaccustomed as I am to public speaking" – hey, sir?' In 1856, as Lord Dufferin explains in Letter VI of his *Letters from High Latitudes* (1857), he addressed a group of Icelanders in Latin: '*Viri illustres*, I began, *insolitis ut sum ad publicum loquendum.*' On 26 July 1897, Winston Churchill made his first political speech at a Primrose League gathering near Bath: 'If it were pardonable in any speaker to begin with the well worn and time honoured apology, "Unaccustomed as I am to public speaking," it would be pardonable in my case, for the honour I am enjoying at this moment of addressing an audience of my fellow countrymen and women is the first honour of the kind I have ever received.' In *c.*1940, Noël Coward opened a Red Cross bazaar at Oxford, beginning: 'Desperately *accustomed* as I am to public speaking . . .'

unbridled passion. General use. An inevitable pairing. Date of origin not known. A cliché by the 1960s/70s.

> It looks, to be honest, like a rather humdrum post-war mansion block, not at all the place for unbridled passion and the reckless disregard for decorum and propriety which lies at the heart of A Greater Love: Charles and Camilla.
> *Observer* (7 August 1994)

> A couple of Wednesdays ago I spent a morning with Bill Giles, the weather man, and an afternoon with Gary Rhodes, the chef, and I realised what it is that carries men of such differing personalities to the top of their respective professions. It's unbridled passion for the job. Lust, almost.
> *Mail on Sunday* (30 April 1995)

under the glare of powerful arc lamps. Journalistic use, mainly. In fact, no matter how glaring or powerful the lamps in question may be, they will certainly not be of the arc variety. E.J. Hatch of Sittingbourne, Kent, advised (1984): 'The last widespread use of arc lamps was for aircraft searchlights during the 1939–45 war; they have been used as theatre spotlights; the other main use is for cinema projectors.' A cliché by the mid-twentieth century.

Sydney Airport in November. An expectant crowd jostles for the best vantage point and the arc lamps for the TV cameras blaze away.
Observer (4 December 1994)

Huge arc lamps are lighting up every one of the course's 16 jumps.
Daily Record (6 April 1995)

Compare **amid the glare of television lights**:

Amid the glare of television lights, the panoply of ecstatic family and friends marking their return, and the flotilla of small boats sounding their klaxons, the fact that the women and their yacht, Heineken, LIMPED IN TO PORT behind the 14 other competitors was an irrelevance.
Mail on Sunday (12 June 1994)

unimpeachable authority. General use. Date of origin not known. A cliché by the mid-twentieth century. Identified as a current cliché in *The Times* (17 March 1995).

The argument of Dr Duffy that drinking more than the 'safe limit' reduces the risk of heart disease, and the suggestion by Dr Duffy and his colleague Professor Plant that it is healthier to drink than to abstain, are supported by the results of research carried out under the unimpeachable authority of Professor Sir Richard Doll at the Cancer Studies Unit in Oxford.
Independent (7 December 1994)

At this season, the peace-dreamers like to press the Christmas message into the service of their causes, with the apparently unimpeachable authority of the words which the angels proclaimed to the shepherds: 'on earth peace, good will toward men.'
Sunday Telegraph (18 December 1994)

unmitigated scoundrel. General use. Date of origin not known. A cliché by 1900? Cited by Ted Morgan in *Somerset Maugham* (1980) as having been used by the writer in his efforts to achieve a 'casual style'.

The state was ruled not by Britain but by the Diwan of Travancore, Sir

Ramaswamy Iyer, of whom it could truly be said that he was an unmitigated scoundrel with no REDEEMING FEATURES.
The Times (26 November 1993)

untimely end.   *See* MEET WITH AN . . .

up and down the country.   Political use. Date of origin not known. A cliché by the mid-twentieth century. Edward Heath, when British Prime Minister 1970–74, would wrap his vowels round the phrase. Michael Foot, the British Labour politician, combined it with another political catchphrase following a by-election victory in April 1983 and said that Labour would, 'Get the spirit of Darlington up and down the country'.

As she did so, a fanfare sounded which was the signal to begin lighting beacons to form a blazing chain up and down the country . . . The airwaves also fell silent as radio stations up and down the country joined the hush.
Scotsman (9 May 1995)

The recognition of winning the award shows that we have been successful in highlighting the efforts of road protesters up and down the country.
Herald (Glasgow) (10 May 1995)

Those battles are likely to be fought up and down the country, as Mr Cavallo cajoles provinces into slimming their state structures and re-activating moribund private sectors.
Financial Times (16 May 1995)

up the wooden hill to Bedfordshire.   Conversational use, meaning 'up the stairs to bed'. Originally a nursery euphemism, this has become part of grown-up 'golf-club slang' and a sort of cliché in the late twentieth century. Sir Hugh Casson and Joyce Grenfell included it in their *Nanny Says* (1972), together with 'Come on, up wooden hill, down sheet lane'. 'Up the Wooden Hill to Bedfordshire' was the title of the first song recorded by Vera Lynn, in 1936. The 'bed-fordshire' joke occurs in a synopsis of *Ali Baba and the Forty Thieves; or, Harlequin and the Magic Donkey* staged at the Alexandra Theatre, Liverpool, in 1868. Indeed, as so often, Jonathan Swift found it even earlier. In *Polite Conversation* (1738), the Colonel says, 'I'm going to the Land of Nod.' Neverout replies: 'Faith, I'm for *Bedfordshire.*' But then again, the poet Charles Cotton had used it yet earlier in 1665.

upturned faces.   *See* SEA OF . . .

usual suspects. General use, especially media, meaning 'the people you would expect, the customary lot'. An allusion to the line 'Round up the usual suspects', spoken by Claude Rains as Captain Louis Renaud in the film *Casablanca* (US, 1942). The Vichy French police chief in the Moroccan city is, in his cynical way, appearing to act responsibly in the light of the fact that a German officer, Major Strasser, has been shot. In 1992 Howard Koch appeared to have conceded the writing of this line to his co-scriptwriters Julius J. Epstein and Philip G. Epstein. It did not, however, catch on as early as some of the film's other lines. A borderline cliché by the early 1990s.

Since the bombing, a Korean has been shot dead by Burmese policemen and two Koreans have been arrested . . . If they are from North Korea, the case against the Kim Il Sung government is indeed strong. But it was not clear whether the Burmese security forces were seriously on to something, or whether this was part of a placatory 'Casablanca'-style round-up of 'the usual suspects'.
Economist (15 October 1983)

The rumour is worth taking seriously for two reasons. The first is that someone is buying Xerox shares aggressively in the market. That might be Hanson, though the mention of the name had an element of 'round up the usual suspects' about it.
Guardian (10 February 1989)

After half-time, Hastings kicked two more penalties and Bachop dropped a goal before another of Scotland's irresistible forward drives orchestrated by Armstrong and involving all the usual suspects – Allen, Weir and White – gave Jeffrey the chance to snatch the ball and dive over from five yards.
Independent on Sunday (20 October 1991)

All the usual suspects will be out at Fontwell tomorrow, when the figure-of-eight chase course will throw up its usual quota of specialist [racing] winners.
Independent on Sunday (17 January 1993)

The Usual Suspects
Title of film (US, 1995)

Orton's script [contained] . . . a lot of clumsy, predictable sniping at the Church, politicians, small-town mentality – the usual suspects.
Independent (1 September 1995)

= V =

vacuum. *See* —— ABHORS A . . .

vagaries of the English climate. General use. The formula (but with 'Spanish climate') was known by 1962. A cliché by, say, 1980.

> Sir, Are weather forecasters an unnecessary luxury? Now being a senior citizen, I survived the vagaries of the English climate long before weather forecasters came to such prominence.
> *The Times* (31 July 1993)

> Running an English vineyard these days may well mean diversifying to make ends meet . . . because of the vagaries of the English climate, which mean that the average annual yield is about 20,000 hecto-litres, are unlikely to be directly affected by the ban.
> *Daily Telegraph* (29 September 1993)

valiant effort. General use. An inevitable pairing. Date of origin not known. A cliché by the mid-twentieth century.

> In a valiant effort to find a kinder term than handicapped, the Democratic National Committee has coined differently abled. The committee itself shows signs of being differently abled in the use of English.
> *Los Angeles Times* (9 April 1985)

Venice/Paris/Athens of the North/South/East/West. Travel writing and journalistic use. Most such phrases date from the nineteenth century. For example, 'the Athens of the North' seems to have been applied to Edinburgh after the 'New Town' was constructed in the early 1800s and the city took on a fine classical aspect. Paris has been called the 'Athens of Europe', Belfast the 'Athens of Ireland', Boston, Mass., the 'Athens of the New World', and Cordoba, Spain, the 'Athens of the West'. A cliché formula by the early twentieth century. In one of James A. Fitzpatrick's 'Traveltalks' – a supporting feature of cinema programmes from 1925 onwards – the commentator said: 'And as the midnight sun lingers on the skyline of the city, we most reluctantly say farewell to Stockholm, Venice of the North . . .' Listed as part of the 'travel scribes' armoury' compiled from a competition in the *Guardian* (10 April 1993). Mentioned by Tom Stoppard in the play *Jumpers* (1972): 'McFee's dead . . . he took offence at my description of Edinburgh as the Reykjavik of the South.'

> All those colorful canals, criss-crossing the city, that had made travel agents abroad burble about Bangkok as the Venice of the East.
> *National Geographic Magazine* (July 1967)

> Vallam is a religious spot, once known as the Mount Athos of the North.
> Duncan Fallowell, *One Hot Summer in St Petersburg* (1994)

veritable ——. General use. Date of origin for this construction not known. A cliché by the 1920s/30s. For example, **veritable pot-pourri**, **veritable minefield**, **veritable inferno** – the last cited as a 'lump of verbal refuse' by George Orwell in 'Politics and the English Language' (*Horizon*, April 1946).

> For the BBC, Tom Fleming could find clichés of his own. He gave us 'the TIME-HONOURED RITUAL of a British royal occasion' . . . and, in front of the Palace balcony, 'a veritable sea' of people.
> *The Times* (30 July 1981)

> It was while she searched through Reggie's wardrobe that she came upon a veritable BONANZA in the form of a Marks and Spencer bag containing an assortment of shirts, underwear and socks.
> Gemma O'Connor, *Sins of Omission* (1995)

vexed question. General use. An inevitable pairing. Known by 1657 in English. Translation of Latin *quaestio vexata*. A cliché by 1900.

> Environment: Throwaway lines – The hour is late and the party's nearly over when Joseph Pisani finds his guests have turned to the vexed question of household waste.
> Headline, *Guardian* (22 May 1992)

vicarage tea-party. *See* MAKE —— LOOK LIKE A . . .

vicious circle. General use, meaning 'reciprocal aggravation as in argument and discussion'. Or a self-perpetuating cycle of aggravation. A term used in logic and known by 1792. A cliché by 1900. Compare the film title *Mrs Parker and the Vicious Circle* (US, 1995), referring to the witty members of the Algonquin Round Table in the 1930s.

We must end the vicious circle of low skill, poor wages, unemployment and national economic decline. Instead for the computer age we must create a new virtue circle of education, productivity, high earning power and national prosperity.
Evening Standard (London) (12 July 1994)

virtual standstill. General use, especially journalistic. Date of origin unknown. Eric Partridge, *A Dictionary of Clichés* (5th edition, 1978) has 'Traffic is (or was) at a virtual standstill' as an American newspaper reporters' cliché, 'dating from ca. 1905'.

Road traffic between Hungary and Austria came to a virtual standstill on Saturday as Hungarian border guards stepped up passport and customs checks following a bomb blast in Budapest.
Financial Times (25 July 1994)

The railways came to a virtual standstill yesterday as train drivers staged the first of six 24-hour stoppages. Union leaders said there was worse to come.
Independent (15 July 1995)

voyage of discovery. General use. Known by the mid-nineteenth century in both the literal and figurative senses. A cliché by the mid-twentieth century.

Around The World In Masterpieces; The National Gallery's 'Circa 1492,' A Grand Voyage Of Discovery.
Headline, *Washington Post* (12 October 1991)

The prospect of writing a book about myself had been depressing me. Now I realised that it could be a voyage of discovery.
Bob Monkhouse, *Crying With Laughter* (1993)

wagging.   *See* CASE OF THE TAIL WAGGING THE DOG.

wall of silence.   General use, especially journalistic. Date of origin not known. A cliché by the 1970s/80s.

> Wall of silence over murder in prison.
> Headline, *Observer* (30 April 1995)

want.   *See* FULFIL A LONG-FELT . . .

warring faction(s).   General use, especially journalistic. Known by 1972. A cliché since that date, if not before.

> The central district came under fire from all sides during the fighting and was devastated though the Riad Solh and the Stock Exchange remain almost undamaged. This was the Wall Street of Beirut, and each warring faction was evidently anxious to preserve its bank accounts.
> *Mail on Sunday* (6 November 1994)

washed down with the local wine.   Travel journalistic use. Part of the 'travel scribes' armoury' compiled from a competition in the *Guardian* (10 April 1993).

> But back to the splendid restaurant in Bergheim. This place was typical of Alsace – good food, served simply but elegantly in generous portions to be washed down with the local wine for which the area is justly famous.
> *Herald* (Glasgow) (10 October 1994)

> We spent our evenings in delightful hotels – one a palace, another set in magnificent gardens – devouring tajines (stews) and couscous and kebabs the size of swordsticks, washed down by local wine and liquid chewing gum (that's sweet Moroccan tea, to you).
> *Daily Mail* (29 April 1995)

——watch. Mostly media use – a suffix designed, apparently, to add dignity and status to almost any vigil, regular study or observation. Used in earnest in the UK from about 1985. It stemmed from Neighbourhood Watch (sometimes Home Watch) schemes, which had been started by police in the UK a year or two before this – schemes in which residents are encouraged to 'police' their own and each other's properties.

The coinage originated, however, in the US in the early 1970s, but as early as 6 July 1975, the *Observer* TV critic could write, 'Camden Council employs a lone inspector to walk the pavement on the lookout for citizens allowing their dogs to foul it. In a sane society he would command a department called Shitwatch.' The comedian Les Dawson had a BBC TV series entitled *The Dawson Watch* by 1980.

In 1985, there were the TV programme titles *Drugwatch*, *Nature Watch*, *Newswatch*, *Crimewatch UK*, *Firewatch*, not to mention a feature called 'Wincey's Animal Watch' on TV-am. In 1986 came *Birdwatch UK* and *Childwatch* (on TV). Since then I have become aware of *Railwatch* (BBC TV, 1989), *Weather Watch* (ITV, 1989), 'Longman Wordwatch', a scheme for readers to contribute to the *Longman Register of New Words*, and something called the Worldwatch Institute in Washington – which seems to be the ultimate in ——watches.

> I'm fed up with Agewatch and Childwatch. I'm thinking of founding a society against potential suicide called Wristwatch.
> Russell Harty, quoted by Alan Bennett in memorial address (14 October 1988)

watery grave. General use, but mainly journalistic. 'Wat'ry grave' occurs in Shakespeare, *Pericles*, II.i.10 (1609). A cliché by 1900.

> [He] was in two bunkers for a double bogey at the eighth. He had a watery grave at the last when he pulled his seven-iron approach into the duck pond.
> *Irish Times* (9 May 1994)

> Political 'photo opportunities' are not supposed to be life-or-death affairs. But the Socialist candidate in the French presidential election, Lionel Jospin, broke the rule on Sunday when he very nearly fell into a watery grave while attempting to board a fishing boat in the Breton port of Concarneau.
> *Evening Standard* (London) (19 April 1995)

we are just good friends. *See* JUST GOOD FRIENDS.

we gave him/her everything ... where did we go wrong? General use. What parents say when their offspring commit offences which attract the attention of the popular newspapers. Clichés by the mid-twentieth century.

> 'When a Jewish child marries a non-Jew, the parents see it as a rejection of their own values and beliefs,' he says. 'They may also feel stigmatised in the Jewish community and angry at their child for shaming them.' But the over-riding emotion is guilt. Rabbi Romain says parents often ask, where did we go wrong?
> *Guardian* (26 July 1994)

> 'We don't understand it, we gave him everything,' say parents to me when they discover that their son has gone off the rails. By 'everything' they mean computer games, video recorders and so forth. They do not mean time, attention or affection.
> *Daily Mail* (24 May 1995)

we have surely learned the lesson of ——. Journalistic use. Listed in the *Independent* (24 December 1994) as a cliché of newspaper editorials.

we must stamp out this evil in our midst. Journalistic use, in campaigning and editorializing. Date of origin not known. In June 1967 Chris Welch of *Melody Maker* wrote: 'We can expect a deluge of drivel about the new people [proponents of Flower Power, peace and love] any day now from the Sunday papers, with demands to "stamp out this evil in our midst".' So, a cliché by that time.

> For each person who advised taking to drink or moving house, there were at least five victors. The tearful letters and the rants about 'the jackboot of ground elder' and the 'evil in our midst' were far outweighed by vigorous calls to action.
> *Daily Telegraph* (8 May 1993)

> For it was the ability to look the other way when evil was at liberty in society that allowed the monster to grow in Germany in the thirties. It is no less a danger for us, even if evil in our midst has no uniform and is not organised behind a common banner.
> *Herald* (Glasgow) (31 July 1993)

we name the guilty men. Journalistic and authorial use. *Guilty Men* was the title of a tract 'which may rank as literature' (A.J.P. Taylor). It was written by Michael Foot, Frank Owen and Peter Howard using the pseudonym 'Cato'. Published in July 1940, it taunted the appeasers who had brought about the situation whereby Britain had had to go to war with Germany. The preface contains this anecdote: 'On a spring day in 1793 a crowd of angry men burst their way through the doors of the assembly room where the French Convention was in session. A discomforted figure addressed them from the rostrum. "What do the people desire?" he asked. "The Convention has only their welfare at heart." The leader of the angry crowd replied, "The people haven't come here to be given a lot of phrases. They demand a dozen guilty men."' The phrase 'We *name* the guilty men' subsequently became a cliché of popular 'investigative' journalism. Equally popular was the similar, 'We name these *evil* men.' A cliché by the 1960s/70s.

> Like all the best Sunday journalists, I name the guilty men, and one guilty woman, if we include Mrs Shirley Williams.
> *Observer* (16 April 1989)

> In this era of 'open government' it is left to Michael Heseltine's department to maintain Whitehall standards and not name the guilty men.
> *Guardian* (23 June 1994)

> Bates is still fuming about the pitch invasion which followed his side's FA Cup defeat by Millwall ten days ago and has appealed to the public to name the guilty men. 'There will be no hiding place for these people,' he raged. 'Not at Chelsea, not at home, and not even in their local pub.'
> *Daily Mirror* (18 February 1995)

we shall not see his like again. Obituary and tribute use. Alluding to Shakespeare, *Hamlet*, I.ii.187 (1600), where the Prince says of his late father:

> A was a man, take him for all in all;
> I shall not look upon his like again.

A cliché by the mid-twentieth century. Dorothy Parker on Isadora Duncan's book *My Life* in the *New Yorker* (14 January 1928): 'She does not whine, nor seek pity. She was a brave woman. We shall not look upon her like again.' In *Joyce Grenfell Requests the Pleasure* (1976), the actress recalls being rung by the United Press for a comment on the death of Ruth Draper, the monologist: 'My diary records: "I said we should not see her like again. She was a genius." Without time to think, clichés take over and often, because that is why they have become clichés, they tell the truth.'

And if Khamaseen gallops to a glorious tenth for Lester, those famous, famished features will be wreathed in the biggest smile the old place has ever seen. Khamaseen supporter or not, we wish him nothing less. We will assuredly never see his like again.
Sunday Times (29 May 1994)

Football: The End Of Rushie: We'll Never See The Like Of This Super Hitman Again Says Emlyn Hughes: Farewell Wembley Appearance For Ian Rush.
Headline, *Sunday Mirror* (2 April 1995)

we will get a result.   Sporting use, especially football – as in 'If we play, we will get a result'. Modern origin. Professor Harold Carter in a letter to the *Sunday Times* (14 January 1990) wondered: 'Presumably if a game is played a result will ensue. Why has "We will win" disappeared? Or, if only a draw is envisaged, "We will not lose"?'

we'll get married just as soon as my divorce comes through.   Seduction use, but probably more apparent in fiction (and parodies of same) than in real life. Registered as a cliché in *Time* Magazine (14 December 1981).

weaves (its own) magic/spell.   Journalistic and promotional use. Date of origin not known. A cliché by the 1960s/70s.

Wembley may indeed be old and cramped, but it carries capital city clout and there is a certain magic about the place that weaves a spell over players and spectators alike.
Evening Standard (London) (7 February 1995)

Life is relaxed. The living is easy. The warm breeze of Morocco weaves its own magic.
Austin Reed Spring Summer (clothing) catalogue (1995)

week is a long time in politics.   General, especially journalistic use. Harold Wilson's famous dictum probably first arose at a meeting between Wilson and the Parliamentary lobby correspondents in the wake of the sterling crisis shortly after he first took office as Prime Minister in 1964. From the late 1980s onwards, Channel 4 TV carried a weekly review with the title *A Week in Politics*, clearly alluding to Wilson's phrase – which provides an easily variable format. In due course, —— **is a long time**

in —— became something of a cliché. Listed in the *Independent* (24 December 1994) as a cliché of newspaper editorials.

[On the outgoing editor of the TV programme *Forty Minutes*]: 'His successor will have to work hard, though, to keep the formula fresh. 2,400 seconds is a long time in television.'
Independent (19 May 1989)

weighty tome. General use, semi-archaic, for a heavy and/or learned book. Date of origin not known. A cliché by the mid-twentieth century.

Recently, book store displays were joined by a weighty tome about little grey aliens with blank eyes abducting large numbers of Americans and forcing them to have sex inside spaceships, followed by lectures on ecology.
Financial Times (23 July 1994)

I run from the house, chaotic basket of beach equipment in hand ... A guilty impulse invariably causes me to snatch some weighty tome with which (in theory) to salve my conscience and (in practice) to muddy the enjoyment of the afternoon.
Times Higher Education Supplement (12 May 1995)

well-deserved/earned break/rest. *See* ENJOYING A . . .

wet and warm. Conversational use. On being offered a drink, one might say: 'I don't mind what it is, as long as it's wet and warm.' *H.L. Mencken's Dictionary of Quotations* (1941) cites as a 'Dutch proverb': 'Coffee has two virtues: it is wet and warm.' I am told that in Kenya, *c.*1950, there was a saying: 'Wet and warm like a honeymoon in Aden.' A borderline cliché.

what about the workers? Political use. Usually written, 'Wot abaht . . .', this is the traditional proletarian heckler's cry during a political speech. It is almost a slogan in its own right, but is now only used satirically. In 1984, in a TV programme to mark his hundredth birthday, Manny Shinwell, the veteran Labour MP, appeared to be claiming that he had been asking 'What about the workers?' – seriously – in 1904, but whether he meant literally or figuratively wasn't clear. He told John Mortimer in *Character Parts* (1986): 'I remember Bonar Law, future Prime Minister and Conservative Member of Parliament for the Gorbals, giving a speech in Glasgow, and it was all about Free Trade or something and they were applauding him! Unemployed men were applauding Bonar Law! So I shouted out, "What about the workers!" . . . I got my picture in the papers.'

If it ever had much circulation outside of parody, then the phrase became a cliché some time after the First World War. It occurs along with other rhetorical clichés during the 'Party Political Speech' (written by Max Schreiner) on the Peter Sellers comedy album *The Best of Sellers* (1958). Also in the 1950s, Harry Secombe as 'Neddie Seagoon' on the BBC radio *Goon Show* would sometimes exclaim (for no very good reason), 'Hello, folks, and what about the workers?!' Later, in the 1970s *Morecambe and Wise Show*, Eric Morecambe incorporated it in a nonsense phrase of sexual innuendo when referring to 'a touch of hello-folks-and-what-about-the-workers!'

what the punters want. Business and journalistic use, referring to purchasers of goods, newspapers, tickets for various forms of entertainment. Date of origin unknown. A cliché by the 1970s/80s. Identified as a current cliché in *The Times* (17 March 1995). Indeed, any talk of people as punters if they are outside the field of betting and gambling looks set to become clichéd.

> The punters were well pleased . . . [but] as far as I was concerned I played crap that night.
> *Record Mirror* (7 May 1977)

> This, after all their radical predictions and experiments, is what constitutes a brand-new house as we head towards the start of the third millennium but it is what the punters want, although the punters have little choice anyway.
> *Sunday Times* (12 February 1995)

> For Duncan, his gizmo is pure fantasy. 'It is what the punters want,' he declared. 'There are 2000 people looking up at you – they want something larger than life.'
> *Guardian* (18 May 1995)

what's a nice girl like you doing in a joint/place like this? Conversational/chatting up use, and now only in a consciously arch way. It is listed among the 'naff pick-up lines' in *The Naff Sex Guide* (1984). I suspect it may have arisen in Hollywood Westerns of the 1930s. It was certainly established as a film cliché by the 1950s when Frank Muir and Denis Norden included this version in a BBC radio *Take It From Here* parody: 'Thanks, Kitty. Say, why does a swell girl like you have to work in a saloon like this?' In the film *Kiss Me Stupid* (US, 1964) Ray Walston strokes Kim Novak's knee and whispers: 'What's a beautiful joint like this doing in a girl like you?' – thus 'reducing the age-old seducer's spiel, while telling the same old story' (as Walter Redfern comments in *Puns*, 1984). In 1973, *Private Eye* carried a cartoon of a male marijuana-smoker with a female, and the caption, 'What's a nice joint like you . . .?'

whatever happened to ──?   Journalistic use. The original conversational query occurs in Noël Coward's song 'I Wonder What Happened to Him?' (from *Sigh No More*, 1945) in the form, 'Whatever became of old Bagot . . .?' But the film title *Whatever Happened to Baby Jane?* (1962) fixed the phrase in the way most usually employed by journalists. Like WHERE ARE THEY NOW?, this became a standard formula for feature-writing on a slack day. In the early 1980s, the *Sunday Express* ran a weekly column, disinterring the stars of yesteryear, sometimes under the heading 'Where are they now . . .?' but more usually, 'Whatever happened to . . .?'

Whatever Happened to . . .? The Great Rock and Pop Nostalgia Book
Title of book by Howard Elson and John Brunton (1981)

Whatever Happened to Romance?
Advertisement for Coty Perfume (*c.*1983)

wheel.   *See* REINVENT THE . . .

wheel has come/turned full circle.   General use, especially in politics. The origin is plainly a passage in Shakespeare, *King Lear*, V.iii.173 (1605). Edmund the Bastard says, 'The wheel is come full circle', referring to the wheel of Fortune, being at that moment back down at the bottom where he was before it began to revolve. A cliché by the mid-twentieth century.

I turned on the wireless and heard the official announcement of Italy's declaration of war on Germany. So now the wheel has turned full circle.
Chips Channon MP, diary (13 October 1943) in *Chips: The Diaries of Sir Henry Channon* (1967)

Full Circle
Title of memoirs by Sir Anthony Eden (1960)

The Vixen in Hytner's production is caught by the Forester as a cub while she is entranced watching a dragonfly; at the end, another cub is doing the same. So it comes full circle . . . It was full circle, too, for some of us at Covent Garden on Tuesday when the original four-act version of Britten's

Billy Budd returned there for the first time since it was toured in 1952, six months after its world premiere.
Sunday Telegraph (4 June 1995)

But we could come full circle. Twenty years after Britain voted clearly in favour of being part of Europe, pressure is growing to involve all the Union's voters in a referendum on whatever proposed changes come out of the IGC.
Scotsman (5 June 1995)

With this, the wheel my father started comes full circle. His mild hero-worship for the likes of PV Doyle has been turned upside down.
Irish Times (5 June 1995)

when all is said and done ... General use. Known by the mid-nineteenth century in the US. Identified as a current cliché in *The Times* (17 March 1995).

When All Is Said and Done
Title of autobiography (1962) by Rose Franken (popular novelist of the 'Claudia' books)

And when all is said and done, that [cricket] cap belongs to all of us. The England team of our imaginations, of our dreams, represents the whole of England from the top to the bottom.
Sunday Times (31 July 1994)

To spice up the winter go for a little bit of animal. PVC may be doing a turn with the under 25s but when all is said and done it is very sticky, hot and uncomfortable.
Herald (Glasgow) (20 September 1994)

when are you going to finish off that dress? Conversational/chatting up/flirting use. Addressed to a woman with skimpy décolletage. Date of origin unknown. Tom Jones can be heard so addressing a member of the audience on the LP *Tom Jones – Live at Caesar's Palace, Las Vegas* (1971).

when the chips are down. General use, meaning 'at a crucial stage in a situation'. The phrase alludes to the chips used in betting games. The bets are placed when they are down but the outcome is still unknown. A cliché by the 1970s/80s. Identified as a current cliché by Howard Dimmock of Westcliff-on-Sea in a letter to the *Sunday Times* (31 December 1989).

If when the chips are down, the world's most powerful nation ... acts like a pitiful helpless giant, the forces of totalitarianism and anarchy will threaten free nations and free institutions throughout the world.
Richard M. Nixon, TV speech (30 April 1970)

There is a substantial body of opinion in Britain – and in Chobham – that holds that Lloyd's Names deserve all the suffering they have got. In a sense, it is this factor that has turned their calamity into a tragedy. Now that the chips are down, communities aren't rallying round.
Independent on Sunday (19 March 1995)

when the —— had to stop. General, especially journalistic use. Popularized by *When the Kissing Had to Stop*, the title of a novel (1960) by Constantine Fitzgibbon about a Russian takeover of Britain, and adapted for TV in 1962. That title derives in turn from Robert Browning's poem 'A Toccata of Galuppi's' (1855): 'What of soul was left, I wonder,/When the kissing had to stop?' A cliché by 1970. In *Keep Taking the Tabloids* (1983), Fritz Spiegl noted these headline uses: 'When the Music had to Stop', 'When the Talking had to Stop'.

—— where are you now?/where are they now? Journalistic use. A popular formula when resurrecting people who have passed out of the headlines – compare WHATEVER HAPPENED TO —— ? The rhetorical question occurs rather differently in Wordsworth's ode 'Intimations of Immortality' (1807):

Whither is fled the visionary gleam?
Where is it now, the glory and the dream?

Where Are They Now? was the title of a radio play by Tom Stoppard in 1970.

Still, this appears to be the week for national treasures so there is no ignoring Roy Hudd. Full Steam A-Hudd (Radio 2, today, Saturday, 7.33pm) features Hudd, the BBC Big Band and a where-are-they-now line-up which includes Frankie Vaughan, June Whitfield, Marion Montgomery, Pam Ayres and Bonnie Langford.
The Times (3 June 1995)

Sport: Where are they now? – Nicola Pietrangeli.
Headline, *Independent* (6 June 1995)

where do we go from here? Political and media use. For example, it is now a pompous way of rounding off broadcasting discussions about the future of almost anything. A possible source was hinted at by Winston Churchill when, in a broadcast to the US from London on 8 August 1939, he said: 'And now it is holiday again, and where are we now? Or, as you sometimes ask in the United States – where do we go from here?' 'Where Do We Go From Here?' was the title of a song of the 1940s, popular for a while in the Army. A cliché by 1967 when it was used as the title of a book by the Rev. Dr Martin Luther King Jr – and the next year when it was the title of a BBC TV programme inquiry in Scotland. Alternatively, the question can be put to an individual (who has just been interviewed about his life and works) in the form, 'Well, where do you go from here?'

In politics, as a theme for debates, it tends to be put even more pompously (though now, with luck, only jokingly) in the form **whither ——?** (e.g. 'Whither Democracy?' 'Whither Europe?' 'Whither the Labour Party?'). A sketch from BBC TV *That Was the Week That Was* (1962–3 series) began: 'Question of the year, the future of our leader. How soon if ever will he be eased out of Admiralty House and into the Earldom of Bromley. After Macmillan – whither?' The first episode of *Monty Python's Flying Circus* (1969) was subtitled 'Whither Canada?'

Whither the BBC?
Headline on leading article, *The Times* (14 January 1985)

which comes first, the music or the words? Journalistic use. An interviewer's inevitable question when faced with a lyricist, composer or songwriter. Having designated it a cliché in my book *The Gift of the Gab* (1985), I found myself interviewing one of the breed on television a short while afterwards and was dreadfully conscious of the error I could commit. And so I asked him, 'Which comes first, the words or the lyrics?'

Ah, well. When Sammy Cahn, the American lyricist who died in 1993, was asked the question, he would ritually answer: 'First comes the phone call.' To Cole Porter is ascribed the similar: 'All the inspiration I ever needed was a phone call from the producer.' On the other hand, what Ira Gershwin is supposed to have replied was: 'What usually comes first is the contract' – quoted at his death, in the *Guardian* (18 August 1983).

In Richard Strauss's opera *Capriccio* (lyrics by Clemens Krauss) (1942), the eternal question of which comes first is argued thus:

Olivier: Prima le parole – dopo la musica!
Flamand: Prima la musica – dopo le parole!

which side one's bread is buttered. *See* KNOW WHICH SIDE . . .

whirlwind ride. *See* RIDE THE WHIRLWIND.

whirlwind romance. *See* RIDE THE WHIRLWIND.

whited sepulchre. General use, meaning a person 'coated in white' who pretends to be morally better than he, in fact, is – also 'holier than thou'. Alluding to Matthew 23:27: 'Woe unto you, scribes and Pharisees, hypocrites! for ye are like unto whited sepulchres, which indeed appear beautiful outward, but which are full of dead men's bones, and of all uncleanness.' A cliché by 1900.

> If the ombudsman cannot do what seems right in circumstances where the courts themselves would regret having to give judgment for the undeserving party, there is no point in having one at all. Worse, the office would be a whited sepulchre.
> *The Times* (21 May 1994)

. . . who did very nicely out of it, thank you. General use. Date of origin not known. A cliché by the 1970s/80s. Gerald Priestland said it in a Channel 4 TV series *Priestland Right and Wrong* (1983).

who redefined ——. Mostly journalistic cliché of compliment on achievement. Date of origin not known. A cliché by the early 1990s.

> Edward Thompson, who died last year, was an intellectual giant . . . Here was a man who redefined history, rescuing from obscurity a host of ordinary people who, in the early nineteenth century, laid the basis for modern democracy.
> *Observer* (8 May 1994)

> The book doesn't follow Elvis into the bedroom . . . This would be a flaw in any serious biography. For a performer who redefined male sexuality with an infusion of narcissism, and whose work was based largely on carnal energy, it borders on the barmy.
> *Sunday Telegraph* (23 October 1994)

> The knives are out for Macaulay Culkin. The child star who redefined

mischief in *Home Alone* might only be 14 years old, but already his days in Hollywood are numbered.
Today (16 December 1994)

If Foley, the charming smallholder who has redefined the meaning of humility, was looking for obscurity and peace he has found it. Except that as the trainer of Danoli, Ireland's new Arkle, he is never more than a telephone call away from contact with the outside world.
Daily Mail (3 January 1995)

whole hog. *See* GO THE . . .

whose —— is it anyway? Journalistic use. A formula derived from *Whose Life Is It Anyway?*, the title of a play (1978; film US, 1981) by Brian Clark. Later a BBC Radio/Channel 4 TV improvisatory game was given the title *Whose Line Is It Anyway?* (by 1989). By 1993, the *Independent* Magazine was campaigning for the abolition of it as a headline cliché.

Whose womb is it anyway?
Northern Echo (9 November 1992)

Whose Queen is it anyway?
Evening Standard (London) (18 March 1993)

why are you telling me all this? Drama use. The agricultural soap opera *The Archers* has been running on BBC national radio since 1951. In 1983, Norman Painting, who has written many of the episodes as well as playing 'Phil Archer' throughout the existence of the series, admitted that a number of expository clichés had crept in, including this one.

wickedly funny. Publishing and promotional use. A cliché by the 1970s.

It is a wickedly funny book, too. The mock lists in 'Etymology' and 'Extracts' guy any too solemn an encyclopaedist. The fart in 'Loomings' confirms the touch of Smollett in Melville, as does his send-up of sabbatarian probity in the Pequod's owners, Peleg and Bildad.
Times Higher Education Supplement (28 April 1995)

A wickedly funny satire on the English legal system, the comic strip Queen's Counsel has been a regular feature on the Law pages of *The Times* for several years.
New books catalogue, Robson Books Ltd (August-December 1995)

wife. *See* PAY TRIBUTE TO MY LONG-SUFFERING . . .; TO MY WIFE, WITHOUT WHOM . . .

wife and family. *See* MY WIFE AND . . .

wife doesn't understand. *See* MY WIFE DOESN'T . . .

wild as a stallion. *See* AS WILD . . .

wild horses wouldn't drag it out of me. General idiomatic use, referring to the old practice of a person being tied to horses pulling in different directions in order to make him reveal information. Date of origin not known. A cliché by the mid-twentieth century.

> Wild horses would not make me tell you anything more about [the Book Prize for Fiction result].
> Libby Purves, *Listener* (September 1983)

wilderness. *See* LAST GREAT . . .

—— will never be the same again. Media use. Any change, however unremarkable, tends to require this plonking approach. Date of origin unknown. A cliché by the 1970s/80s. 'ONE THING IS CERTAIN. Things will never be the same again' – cited by Malcolm Bradbury in an article on clichés in *Tatler* (March 1980).

> The Broadway musical would never be the same again.
> TV promo, New York (1983)

> Life for George Bush will never be the same again.
> Tim Ewart, ITN news (20 January 1989 – the day of the President's inauguration)

> [Keith Joseph] was irreplaceable; somehow politics would never be the same again.
> Margaret Thatcher, *The Downing Street Years* (1993)

> Many families were faced with the fact that someone they loved would not return home. Life would never be the same again.
> Rev. Pat Crashaw, *Kensington and Chelsea Post* (4 May 1995)

> Rugby union's backdrop looked much the same as ever . . . It was Day One, though, of the new order – the game would never be the same again.
> *Observer* (25 June 1995)

will the last person to leave —— please turn out the lights. Journalistic use, mainly. 'Would the last person to leave the country please switch off the lights' – included in *Graffiti 2* (1980). On 9 April 1992 this line suffered a revival when on the day of the British General Election, the *Sun* newspaper's front page headline was: 'If Kinnock wins today will the last person in Britain please turn out the lights.'

> Will the last person to leave Broadway, please turn out the lights.
> Headline, *Independent* (10 June 1995)

wind of change. General, but especially political, use. Speaking to both Houses of the South African parliament on 3 February 1960, the British Prime Minister Harold Macmillan gave his hosts a message they cannot have wanted to hear: 'The most striking of all the impressions I have formed since I left London a month ago is of the strength of this African national consciousness. In different places it may take different forms, but it is happening everywhere. The wind of change is blowing through this continent. Whether we like it or not, this growth of national consciousness is a political fact.' The phrase 'wind of change' – though not original – was contributed to the speechwriting team by the diplomat (later Sir) David Hunt. The *Oxford English Dictionary* (2nd edition) acknowledges that use of the phrase 'wind(s) of change' increased markedly after the speech. When Macmillan sought a title for one of his volumes of memoirs he plumped for the possibly more common, plural, usage – *Winds of Change*.

In a similar windy metaphor Stanley Baldwin had said in 1934: 'There is a wind of nationalism and freedom round the world, and blowing as strongly in Asia as elsewhere.' President George Bush made 'a new breeze is blowing' the theme of his inauguration speech on 20 January 1989. A cliché since 1945 states Eric Partridge in *A Dictionary of Clichés* (5th edition, 1978).

winter holds —— in its icy grip. General use, especially journalistic. Described as an American journalistic cliché by one Frank Sullivan, and included by Eric Partridge in *A Dictionary of Clichés* (5th edition, 1978).

> Pickets mount lonely vigils at pit gates down leafy lanes resplendent in the golds and russet-reds of autumn, but soon to be in the icy grip of an Appalachian winter.
> *Daily Telegraph* (1 November 1993)

Sweden ran out of influenza vaccine this month, well before winter had exerted its icy grip.
Financial Times (8 November 1993)

As Britain shivers in the icy grip of winter, people's thoughts have inevitably turned to that annual pilgrimage to the holiday sun.
Today (3 January 1995)

winter of discontent. Political and journalistic use. Shakespeare's *Richard III* (1592) begins, famously, with Gloucester's punning and original metaphor:

Now is the winter of our discontent
Made glorious summer by this son of York;
And all the clouds that lour'd upon our House
In the deep bosom of the ocean buried

even if the editor of the Arden edition does describe the entire image as 'almost proverbial'. The phrase 'winter of discontent' suffered the unpleasant fate of becoming a politicians' and journalists' cliché following the winter of 1978/9, when British life was disrupted by all kinds of industrial protests against the Labour government's attempts to keep down pay rises.

The first actual use I have found is in the *Sun* (30 April 1979). As part of a series on the issues in the forthcoming election, in the week before polling, the paper splashed across two pages the words: 'Winter of discontent. Lest we forget . . . the *Sun* recalls the long, cold months of industrial chaos that brought Britain to its knees.' (Sir) Larry Lamb, editor at the time, suggested in a Channel 4 TV programme *Benn Diaries II* (29 October 1989) that he had introduced the phrase 'in a small way' during the winter itself (it was imitated by others), then 'in a big way' during the election. James Callaghan, the Prime Minister who was destroyed by the phrase, seems to have claimed that he used it first (recalled in a TV programme, December 1991).

There is little new under the *Sun*, of course. J.B. Priestley, writing of earlier much harder times in *English Journey* (1934) ended his fourth chapter with: 'The delegates have seen one England, Mayfair in the season. Let them see another England next time, West Bromwich out of season. Out of all seasons except the winter of discontent.' Not a cliché, however, until 1979.

Poles face LONG HOT SUMMER of discontent.
Headline, *Independent* (5 June 1995)

wish you were here! Holidaymakers' use in correspondence. 'I am learning Dutch, and wish you were here ... to mynheerify with me' – Southey, *Letter to Lieut. Southey* (1804). This cliché of holiday correspondence has been used as the title of songs (reaching the charts in 1953 and 1984) and of a British ITV travel series (from 1973 onwards). In the full form, '**Having a wonderful time**, wish you were here,' Eric Partridge in his *Dictionary of Catch Phrases* suggests a beginning in Edwardian times. But why not earlier, at any time since the introduction of the postcard in Britain, which was in 1870? To be sure, cards on which you wrote your own message did not come on the scene until 1894 and the heyday of the picture postcard was in Edwardian times. In the early days, perhaps the message was already printed on the card by the manufacturer? Nowadays, probably, the wording is only used in jest or ironically.

Having Wonderful Time, a play about a holiday hotel in the Catskills, by Arthur Kober (1937) became, in an exchange of phrases, the musical *Wish You Were Here* in 1952. *Wish You Were Here* was also used in 1987 as the title of a British film about sexual awakenings in a seaside resort. Clichés both by, say, the 1920s/30s.

witching hour (of midnight). General use. This cliché seems to have grown out of a blend of such lines as: "Tis now the very witching time of night,/When churchyards yawn ...' – Shakespeare, *Hamlet* III.ii.379 (1600) and 'It was now the witching hour consecrated to ghost and spirit' – Lord Lytton, *Rienzi* (1835). *The Witching Hour* was the title of a play by Augustus Thomas (*c.*1915; filmed US, 1921 and 1934). A cliché by the mid-twentieth century.

9.45pm Drop in to The Midnight Shop (223 Brompton Road, SW3), which, as it's name suggests, stays open until the witching hour. It claims to be London's original late-night store, and is a well-stocked grocers and delicatessen.
Daily Mirror (3 December 1994)

—— with a difference. Promotional use – 'the club/disco/hotel/car/ anything ... with a difference'. The phrase was current in the nineteenth century. 'So also at Westminster – with a difference' – Anthony Trollope, *The Three Clerks* (1857). A cliché by the 1960s/70s.

Earth in Orbit is a geography book with a difference. It is the first programmed textbook of English origin.
Guardian (15 January 1963)

On Sunday there is to be a sponsored pub crawl with a difference.
Presenter, Radio Clyde (1983)

(with an) iron fist/hand. General use, for ruthlessly, firmly. 'Iron fist' was known by 1740. Both clichés by 1900. Some connection with the phrase 'An iron hand/fist in a velvet glove.' Napoleon is supposed to have said, 'Men must be led by an iron hand in a velvet glove', but this expression is hard to pin down as a quotation. Thomas Carlyle wrote in *Latter-Day Pamphlets* (1850): 'Soft speech and manner, yet with an inflexible rigour of command ... "iron hand in a velvet glove", as Napoleon defined it.' The Emperor Charles V (1519–56) may have said it earlier. Here the image is of unbending ruthlessness or firmness covered by a veneer of courtesy and gentle manners. Compare MAILED FIST.

Once upon a time, the judiciary was criticised for using an iron fist against the poor and a velvet glove against the wealthy and powerful.
Observer (17 July 1994)

Hard man in a time of soft-spoken clichés – Ronald Payne sees popular support for the French interior minister's iron fist – but some distrust his political ambitions.
By-line, *European* (19 August 1994)

This would have the great merit of ending opposition or indifference to the alliance within Bill Clinton's administration while maintaining America's role as leader. It would, however, mean Nato having to accept becoming the servant of the UN instead of the iron fist of the West.
Sunday Times (2 October 1994)

with the added bonus. General use. An almost tautological inevitable pairing. Date of origin not known. A cliché by the 1960s?

The Gossamer Cord (HarperCollins £14.99) is the latest in Philippa Carr's Daughters of England series, 'a sweeping saga of the history of England' and the fiction equivalent of painting by numbers ... Grab volume five and you can bone up on 'the tumult of Restoration, Plague and Fire' with the added bonus of being right-on and politically correct.
Sunday Times (12 July 1992)

The changes wrought in Compass will 'simply be replicated in the US', says

Mackay, with the added bonus of acquiring new catering franchises with the Canteen acquisition.
Evening Standard (London) (3 May 1994)

Game wardens feed the crocodiles every night – it is an entertaining distraction for the tourists before dinner – but this time the leopard was an added bonus.
Evening Standard (3 May 1994)

with the gloves off.   *See* GLOVES ARE OFF.

within a hair's breadth.   General idiomatic use. Known by 1584. A cliché by 1900.

Black was beaten by a hairsbreadth in a blanket finish for the silver and bronze medals.
The Times (1 September 1960)

The first half ended with Brian McLaughlin missing a Hay cross by a hairbreadth and then Andy Walker forcing a great save from Snelders. Immediately, a Billy Dodds run and shot forced Bonner to give away a corner.
Herald (Glasgow) (27 December 1994)

A further reason why Mr Blair is wise not to tolerate any complacency among his supporters is the formidable, but often underestimated, height of the electoral hurdle facing Labour. The party needs a swing of 4.5% to achieve even a hairsbreadth overall majority.
Economist (6 May 1995)

without causing a ripple.   General use, mainly journalistic. Date of origin not known. A cliché by the 1980s. Identified as a current cliché in *The Times* (17 March 1995).

All the same it is difficult to raise the question of constitutional status in any part of the UK without causing a ripple effect elsewhere.
Herald (Glasgow) (22 September 1994)

Picture, if you please, a swan, gliding serenely across the water, barely causing a ripple. That's presenters Richard Keays and Andy Gray grinning at the camera. Underneath the water, the other 78 bods are paddling away like the Waverley with a turbo charger.
Sunday Mail (1 January 1995)

without further ado.   General use, often when speaking aloud in public, and consciously archaic. Meaning 'without further delay or messing about'. Date of origin not known. A cliché by the 1960s/70s.

At the airport he was stopped by a pimply young border guard who demanded who he was. 'I am Rostropovich,' the great cellist replied imperiously. After disappearing to consult a superior, the nervous guard let him through without further ado, and Rostropovich went straight to join Boris Yeltsin on the barricades.
Independent (17 June 1994)

For a change, I thought I would review the events of the last 12 months and give my own awards for achievements great and small . . . I am sadly not joined today by Kim Basinger to present the awards with me. So without further ado, here are the results: Best British Success of the Year . . .
Daily Telegraph (31 December 1994)

without whom.   *See* TO MY WIFE . . .

wolf.   *See* KEEP THE WOLF FROM . . .

wooden hill.   *See* UP THE . . .

workers.   *See* WHAT ABOUT THE . . .

World War.   *See* IT WAS WORSE THAN THE BLITZ.

worse before it gets better.   *See* IT'S GOT TO GET . . .

writ large.   General use, meaning 'in enlarged, grand, more prominent form'. John Milton's 'On the New Forcers of Conscience under the Long Parliament' (1646) has 'New *Presbyter* is but Old *Priest* writ Large'. A cliché by 1900.

In her spring or even summer, one might easily have penned the Thatcher speech: simple virtues, simple prescriptions, Great Britain plc as the family grocery writ large. But yesterday – in a speech no ghost could have written for her – there was a new autumnal, even elegiac Thatcher.
Guardian (27 September 1989)

The Royal Family is an ordinary family writ large. That has always been its attraction . . . They provide a universal topic of conversation, a frame of reference, and offer proof that, even though they live in bigger houses, wear

better clothes and take more glamorous holidays, they are as prone as the rest of us to making mistakes.
Independent (7 January 1995)

The British documentary tradition ... became more accessible to the general public when fused with the melodrama of everyday life in a succession of wartime films like *Millions Like Us* and *This Happy Breed*, which created an image of an integrated community – the family writ large – characterised by distinctively British virtues: service and sacrifice, restraint, tolerance and decency.
Sunday Telegraph (23 April 1995)

writing (is) on the wall. General use, meaning that a hint, sign or portent (often doom-laden) is apparent. The idea – though not the phrase – comes from the Bible (Daniel 5) where King Belshazzar is informed of the forthcoming destruction of the Babylonian Empire through the appearance of a man's hand writing on a wall. Jonathan Swift used the precise phrase in *c*.1720. Note also: 'Here, while the national prosperity feasts, like another Belshazzar, on the spectacle of its own magnificence, is the Writing on the Wall, which warns the monarch, Money, that his glory is weighed in the balance, and his power found wanting' – Wilkie Collins, *No Name* (1862). In a BBC broadcast to resistance workers in Europe (31 July 1941), 'Colonel Britton' (Douglas Ritchie) talked of the V for Victory sign which was being chalked up in occupied countries: 'All over Europe the V sign is seen by the Germans and to the Germans and the Quislings it is indeed the writing on the wall ...' A cliché by the 1960s/70s. Listed by Keith Waterhouse in *Daily Mirror Style* (1981). Listed in the *Independent* (24 December 1994) as a cliché of newspaper editorials.

The 'eighties and 'nineties were the GOLDEN AGE ... [of music-hall]; and in 1905 the writing was on the wall ... Musical comedy, the cinema, television all hastened its decline.
Listener (2 December 1965)

And it was about this time that Nigel Rees saw the writing on the wall [as graffiti collector] ...
Derek Batey, Border TV *Look Who's Talking* (30 November 1983)

wrong. *See* WE GAVE HIM/HER EVERYTHING ...

= Y =

yawning gap. General use. An inevitable word pairing. Date of origin not known. A cliché by the mid-twentieth century. Listed in the *Independent* (24 December 1994) as a cliché of newspaper editorials.

> A reflation stimulus is urgently needed now to fill the yawning gap in consumer demand.
> *New Scientist* (10 June 1971)

> Mr Norman Ireland, of Reuters Business Information, said the results showed a 'yawning gap' between the recognised value of information and the way in which it was managed as a proper asset.
> *Financial Times* (16 May 1995)

> Nevertheless there is a yawning gap between the visionary 'guiding idea' of the production, nurtured presumably by Crowley, and the actual monologues (each supported by the other actors in indifferent impersonations), which are mostly student humour about the vicissitudes of innocents abroad.
> *Financial Times* (16 May 1995)

years. *See* MORE YEARS THAN . . .

— years young. Disc jockey and radio presenter use – 'She is 97 years young', etc. Slightly facetious and self-conscious avoidance of ' – years old'. A cliché by the 1960s/70s.

> To be fair they also twice worked a player free with nobody between him and the line 60 metres away; unfortunately the player was Jeff Probyn, 38 years young and not, at the best of times, built for speed.
> *The Times* (10 October 1994)

yeoman service. General use, meaning 'useful service as rendered by a faithful servant'. 'It did me yeoman's service' – Shakespeare, *Hamlet* V.ii.36 (1600). A cliché by 1900.

Sir, – Your correspondent, Frank McDonald, who has given yeoman service to the protection of our environment, has been misinformed to a degree in regard to the objections to the High Speed Service (HSS) scheme for Dun Laoghaire Harbour.
Letter to the editor, *Irish Times* (9 June 1994)

yesteryear. *See* —— OF YESTERYEAR.

yield to public pressure. Journalistic use. The phrase 'public pressure' on its own was known by 1815. Listed in the *Independent* (24 December 1994) as a cliché of newspaper editorials.

Montgomery later said his forces were short of ammunition and troops . . . 'It would have been very easy for me to yield to public criticism and American pressure and to have made greater efforts to gain ground on this flank.'
Independent (3 June 1994)

'It brought it into their living rooms, and with the protests, people saw that public pressure, people power, can yield results. They have realized that they can make a difference.'
Herald (Glasgow) (8 February 1995)

you can take the —— out of ——, but you can't take the —— out of ——. General use. A modern proverbial observation, current in the late twentieth century, e.g. 'You can take a boy out of the slums but not the slums out of the boy', 'You can take the man out of Essex but you can't take the Essex out of the man.' Origin unknown. Something of a cliché by 1995.

You can take the girl out of Richard Shops, but maroon me in Harrods' Cruisewear Department and a congenital reluctance to splash out £275 on diaper-sized designer sarongs proves irrefutably that you can never quite take Richard Shops out of the girl.
Vanessa Feltz, *Mail on Sunday* Review (14 May 1995)

You can take me out of Europe but you can't take Europe out of me. I have to have my cappuccino every morning.
Isabella Rossellini in 'Milk. What a surprise!' advertising (US) (1995)

you have to spend a buck to make a buck. General use. An American business maxim (and very sensible) dating from, say, the 1920s/30s but curiously unrecorded in US reference works. A borderline cliché by the 1990s.

The Opposition rejected the simplistic view that there was always merit in reducing public spending as a percentage of national income. Public spending should be judged on a balanced assessment of need and what prudently could be afforded, bearing in mind 'that you have to spend a buck to make a buck.'
The Times (14 February 1990)

. . . you name it. General slangy use. A closing phrase to prevent a list from going on too long. Date of origin not known. American? A cliché by the 1980s.

They – or, more likely, producer David Morales (of New York club fame) – loaded the songs with bells, beeping brass, you name it, arranging the lot around sultry basslines.
Guardian (5 May 1995)

We're in a very competitive environment now, for our ears and our eyes, there's TV, video, cinema, tapes, you name it it's available and for live music to compete with that, we have to promote what we're doing.
Irish Times (11 May 1995)

you only want me for my body. Lovers' use, possibly only in fiction. A cliché by the 1950s/60s.

And I said, 'You don't love me. You don't love me – you only love my body – [or] my mind.'
Character played by Lee Remick in the film *No Way To Treat a Lady* (US, 1967)

you would never believe it would be possible! In *Are You a Bromide?* (1907), the American writer Gelett Burgess castigated people who spoke in clichés. Of the observation, 'If you saw that sunset painted in a picture, you'd never believe it would be possible!', he wrote: 'It is not merely because this remark is trite that it is bromidic, it is because that, with the Bromide, the remark is inevitable.'

you'd better come in. Drama use. Standard line to a visiting policeman, observed by Fritz Spiegl in an article on drama cliché lines in the *Listener* (7 February 1985).

you'd better try and get some sleep. Drama. After receiving bad news, a character is invariably told this. Observed by Fritz Spiegl in an article on drama cliché lines in the *Listener* (7 February 1985).

you'll have to take pot-luck . . . Conversational use. In *Are You a Bromide?* (1907), the American writer Gelett Burgess castigated people who spoke in clichés. Among the 'Bromidioms' he listed was: 'Come up and see us any time. You'll have to take pot-luck, but you're always welcome.'

you're going out a youngster —— but you've *got* to come back a star! Mainly show business use, but only in parody. Not a cliché when new-minted in the film *42nd Street* (1933). Warner Baxter as a theatrical producer said the line to Ruby Keeler as the chorus girl who takes over at short notice from an indisposed star.

your earliest convenience. A cliché of correspondence – especially formal, business letter writing – since the nineteenth century.

> You will perhaps oblige me with a line at your earliest convenience.
> Charles Dickens, letter (30 July 1832)

your policemen are wonderful. Mainly show business use. What visiting stars (especially American ones) traditionally say to British interviewers. A cliché by the mid-twentieth century, but note the date of the first citation:

> *Magistrate*: 'Have you anything to say for yourself?'
> *Prisoner*: 'Yus, I fink your London police are wonderful.'
> Caption to cartoon by Edmund J. Sullivan in *Punch* (25 January 1933)

> 'Oh, but we're not so *very* wonderful, really!'
> Bashful London policeman to tourists in *Punch* cartoon (30 May 1938)

> When Kristina Wayborn [actress in James Bond film] said that she loved British fish and chips it seemed a simple kindness to ask what she thought of our policemen. 'They are so wonderful. They make you feel so secure,' she replied in the best possible taste.
> *Guardian* (4 June 1983)

> Thriller writer, Max Byrd . . . almost said that our policemen are wonderful, but stopped himself and touched his shoulder holster.
> *Guardian* (13 July 1985)

> I have yet to see one of your crazy drivers pulled over for a traffic violation. Your policemen are wonderful, but why don't they throw away that halo and get on to a little ticket-writing?
> Letter to the editor, *Today* (20 January 1987)

The British are hypocritical, racist, secretive, arrogant, violent and boorish in drink. They treat old people abominably ... They have the best and the worst press in the world, the silliest scandals and the most honest taxi drivers. Their policemen are wonderful – up to a point.
Guardian (3 April 1989)

'Your policemen are wonderful' is the stock remark of all visitors to London, to all interviewers; but our own policemen, the Garda Siochana are equally deserving of praise.
Irish Times (26 January 1994)

DATE DUE
